JESUS AND THE CHURCH
The Beginnings of Christianity

Willi Marxsen

Selected, Translated, and Introduced
by Philip E. Devenish

TRINITY PRESS INTERNATIONAL   PHILADELPHIA

First Published 1992

Trinity Press International
3725 Chestnut Street
Philadelphia, PA 19104

Translation © 1992 Philip Devenish

Cover design—Brian Preuss

Library of Congress Cataloging-in-Publication Data

Marxsen, Willi, 1919-
    Jesus and the Church : the beginnings of Christianity / Willi
Marxsen ; selected, translated, and introduced by Philip E.
Devenish. — 1st ed.
        p.   cm.
    Essays translated from the German.
    Includes bibliographical references.
    ISBN 1-56338-053-6 :
    1. Jesus Christ—History of doctrines—Early church, ca.
30-600.
    2. Church—Biblical teaching.   3. Bible. N.T.—Criticism,
interpretation, etc.   I. Devenish, Philip E.   II. Title.
BT198.M39635   1992
232—dc20
                                                    92-33155
                                                    CIP

Printed in the United States of America
92 93 94 95 96   6 5 4 3 2 1

CONTENTS

FOREWORD

Although the essays presented in this volume are available for the first time in English translation, Willi Marxsen's work has by no means remained unknown to readers in the English-speaking world. From 1968 to the present, more than a dozen of his books and articles have appeared in English. These include his *Introduction to the New Testament* (Fortress Press, 1968), through which thousands of college and seminary students have been introduced to the earliest writings of the Christian movement. They include, as well, his pioneering redaction-critical study of the Gospel of Mark, *Mark the Evangelist* (Abingdon Press, 1969), his important discussion of the traditions about Jesus' resurrection, *The Resurrection of Jesus of Nazareth* (Fortress Press, 1970), and his classic, *The New Testament as the Church's Book* (Fortress Press, 1972). A number of his publications, including those available in English, are devoted to the question of the historical Jesus and christology. The most recent of these are the lectures that were prepared specifically for delivery in the United States, *Jesus and Easter* (Abingdon Press, 1990).

The nine short studies carefully selected and translated by Philip Devenish for this volume are all responsive, in one way or another, to the question posed in the title of chapter 5, "When Did Christian Faith Begin?" Thus, as the volume's own title indicates, these studies all have to do with Jesus and the beginnings of Christianity. This is a topic of fundamental importance for anyone who wishes to understand the history of Western civilization, as well as for every present-day Christian. It is, moreover, an issue that demands of investigators both skill in the application of the appropriate historical methods and theological acumen. Professor Marxsen's work, as the following essays demonstrate, is distinguished in each respect. He is an able and knowledgeable New Testament scholar who, at the same time, is a discerning theologian. Indeed, one is tempted to say that as such, he belongs to an "endangered species."

It will be noted that the earliest of these essays was originally published in German in 1966, and the latest in 1978. In most respects, however, the essays remain as fresh and up-to-date as when they were first written. This is the case, in part, because the specific topics to which they are devoted are such fundamental ones that they continue to be the subject of investigation and discussion. This is shown very well by Professor Devenish's insightful introduction. That these essays still have so much to offer is, above all, a tribute to Marxsen's own sound scholarship and keen insight. In particular, he is able to identify and to articulate with exceptional clarity the key questions and the most critical issues. Thus, even where one may not agree with the conclusions, one is informed and challenged by the lines of inquiry that Marxsen opens up. As a result, readers will often find themselves thinking about familiar topics in new ways, reexamining matters that they may have long since regarded as settled, and in the process gaining greater clarity about their own views.

Three particular distinctions of Marxsen's work are evident in the essays collected here. First, these studies of Christian origins manifest his concern to understand the meaning and significance of Christian faith itself. His interests thus move beyond the rather narrow boundaries observed by many New Testament scholars today. Indeed, he once remarked that he considers himself more a "theologian" than a "New Testament scholar," at least as New Testament scholarship is often conceived. Yet his theological inquiries proceed on the basis of and in association with his historical and exegetical investigations. For this reason his work can contribute in an especially fruitful way to wider theological discussion. How this has been true and how it may continue to be is the particular subject of the editor's introduction in the present volume.

It is a further distinction of Marxsen's work, including the essays offered here, that it cannot be easily identified with any particular "school of thought" or hermeneutical approach. This is not to suggest that it is in any way idiosyncratic, or that it is out of touch with mainstream scholarship. Marxsen has by no means neglected

FOREWORD

the work of other interpreters. He knows it well and engages it critically and appreciatively. Yet he has steered his own course, examining texts and thinking through issues without feeling beholden either to the current scholarly consensus or to the latest scholarly innovations. A recent volume of essays presented to him on the occasion of his seventieth birthday demonstrates this impressively (*Jesu Rede von Gott und ihre Nachgeschichte im frühen Christentum*, edited by D.-A. Koch, G. Sellin, and A. Lindemann, 1989). Its contributors represent not only several different confessional traditions, countries, and scholarly disciplines but also several distinct approaches to the study of the New Testament and to "doing theology."

Finally, readers of the following essays will come away with an appreciation of Professor Marxsen's concern for the faith and witness of the Christian church. This does not mean that his approach or interests are in any way sectarian. Nor can it be claimed that his views have always found favor even within his own confessional tradition. But there is no question that his published work, and also his university teaching and lectures to Christian laity, show him to be a scholar who *cares* about the gospel by and for which the church exists. He writes with great clarity and with evident commitment on behalf of this gospel. What he provides, however, is not a traditional "defense of faith" or of some particular doctrinal formulation of it. He offers what many will regard as a better and more lasting gift: studies that are in themselves compelling examples of "faith seeking understanding."

Victor Paul Furnish
Perkins School of Theology
Southern Methodist University, Dallas, TX

Introduction

THE JESUS-KERYGMA
AND CHRISTIAN THEOLOGY*

Translating essays from a previous generation of scholarship calls for special justification.[1] There are several reasons why the following essays by Willi Marxsen should be made more widely available, especially at this time.

In the essays collected here, Marxsen focuses on the earliest stratum of tradition that can be reconstructed from the synoptic gospels. This material constitutes the greater part of our most direct evidence for encounters between Jesus of Nazareth and his contemporaries, encounters that Marxsen argues should be regarded as the founding events of what in time came to be called the Christian church. As such, this stratum of tradition and the situations it reflects are of special importance to the work of theologians and historians.

Understanding these presynoptic traditions has fundamental importance for accomplishing the task of Christian systematic theology if, as Schubert Ogden has joined Marxsen in arguing, it is this earliest stratum that constitutes the source for reconstructing that "Jesus-kerygma" which is the true "canon before the canon" or "norm of appropriateness" for Christian claims.[2] Ogden has followed Marxsen's lead in arguing with great power and precision for this revisionary alternative to classical Protestant and Roman Catholic interpretations of canonicity in terms of "scripture alone" and "scripture and tradition," respectively. If their arguments for for-

---

*Numbers in parentheses refer to specific page numbers in this volume.

mally identifying the canon in this way are valid, the task of determining the appropriately Christian character of a given claim evidently presupposes understanding the material content and meaning of the presynoptic traditions that comprise this norm. Here Marxsen's work is invaluable, for, as we shall see, he has paid sustained attention to the subject-matter of the Jesus-kerygma in the essays that follow.

Marxsen's explorations in the presynoptic Jesus-traditions are also especially significant in two particular respects for New Testament scholarship at the present time. In the midst of a resurgence of explicitly historical interest in Jesus of Nazareth, Marxsen makes clear that the Jesus who is accessible to historical reconstruction is the always interpreted Jesus of the Jesus-kerygma, rather than a so-called historical Jesus (in the sense of "Jesus without and before any interpretation." [58][3]). This recognition of the "form critical reservation" imposed by the character of our sources serves as a reminder of the limits, as well as of the proper object of historical reconstruction. Secondly, given contemporary emphasis on the narrative character of scripture, including both the gospel genre and pregospel passion accounts, Marxsen's pursuit of the "canon before the canon" to its source in independently circulating Jesus-kerygmata, not all of which have a narrative character, properly relativizes claims to canonical primacy on behalf of narrative as such.

Finally, Marxsen offers several absolutely basic insights into both the logical structure of the remarkably diverse interpretive witnesses to Jesus and the actual processes by which such witnesses were generated. He suggests how and why a wide variety of titles were ascribed to Jesus, how a new and different interest in his "person" came about, and how ritual practices such as baptism and the Lord's Supper took on disparate shapes and meanings. Marxsen's work on these topics has far-reaching implications for both Christian theology and worship.

As we have indicated, Marxsen's work as a whole serves to challenge not only Christian witness, but also the method and content of Christian theology at the most basic level. We might put this somewhat pointedly by saying that his work has proven so far to be too theological for contemporary theology and too exegetical for contemporary exegesis. Indeed, this introductory essay is intended

INTRODUCTION

to clarify and at least partially to justify this polemical claim. In it, we shall first investigate Marxsen's treatment of what he calls the "Jesus-kerygma" contained in the earliest presynoptic traditions, asking what this can tell us about the earliest Christian events. We shall then make explicit some implications of this treatment for both the logical structure and the historical development of Christian witness and theology.

The Jesus-kerygma and the Beginnings of Christianity

What can we learn from extant sources about the earliest traditions of what came to be called "Christianity" and "the church"? This is in the first instance a literary question, insofar as it is directed to texts. Two sets of issues should be mentioned by way of prolegomena.

In the essays collected here, Marxsen directs his attention almost exclusively to the texts collected in the New Testament, which he treats as data for reconstructing traditions and the situations and events they in some way reflect. Since Marxsen does not concern himself with other materials that have recently been claimed to be important to the question he seeks to answer, one will have to take account of any limitations this may impose on his findings in assessing their value.[4]

In addition to the issue of overall approach and the range of his "database," there is the important matter of a method for reconstructing what are widely agreed to be the specifically oral traditions that have come to be incorporated in extant written texts. Marxsen does not address issues related to orality, and only his characteristic caution in drawing conclusions from what are perhaps the inappropriately literate presuppositions of classical form criticism can serve to minimize whatever effects one may take such presuppositions to have upon his work.[5] In short, Marxsen's achievement is intimately tied to his appropriation of form criticism. Its limitations are such as can be shown to inhere in the approach and method this comprises, and these we must leave the reader to decide. Similarly, however, the value of Marxsen's achievement consists in the extent to which he has consistently seen the form critical project through to its logical conclusions. This value, we shall argue, is considerable.

INTRODUCTION

We are now in a position to consider Marxsen's own critical-constructive project. Perhaps most fundamental to it is the use to which he puts a judgment independently arrived at and given powerful mutual corroboration by the so-called kerygma theology inaugurated by Karl Barth and form criticism, particularly in the hands of Rudolf Bultmann: namely, that early Christian traditions have the character of "kerygma," that is, proclamation or, more broadly, witness. These early traditions functioned (and by implication may still do so) to address people in order to call them to the kind of integral, personal response that Bultmann, for example, sought to clarify by critically appropriating the existentialist philosophical anthropology of Martin Heidegger. To speak of such traditions as "kerygma" is therefore to make both a literary or rhetorical judgment about their form or genre (the emphasis of form criticism) and a substantive judgment about their point or meaning as call or witness (as emphasized by kerygma theology).

Marxsen pursues this twofold interpretive judgment more consistently than did either the kerygma theologians or the form critics. In the process, he displays its deeper and broader significance for understanding the earliest Christian texts and their history. In particular, he shows what it means to recognize that the earliest presynoptic traditions have the character of Jesus-kerygma and to treat them consistently as such.

Marxsen clarifies the concept of Jesus-kerygma positively as well as negatively, by specifying both what it does and does not include and imply. In so doing, he addresses basic issues of rhetorical genre, substantive purpose, and, most especially, material content. He points out that, as a category in genre criticism, the concept of kerygma as such has proven useful in understanding the Hebrew Bible. In this rhetorical respect, it is a category neither of Christian religion nor of Greek language (79). He also argues that, in applying the concept to specifically Christian texts, both kerygma theology and form criticism typically equated kerygma as such with distinctively Easter-kerygma, thereby assuming rather than arguing for the presence of the particular material content such an identification implies (78). It is well known that, in contrast to this assumption, the traditions contained in the reconstructed sayings-source Q, for instance, speak neither of cross nor resurrection, yet are substantively kerygmatic in calling people to response.

INTRODUCTION

Moreover, however the events after Jesus' death referred to by the term "Easter" are to be understood, one must not only distinguish the issue of their *causal* influence on presynoptic traditions from that of their influence on the *material content* of such traditions, but must also recognize that both issues are independent of the *date* when these traditions arose and were written down. That various traditions may have been (and probably were) put into written form *after* Easter implies neither that they were formulated *because of* Easter nor that *their contents were shaped* by it. Such influence needs to be shown rather than assumed, as is usual. However, it is by no means clear that much of the presynoptic material shows either causal or material influence by events that occurred after Jesus' death. On reflection, these are basic logical points. And yet it has taken Marxsen's patient pursuit of what speaking of kerygma does and does not imply to make them. Such fundamental considerations open the way to recognizing that presynoptic traditions are kerygmatic in form and substance, even though they may exhibit neither causal nor material influence by the crucifixion or Easter. In other words, there are good reasons to think that there is Christian kerygma, as well as Christian faith, before and also apart from Jesus' death and Easter. But just what does it mean to say this?

Marxsen addresses this question by distinguishing what he calls the "Jesus-kerygma" reflected in the independently circulating presynoptic traditions identified by form criticism from both the "Christ-kerygma," typically represented by prePauline and Pauline materials, and the "Jesus Christ-kerygma" of the synoptic texts themselves. He finds the clue for distinguishing these three forms of early Christian kerygma in the ways various traditions understand and speak of their subject-term as they bear witness to Jesus. This is a material as well as a semantic point. Thus, various presynoptic kerygmata characteristically summon people to response by confronting them in diverse ways with Jesus before his death. The subject-term of such Jesus-kerygma is this "Jesus." To this, Marxsen contrasts a Christ-kerygma, in which traditions about Jesus before his death play less, if any role. Such Christ-kerygma is oriented to the mere fact (the "*dass*") of what is testified to in the Jesus-kerygma, rather than to the Jesus who is its content (the "*was*"). The subject-term of this Christ-kerygma is "Christ." Finally, at the level of the synoptic texts, one reads of the deeds and words

xv

of Jesus Christ. Here, a linguistically mixed form of "Jesus Christ-kerygma" has been created by combining the honorific title "Christ" (= "Messiah"), which has come to be employed as a proper name in the Christ-kerygma, with the one (Jesus) to whom this title has been ascribed.[6] In the essays collected here, Marxsen employs this threefold analysis to relate the history of transmission of early Christian witness to the types of events from which this witness emerged.

We shall focus here on Marxsen's analysis of the presynoptic Jesus-kerygmata for two reasons. These provide what access we have to the originating historical events of what comes to be called Christianity and the church. Moreover, as we have said, Marxsen and Ogden have argued powerfully that it is the meaning to be discerned in these events by which all subsequent claims to pass on this meaning appropriately are ultimately to be judged.

Form criticism (or, in the literal meaning of *Formgeschichte*, form history) has demonstrated that the Jesus-kerygmata arose and circulated as independent units before being incorporated into collections and narratives. Negatively, this means that "it is not as if we only really have the whole once we have the sum of the independent traditions"; positively, it means that "each tradition by itself expresses the whole" (126). Thus, each such Jesus-tradition functions as a discrete, atomic unit, presenting a content sufficient to its kerygmatic purpose.

Marxsen's work permits us to construct a threefold typology of Jesus-kerygmata. This in turn presupposes a more basic twofold analysis of how various presynoptic Jesus-traditions treat their subject-matter, as well as how they communicate it. Anticipating further elaboration and clarification, we can represent the various types of Jesus-kerygma schematically in this way:

subject-matter (*what regarded*)	Jesus-kerygma treatment (*how regarded*)		communicative mode (*how expressed*)
kerygmatic Jesus	distributively as praxis	(1)	sacramental
kerygmatic Jesus	distributively as praxis	(2)	explanatory
kerygmatic Jesus	collectively as person	(3)	explanatory

Thus, we can identify (1) a "praxis-sacramental" type of Jesus-kerygma that communicates situations of encounter with Jesus by representing particular words and deeds expressly as his; (2) a "praxis-explanatory" type in which concepts and symbols are employed in an expressly explanatory manner to interpret encounters with Jesus; and (3) a "person-explanatory" type that reflects acts of ascribing one or another honorific title to Jesus. For the moment, we may simply note that all three types share a common subject-matter that we shall call the "kerygmatic Jesus," although they treat and communicate this in distinctive ways. Marxsen argues, moreover, that all arise directly out of encounters with this Jesus, and that such encounters are the originative Christian events.

It is important to insist that the basic heuristic function of this typology is to serve as a tool for explicating the substantive and rhetorical character of presynoptic Jesus-traditions. The typology may also indirectly serve the related goals of classifying genres and understanding tradition-history.

The "Praxis-Sacramental" Jesus-kerygma

One type of Jesus-kerygma consists in presenting a particular deed or word referred to Jesus as a summons or call to response. Precisely what this "reference to Jesus" entails will become clear as we proceed. For the moment, it is important to note that the concept of Jesus-kerygma presupposes such reference, even if this is not explicitly made but only implied. A word or deed of Jesus might be presented with knowledge of, but without explicit reference to him; this is common in the case of wisdom sayings, for example. Moreover, as nonlinguistic actions, deeds cannot simply by themselves bear such explicit reference. Thus, such words and deeds might well be presented as kerygma, and yet it is only by being brought into connection with Jesus that they can become Jesus-kerygma.[7]

The basic subject-matter of traditions of this first type of Jesus-kerygma is, then, a particular event or situation of praxis, whether an enacted deed or spoken word, and this as referred to Jesus. Marxsen emphasizes that among the earliest presynoptic traditions we can identify two structurally identical versions of this type of witness. Some of these kerygmata focus on *deeds*. For instance, they present Jesus as engaging in table fellowship with unacceptable elements in contemporary society, or performing an exorcism, or breaking the sabbath. In other words, a discrete act is selected as decisive and presented for kerygmatic purposes. Other traditions of this type focus on *words*. These present Jesus as preaching and teaching, perhaps as engaging in a particular situation of controversy or as speaking by means of a parable. In traditions such as these, a saying (perhaps because of its striking content) or a situation of teaching or prophesying (perhaps because of its memorable character) is similarly proclaimed as decisive for its hearers. Thus, each version lifts up a specific feature (whether of behavior or language) of a particular event or situation and presents the Jesus inherent in it, whether "Jesus-in-action" or "Jesus-as-proclaiming." Moreover, as Marxsen observes, "*each* independent tradition contains the *whole*, even if from a differing perspective in each case" (67). And, since "each interprets the other—the proclamation the activity, and the activity the proclamation," what we are introduced to is "in the broadest sense Jesus—not merely his proclamation. This is precisely why I entitle it 'Jesus-*kerygma*' " (131, 82). This type of Jesus-kerygma presents Jesus-as-praxis. As Marxsen puts it, such traditions make reference to "Jesus of Nazareth: An Event" (chap. 4).

Recall that on Marxsen's analysis, each such independent tradition gives expression to a discrete situation of praxis. So also the "whole" or material content of each such kerygma is the Jesus of the concrete occasion of praxis it re-presents—e.g., Jesus here and now plucking grain on the sabbath, there and then uttering a particular saying, and so forth. This type of Jesus-tradition regards its subject-matter, Jesus, in what we may call a particularizing or "distributive" fashion. This point can be made in both specifically grammatical and logical terms. When Jesus is expressly identified as the grammatical subject to whom such deeds and words are attributed or referred, the noun "Jesus" functions as a generic or "collective" term that both derives from and refers to "wholes" made up of such occasions of praxis.[8] From a specifically logical perspective, such deeds and words are the concrete particulars from which the term "Jesus" is abstracted and for which it serves as the generic universal.

Marxsen's account of these Jesus-kerygmata suggests several reasons why they are best understood as a properly "sacramental" communicative medium. On his view, they seek precisely to re-present a concrete occasion of praxis on Jesus' part precisely as a "sign-act" in which, as Marxsen puts it, "Jesus enacts an act of God" (60).[9] In other words, their purpose is to retrieve the concrete, earthly Jesus as word and deed and, in Marxsen's precise sense, "kerygmatically" to pass him on. As Marxsen makes clear, just as it is Jesus in this "broadest sense" who is recalled, so too he can be re-presented by way of speech as well as by way of action. Indeed, this is just what Jesus' followers prove to have done. They engage in this process of memory and tradition both by recounting him as word and by reenacting him as deed. Thus, this type of Jesus-kerygma takes the form of verbal recounting on the one hand, and of ethical-ritual reenactment on the other. For instance, Marxsen makes clear how, just as Jesus engages in striking forms of table fellowship during his life, so the community of his followers "'remembers' just these meals of Jesus, and what was offered to it by Jesus becomes a reality once more" (143). Likewise, Paul calls people who have already been baptized to retrieve such a sign-act for the sake of its implications for ethics (chap. 9). "Word," "sacrament," and "ethics" therefore interpret one another, each form of activity containing the whole and presenting it from a different perspective. Each praxis-sacramental Jesus-kerygma is, then, a sign-act for communicating as concretely as possible the kerygmatic, earthly Jesus.

The "Praxis-Explanatory" Jesus-kerygma

In the essays collected here, Marxsen treats extensively (though he does not explicitly identify) a second basic type of Jesus-kerygma that is relatively yet really distinct both from the praxis-sacramental type we have just considered and from a third type to which we shall turn shortly (one reflected in traditions that transmit the attribution of honorific titles to Jesus). This "praxis-explanatory" type of Jesus-kerygma, as we shall call it, not only shares a single subject-matter with the praxis-sacramental type, namely, Jesus as an event of word and deed, but even treats this in the same distributive way. However, Jesus-kerygmata of this second type differ from those specifically sacramental kerygmata in putting one or another concept or symbol to a distinctly explanatory use in communicating the same kerygmatic Jesus of praxis. For instance, as Marxsen emphasizes, a variety of presynoptic traditions either employ or presuppose terms such as "God's rule (or kingdom)" (*Gottesherrschaft*) and "the finger of God" in the process of communicating the event-character of Jesus' kerygmatic praxis and of encounter with it. Throughout these essays, Marxsen attends to the explanatory use of a wide variety of such terms, including *metanoia* (as "turnabout" or "about-face" [*Umkehr*]), "resurrection of the dead" (and especially its relation to "faith" in chap. 6), and the diverse concepts and symbols employed to explain the significance of Jesus' activity at meals (chap. 8) and of his crucifixion (chap. 7).

This second type of Jesus-kerygma exhibits a more complex logical and hermeneutical structure than that of the sacramental mode of communication we have just considered. At the most formal level, this structure results from its use of distinctively religious concepts and symbols for explanatory purposes. This praxis-explanatory Jesus-kerygma obtains its particular material character through its employment of specifically theistic concepts to explain Jesus-praxis. In order to illustrate both the differences and the similarities between the sacramental and explanatory types of Jesus-kerygma, let us compare two traditions oriented to Jesus-as-word.

First, consider the praxis-sacramental tradition that consists in the proclamation, whether explicitly or implicitly referred to Jesus, of a comparison between plants and their fruit on the one hand and human agents and their acts on the other.[10] Such a comparison makes what I shall call a "connective" use of "first-order" terms regarding plants and persons. For the kerygmatic recounting of this tradition to succeed as a communicative event, the hearer must grasp the relevant connection(s), which in this instance involves a comparison of an existential-ethical character. What we have called the sacramental mode of communication involves such a broadly interpretive act.

With this, compare the independent tradition recorded as Luke 11:20, "(But) if it is by the finger of God that I cast out demons, then God's rule has just come upon you" (my translation). Like the tradition we have just considered, this example of Jesus-kerygma refers (explicitly) to Jesus-as-praxis (Jesus as the "I" in question). However, the concepts or symbols involved have an intrinsically different character and function in a correspondingly different manner. "Finger of God," "demons," and "God's rule" are all what we may call "second-order" terms that are here put to specifically explanatory use. By this I mean two things: (1) that such terms all more or less directly express what Clifford Geertz has called that specifically "religious" combination of cognitive "world-view" and evaluative "ethos," and that, therefore, (2) one must (cognitively) understand the way in which they are used to explain the subject-matter in question in order (evaluatively) to be summoned by the kerygmatic tradition in question.[11] "Finger of God," "demons," "rule of God" are all such cognitive-normative second order terms, in this case of a distinctively theistic character. The tradition under consideration assumes an evaluative understanding of the concept "demons" in presenting its subject-matter as an exorcism, in order to assert a certain assessment of this event of Jesus-praxis. Such an assessment in turn implies the same evaluative understanding of the concepts "finger of God" and "God's rule" that it employs to explain this event. The peculiar character of such an act of religious interpretation, reflecting as it does the specifically explanatory use of second order terms, warrants the distinction of this explanatory type of Jesus-kerygma from the sacramental type discussed earlier. Moreover, it is just this specifically explanatory character which links this type of Jesus-kerygma to a third type reflected in materials that express the act of bestowing an honorific title upon Jesus. To this we now turn.

The "Person-Explanatory" Jesus-kerygma

On Marxsen's showing, this third basic type of Jesus-kerygma deals with the same subject-matter as that of the praxis-sacramental and praxis-explanatory forms, namely, the kerygmatic Jesus. We shall designate this the "person-explanatory" type of Jesus-kerygma in order to distinguish its treatment of this subject-matter from that of the two praxis-types on the one hand, and to express its affinity with the specifically explanatory-type of praxis-kerygma on the other.

Marxsen argues that this type of Jesus-kerygma, like the other two, is reflected in traditions that were originally independent rhetorical units and that have become incorporated into more complex traditions at both presynoptic and synoptic levels. Moreover, he holds such acts of ascribing titles to Jesus reflect the same sort of originative encounter as that exhibited by the praxis-traditions.

Nonetheless, these naming-kerygmata differ significantly in their structural character from both types of praxis-kerygma, even as they share an explanatory approach to communicating their subject-matter with the praxis-explanatory type of Jesus-kerygma we have identified. It will prove important to specify these relations of difference and similarity rather precisely. For, as Marxsen himself explicitly indicates and as his treatment of these issues implies, misunderstandings on this score have led to exegetical and theological confusion of the most basic and serious kind.

Consider for the moment Marxsen's summary reconstruction of the type of situation reflected in traditions such as those incorporated in Mark 8:27-29, in which Peter is presented as ascribing the title "the Christ" to Jesus.

> Various people stand face to face with Jesus. They hear him speak; they see him do something. This speaking and acting of Jesus quite obviously makes different impressions on the witnesses. Some are moved by it; others it leaves cold; still others are repulsed or angered by it. The same speaking and acting of Jesus has completely different effects on those who experience it. And now these people reflect; they consider. They experience Jesus speaking and acting, but it has different effects on them. Still, on the basis of these different effects, they reason back to the one from whom the effects proceed. And now they give Jesus different names: positive, neutral, or even negative (4).

Note that this situation is the same as those reflected in the praxis-traditions. People meet Jesus, which is to say they encounter the praxis of a variety of particular deeds and words: exorcisms and other healings, conduct involving choice of companions and ritual matters, pronouncements of various kinds, and the like. We are presented with a dipolar event of encounter between Jesus and people, people and Jesus. Certain people who are positively moved by such praxis then respond by giving him a name or title: "You are the Christ" (Mark 8:29).

To be sure, Mark presents such an originative act of ascribing a title (not to be fused or confused with subsequent acts of employing and transmitting titles) as something that occurs in the immediate presence of Jesus before his death (as distinct from his corporeal absence, whether before or after his death). Mark also presents this act as paradigmatic, and as in service of his own material interpretation. In his reconstructive analysis of the naming-traditions, Marxsen is able effectively to prescind from all three features. Moreover, Mark's presentation of the proximity and dating of such encounters may or may not be historically accurate. In any event, unless one takes the extreme view that the kerygmatic impact of Jesus' words and deeds is strictly inseparable from this immediate corporeal proximity (and thus must be strictly contemporaneous), these circumstantial factors cannot be regarded as essential to either its constitution or its continuation. In this respect, it is unimportant whether people ascribed titles to Jesus in immediate encounter with him before his death or did so by retrieving him through memory in his corporeal absence after (or even before!) his death. What is decisive, rather, is how the Jesus who is the referent of such acts of naming is understood—this Jesus who must also be the criterion of interpretive validity for any subsequent act of naming, insofar as it means to refer to this same Jesus. It is this Jesus, the Jesus of praxis, who is the criterion, if not always the occasion for the ascriptions of titles. And this remains the case even if such a Jesus is only ever known to us by way of Jesus-kerygma.

Marxsen makes clear that the Jesus who is the subject-matter of such originative acts of naming is identical to the one attested in the praxis-oriented kerygmata, even if these traditions regard Jesus in a different way. As we have seen, praxis-sacramental kerygmata in particular re-present the kerygmatic Jesus by reenacting and retelling various particular deeds and words that communicate him. Marxsen's reconstruction makes clear how the entitling-traditions in their earliest forms comprise responses to and proclaim the same Jesus. They differ from both types of praxis-kerygma insofar as they proclaim the person Jesus, rather than particular events of praxis. Here we recall a point made earlier in both grammatical and logical terms. The subject-matter of the entitling-traditions is Jesus taken "collectively" as person, whereas that of both types of praxis-kerygma is Jesus taken "distributively" as particular words and deeds. And yet it is in how they construe Jesus, not in the Jesus they construe, that the difference consists. More precisely, the person- and praxis-kerygmata share an identical referent; they differ only in how they refer to this referent. Since such entitling-traditions proclaim the person Jesus, not Jesus-as-praxis, they constitute a "person-type" of Jesus-kerygma. For all this, the person- and praxis-types of Jesus-kerygma share the same subject-matter, namely, the (person) Jesus of kerygmatic word and deed.

These person-oriented traditions differ from the sacramental type of Jesus-kerygma in the way they communicate Jesus, and this different mode of communication is what they share with the praxis-explanatory traditions. Strictly speaking, titles (such as "the Christ") properly function not simply as "names" that ostensively denote Jesus, but precisely as concepts or symbols used to explain his decisive significance in the service of communicating him (chap. 1). Like other such terms used directly to explain praxis, titles must be both understood and connected to their referent, the person Jesus, in order thereby indirectly to explain Jesus-as-event.

Finally, Marxsen argues that, like the praxis-kerygmata, these entitling-traditions comprise discrete and independently circulating units of presynoptic tradition. Thus, as each of the independent praxis-traditions "contains the *whole*, even if from a differing perspective in each case," so, "each particular title serves to make *the same* statement," namely, that "people who encountered Jesus had experiences that they really could only have expected from God" (67, 7). Moreover, as each sacramental kerygma at first independently re-presents a situation of Jesus-as-praxis by reenacting and recounting words and deeds as his, and as each praxis-explanatory tradition communicates such an event by employing terms such as "God's rule" and "saving well-being" (*Heil*), so, too, the presynoptic person-kerygmata employ various titles in explaining the significance of this same kerygmatic, earthly Jesus. All three types of Jesus-kerygma not only share a common subject-matter and form history, but also bear witness to a common set of originative events. Each unit of Jesus-tradition is an independent variation on a single theme, and this theme is people's encounter with Jesus.

The Jesus-kerygma and Its Interpretation

While in these essays Marxsen's primary focus is the exegesis of the Jesus-kerygma, he also suggests the broader significance of this contribution for both the history of doctrine and systematic theology. To this dual end, he (1) engages the history of research in order to propose conceptual resources that are more adequate to understanding the Jesus-kerygma, and (2) clarifies the structural developments and transformations it undergoes in the earliest Christian period. We shall briefly consider each topic in turn.

The History of Research

The recognition that it is the kerygmatic Jesus of word and deed who is the subject-matter of the diverse Jesus-kerygmata is the basis for a variety of critical analyses and constructive proposals that Marxsen puts forward in these essays. Thus, for instance, he engages the history of research to argue that so-called orthodox, liberal, and kerygma theology alike have formulated a "false set of alternatives" in asking whether Jesus is the "bearer or content" of the gospel (chap. 3). Such a dichotomy only reflects basic confusions that haunt both exegesis and christology, because it implies *a forced choice between two misunderstandings* of Jesus. Since it presents two equally misguided approaches as the exclusive options for interpretation, it ironically prevents the approach embodied in the Jesus-kerygma from even being considered.

The first approach interprets Jesus as the "content" rather than the "bearer" of the gospel. Whether it finds expression in more traditional or more modern terminology, the entire line of christological reflection typical of classical orthodoxy draws a distinction between the "person" and "work" of Jesus (Christ) that implies a different understanding of Jesus from the one reflected in the Jesus-kerygma. For, whereas the Jesus-kerygma looks either to Jesus-as-praxis or to the person Jesus, classical christology looks to a "person of" Jesus that is different from, because additional to, this. As we have seen, the praxis-oriented kerygmata regard Jesus distributively as word and deed, and the person-oriented kerygmata regard Jesus collectively as generalized from word and deed. However, classical christology in all its forms takes as a constitutive feature of its subject-matter Jesus "in his person," which is to say, Jesus as "behind" or in one way or another inferred from word and deed. This is a fundamental ontic as well as epistemic point, as I will now seek to clarify.

On the one hand, the point is ontic because such an approach looks to a different subject-matter from that of the Jesus-kerygma.

As we have seen, the subject-matter of all types of Jesus-kerygma is Jesus in relation to people—what we have called the kerygmatic Jesus. Even the person-oriented entitling-kerygmata proclaim not the person of, but rather the person, Jesus. For the Jesus of the Jesus-kerygma in all its forms is not simply a source of or agent behind praxis, but rather is the directly encountered praxis or person himself. As the Jesus-kerygma presents him, the relevant Jesus is the related Jesus. In the technical terminology of classical dogmatics, the Jesus of the Jesus-kerygma *in se* is not (as in classical christology) Jesus *a se* or *pro patri*, but rather Jesus *pro aliis*. If the subject-matter of the Jesus-kerygma is itself a relation, then this is intrinsically (*in se*) relational. The recognition of this fundamental logical point serves not to deny, but critically to test such theologoumena as the *vere homo-vere deus* for their appropriateness to the Jesus-kerygma. As Marxsen puts it, this ancient christological confession "is not to be treated in isolation as a statement about the character of the person." The point of the Jesus-kerygma is rather to communicate (and here, to explain) that "through a human being (who was a human being, really human and nothing but human), there breaks in the rule of God that only God can bring. And as the one who brings God's rule, this human being is experienced really and entirely as God" (34f). To speak of Jesus as *vere homo-vere deus* is therefore to assert this of the person Jesus in relation to people, but not (and not also) of the person of Jesus in relation to God (the Father). To do so would be to introduce a new, because additional, datum into the subject-matter at issue.

From an epistemic point of view, access to such an additional datum requires what could never be anything besides an inference regarding Jesus' relation to God based on words and deeds. For as analysis of the Jesus-kerygma shows, it is these alone that people ever did or ever do encounter. Naturally, such an inference implies a justificatory procedure appropriate to it. As it happens, two basic types of justification have been attempted. On the one hand, there is the inductive approach that characterizes historical-hermeneutical "quests" for Jesus, whether old or new. On the other hand, there are the various deductive approaches that characterize classical dogmatic christology as such, whether this be of the traditionally a priori or more modern "transcendental" type. However, not only are these two approaches logically incompatible (contingent facts and conceptual necessities cannot both justify the same assertion) but, as Marxsen points out, each leads to its own misunderstanding of response to Jesus. For, as Marxsen makes clear, the Jesus-kerygmata regard response to Jesus as personal acts of "risk" (*Wagnis*), of "giving oneself over to" (*sich einlassen auf*) Jesus, or of "being moved" (*betroffen*) by him. As the kerygma theology of both Barth and Bultmann rightly saw, the attempt "to insure the content of the confession of faith by way of historical investigation detracts from the risk of faith. However, this corrupts faith completely; it is no longer faith at all" (48f). But deductive approaches commit their own version of the same error, the only difference being that their assertions claim necessity rather than probability for themselves. Thus, both forms of classical christological argument misrepresent the logic of the epistemic act of direct personal response to the person Jesus, because both alike misrepresent the ontic correlate of this act as the person of Jesus, which can only be indirectly inferred from encounter with him. Such classical approaches therefore miss the "point of christology."[12] In contrast, Marxsen seeks to ward off such misunderstandings by speaking of faith's object as "Jesus of Nazareth: An Event" (chap. 4) and of "Christian Faith as Resurrection of the Dead" (chap. 6).

Marxsen is also clear that treating Jesus as the "bearer," rather than the "content," of the gospel has led to a related set of errors which, in this case, characterizes liberal or revisionary forms of christology. As we have seen, whereas for the Jesus-kerygma, "person" and "praxis" are two analytically distinct ways of speaking about a single and integral subject-matter, to regard Jesus as the "bearer" of a "gospel" is rather to envisage two really separable subject-matters. Thus, as "bearer," Jesus is understood now as "example," "paradigm," "hero," "martyr," or "great personage," as the "author" or "agent" who "bears" a "content" taken to comprise a "message," "teachings," or "social program." Such approaches misdirect attention either toward a "who" it is that happens to bear certain words or deeds, or to a "what" that happens to be said or done. In contrast, the Jesus-kerygma regards Jesus and gospel as inseparable. For the Jesus of the Jesus-kerygma is the person Jesus as acting and speaking; the gospel of the Jesus-kerygma is this same Jesus-as-praxis.

This fundamental insight also lies behind Marxsen's effort in chapter 2 to clarify his claim that "the Jesus-business (*die Sache Jesu*) continues" and, thereby, to defend it against what he alleges are misunderstandings. A word about this translation of the concept *Sache Jesu* will serve to make this point. I have chosen the phrase "the Jesus-business" in an effort to express that what is at issue is a single, atomic "whole," the "event" of Jesus as a sign-act of enacted word or spoken deed. Thus, the basic point is not how the word *Sache* is translated, but rather that the phrase *die Sache Jesu* be rendered in such a way as to indicate that the datum or subject-matter to which it refers is an integral and noncomposite reality. Translations such as the "cause" or "purpose of Jesus," or even the "work" or "ministry of Jesus," only mirror the kinds of misconstruals we have just considered—misconstruals that lead to the sorts of false alternatives that Marxsen deplores and seeks to overcome.[13] However, the "Jesus-business" properly "continues" precisely and only insofar as concrete events of kerygmatic praxis are reenacted in similarly kerygmatic words and deeds of his followers. Then, and only then, does Jesus "still come today" (18).

The Development of the Jesus-kerygma

To this engagement of the history of research correspond Marxsen's efforts to identify, to account for, and to assess a variety of developments and transformations of the Jesus-kerygma. While these must be regarded as very fluid and complex processes that have not been at all adequately investigated historically, we can at least point to some of what Marxsen takes to be the most fundamental features of such change.

As we have seen, Marxsen uses the insights of form history and criticism to identify a presynoptic Jesus-kerygma that was influenced neither by the language of Easter nor by faith *in* Jesus (Christ). However, at the level of the synoptic texts themselves, as well as in the remaining literature of the New Testament, we do note one or both such kinds of influence (even if only at Matt. 18:6 and 27:42 in the latter respect). Moreover, it is striking that, "the branch of tradition which, *expressis verbis*, takes its bearings from faith in Jesus (Christ), for all practical purposes completely ignores the Jesus-traditions" (86). In order to account for these phenomena, Marxsen argues that, "the explanation closest to hand (and plainly demanded by the fundamental insights of form criticism) remains that of supposing that there were two early communities (*Urgemein-den*)" (86). One such community seems to originate in encounter with the earthly Jesus before his death and to proclaim and enact what it understands as his kerygmatic praxis. The Jesus-kerygma is our primary evidence for this community. A second community seems to have originated with Easter-experiences subsequent to Jesus' crucifixion. For this, the earliest reconstructable traditions of the so-called Christ-kerygma are our primary evidence. How are we to understand these two communities and their witness in relation to each other?

In the essays collected here, Marxsen restricts himself to the latter aspect of this question.[14] He is clear that we can compare such traditions only by identifying the subject-matter at issue in each case, not by simply comparing the terms and concepts in which the subject-matter is presented. This is a basic, logical point. Since it is these terms and concepts that we seek to compare, we need a variable or *tertium comparationis* of which they are specific values.

As we have seen, Marxsen argues that, in the case of the Jesus-kerygma, this subject-matter is understood formally as "a faith that was initiated by Jesus," and more substantively as "an event of being moved" (*betroffen*) (88). Indeed, it is the very pervasiveness of disagreement and controversy reflected in the Jesus-kerygma that confirms this understanding of the subject-matter at issue. As he says, "in the manner, speaking, and acting of Jesus there was evidently an element that forced one to engage in criticism and, in so doing, to form an opinion" (5). For example, while some were moved positively and explained his exorcisms and healings in terms of "the finger of God," others invoked the name of Beelzebub in order to explain their negative reaction. Some people followed him, while others managed to dispose of him by means of crucifixion. Overtly contradictory evaluations of Jesus therefore contend with each other from the outset.

However, Marxsen also mentions a third response. Recall that, while some react positively or negatively to Jesus, others he "leaves cold" (4). Indeed, Marxsen suggests that the parable of the ten lepers in Luke 17:11–19 is meant to indicate that such a neutral response precisely fails to grasp that kerygmatic character of encounter with Jesus to which both his followers and opponents bear witness, each in their own way (69,110). Such traditions show that it always was—and still is—possible to miss, even if perhaps only by resisting, this kerygmatic point. The diversity of response indicates that we should not take for granted a common basis of approach to Jesus. But then, neither should we take for granted a corresponding continuity among traditions that develop over time.

As we have seen, Marxsen argues that all types of Jesus-kerygma share a common understanding of a single subject-matter, namely, the kerygmatic Jesus. They regard encounter with Jesus as *an indivisible, as well as an inherently kerygmatic event*. Such an understanding finds expression in sacramental modes of communication, in the way symbols such as "God's rule" and "turnabout" (*metanoia*; *Umkehr*) are used to explain this encounter, and in acts of ascribing titles to the person Jesus. Marxsen also argues throughout these essays that some, though by no means all, of the expressions of Christ-kerygma and Jesus Christ-kerygma also share this same subject-matter of the kerygmatic Jesus. Such traditions may speak of "appearances" of the "exalted" or "risen" one who was crucified; of the Jesus whose "parousia" could only be awaited anew; of him, encounter with whom brings "eternal life," "resurrection from the dead," "justification," "reconciliation," "new creation." In so doing, Marxsen illustrates how a wide variety of current forms of expression were enlisted to formulate appropriate expressions and explanations of this shared subject-matter. To the extent that such appropriate lines of development do in fact emerge, the traditions which come from and develop out of the two early communities converge and corroborate each other in witnessing to an indivisible and inherently kerygmatic event of encounter with Jesus.

However, Marxsen also shows that people did not always treat encounter with Jesus as the indivisible and kerygmatic subject-matter both his followers and his opponents took this to be, nor did they always go on subsequently to understand it in this way. While we can only briefly and selectively illustrate Marxsen's interpretation of how this did and did not occur, both the illustrations and their implications are remarkable.

1. *"God's rule."* Marxsen argues that, as the Jesus-kerygma employs this concept, "it belongs to the essence of the rule of God not to be a state of affairs, but rather to break in again and again" (63). To this, he contrasts another explanatory use of the same term, which he accordingly translates "kingdom of God" in order

to signal that, on this view, "God will establish a new state of affairs, at the beginning of which the dead will be raised and the living and (raised) dead will be judged" (63). What some either take or employ as a way of explaining *indivisible events* of kerygmatic encounter, others use to describe intrinsically *divisible states of affairs*.

2. *Jesus' crucifixion and death.* People either witness or learn about the crucifixion and death of Jesus. However, as Marxsen indicates, they proceed to view and to explain this subject-matter in incompatible ways. On the one hand, it is properly regarded as an indivisible, kerygmatic challenge, like other encounters with Jesus in these basic respects. Thus, it may be explained either with recourse to the terminology of atonement as a "salvation-event" or as paradigmatic of encounters with Jesus before his death, always themselves "*on the brink of* the cross" because of the risk they involved (122,135). On the other hand, Jesus' death can also be inappropriately treated as a *discrete* item in an *additive sequence*: namely, as the last event in Jesus' career, now understood in relation to this telos. Thus, one may look to the course of Jesus' life, perhaps regard its components as complementary "stations" on the "way unto death" of a martyr, or even make inferences about the person of Jesus, whether concerning his relation to God or to his own "fate". Here, however, we are confronted with a subject-matter that is composite and inferential. Such explanations are discrepant with the subject-matter of the Jesus-kerygma.

3. *Titles of Jesus.* As we have seen, the Jesus-kerygma reflects diverse acts of ascribing titles to the person Jesus in response to events of praxis. Thus, "each independent title serves to make *the same* statement. For in all the titles what is aimed at is precisely that they identify a bearer who has a specific commission from God" (8). Insofar as such acts keep to what Marxsen calls the "direction" of movement *from* the encounter with Jesus *to* the particular title used to explain his role in occasioning it, they are structurally appropriate to their subject-matter, however conceptually diverse they may be (11). However, this direction can be—and not infrequently is—reversed, so that one reasons from *title* to *subject-matter*, as if the title itself, not Jesus, were the starting point. Such an approach is discontinuous with the person-oriented Jesus-traditions, for one infers from various titles discrete qualities taken compositely to

characterize the person of Jesus, independent of the person Jesus in some actual relation of encounter. Thus, both the integrity and the kerygmatic character of the subject-matter are lost.

4. *The Lord's Supper.* Marxsen understands the activity of followers of Jesus to have included (and here he points to a Jerusalem community oriented to Easter-experiences) "gathering at a common meal, which was the distinctive way in which they had experienced communion with God and each other anyway" (141). He argues that people "remember" kerygmatic encounter with Jesus at meals during his life by sacramentally reenacting it in the acts of breaking and circulating bread and passing a cup around the table, and by explaining such "saving activity" in language drawn variously from sacrificial covenant terminology ("blood"), political philosophy ("body"), and apocalypticism (*maranatha*, "Come, Lord") (142f.). Whether such a retrieval of encounter with Jesus occurs temporally by way of "memory," or comes to be explained materially by way of sacred food, insofar as it is oriented to the re-presentation of this subject-matter it is congruent with the content of the Jesus-kerygma. In either case, it is not the explanatory concepts themselves, but the encounter with Jesus to which such traditions testify. As in each of these examples, discrete and diverse explanations are not to be confused with and thereby objectified into substitutes for the event they are meant to explain. "God's rule" is not a "state of affairs"; Jesus' death is not an "atoning sacrifice"; to call Jesus "Son of God" is not to infer discrete qualities of his person; to speak performatively of bread and wine as "body" and "blood" is not to refer to "elements."

5. *Doctrine and ethics.* Finally, the Jesus-kerygma concerns Jesus as deed and word or, more inclusively, Jesus-as-praxis. It is this that is the "Jesus-business." However, "Jesus' message can be turned into doctrine, and this doctrine into a program" (130). The event of being moved by Jesus, explained as a "resurrection of the dead" that puts all worldly laws "at risk," can be transformed into such moral rules as make prediction and calculation possible in human affairs (112). However, if the Jesus-business is to continue and if Jesus is still to "come today," this can happen only *as* praxis and as risk *in response to* such praxis. Once again, what is an indivisible encounter is not to be transmuted into a composite of beliefs or rules. For it is not so in the Jesus-kerygma. As Marxsen puts the

point succinctly, "*each* independent tradition contains the *whole*, even if from a differing perspective in each case. In this way, each tradition both expresses and invites one into the experience of the whole" (67).

Not only from the outset, but also as traditions developed, various ways emerged of understanding and misunderstanding such "wholes." These traditions do not display any uniform line of development. However, the illustrations we have identified all do exhibit a common structural logic. In each, *what is properly an explanation of something else becomes itself something to be explained.* "The kingdom of God," the crucifixion as one in a sequence of saving events, titles as bases for inference about the person of Jesus, eucharistic "elements," or Christian praxis as doctrinal beliefs and moral rules—all are examples of this fallacy of "reified explanation," whereby an indivisible "whole" of encounter is transformed into a logically different subject-matter made up of composite data.

It is these "wholes," these events of encounter with the kerygmatic Jesus that certain people took as decisive for their lives and explained to others in concepts that include or presuppose the word "God," that Marxsen is concerned to clarify and also to re-present in the essays that follow. And it is to such experiences of understanding and encounter that the reader is now invited.

NOTES

1. The three volumes of collected essays are: *Der Exeget als Theologe: Vorträge zum Neuen Testament* (Gütersloh: Gütersloher Verlagshaus Gerd Mohn, 1968), *Die Sache Jesu geht weiter* (Gütersloh: Gütersloher Verlagshaus Gerd Mohn, 1976), and *Christologie—praktisch* (Gütersloh: Gütersloher Verlagshaus Gerd Mohn, 1978). Only one essay from among the three collections, "Die sogennanten Heilsereignisse zwischen Karfreitag und Pfingsten" (*Die Sache Jesu geht weiter*, 72–81), has been published in English, as "The So-called Saving Events between Good Friday and Pentecost," *Australian Biblical Review* 27 (October 1979): 15–23.

2. See especially Willi Marxsen, *Das Neue Testament als Buch der Kirche* (Gütersloh: Gütersloher Verlagshaus Gerd Mohn, 1966). ET *The New Testament as the Church's Book*, trans. James E. Mignard (Philadelphia: Fortress, 1966). Also Schubert M. Ogden, *On Theology* (San Francisco: Harper & Row, 1986), 45–68, and "Sources of Religious Authority in Liberal Protestantism, *Journal of the American Academy of Religion* 44 (1976): 403–16.

3. *Jesus and Easter: Did God Raise the Historical Jesus from the Dead?* trans. Victor Paul Furnish (Nashville: Abingdon, 1990), 16.

4. See, for instance, Helmut Koester, *Ancient Christian Gospels* (Philadelphia: Trinity Press International, 1991), which employs such materials and seeks to assess their significance for this task.

5. On this point, see especially Werner H. Kelber, *The Oral and the Written Gospel* (Philadelphia: Fortress, 1983).

6. Marxsen addresses these issues at length in his substantial article, "Christology in the N.T." in the supplementary volume of the *Interpreter's Dictionary of the Bible* (Nashville: Abingdon, 1976), 146–56.

7. Indeed, praxis must itself be referred (even if such a reference is only implicit) to Jesus in order for such a tradition to be regarded as *Jesus*-kerygma at all. In this respect, such a connection is functionally equivalent to the attribution of words and deeds to Jesus in praxis-sacramental kerygmata. Thus, even if one were able not only to identify, but also effectively to employ a criterion for distinguishing the "authentic" praxis of Jesus—a condition that is scarcely to be assumed to be met, since we lack precisely

the sorts of autographs that would seem to be presupposed by such a criterion (see 26;57;93;125)—such praxis could only be regarded as Jesus-kerygma if it at least made this reference to Jesus. In this case, so far as Jesus' own praxis is concerned, only that which were self-referential (such as might perhaps be taken to be exemplified, for instance, in the "Son of Man" sayings) could constitute Jesus-kerygma. Absent such reference, the kerygma of Jesus is not to be regarded as Jesus-kerygma and, as such, is not to be called "Christian." This interpretation of the validity conditions of Julius Wellhausen's famous dictum that, "Jesus was not a Christian, but a Jew" differs from that presupposed by Marxsen, who argues that Jesus "precedes all Christian faith. However, he precedes it in such a way that, as 'pioneer' of the very same event of being moved, he also always belongs to this faith. . . . But in this case, one can also venture the claim that Jesus was the first Christian" (95). On my view, once we have Jesus-kerygma, but only then, do we have "Christianity," in the sense implied by Wellhausen's remark. Whether such Christianity remains a "Judaism" seems to me to be now (even as it was then!) a decision precisely for Jews, not for Christians. For a wide-ranging examination of this complex of issues that admits the view proposed here, see Hans Dieter Betz, "Wellhausen's Dictum, 'Jesus was not a Christian, but a Jew' in Light of Present Scholarship," *Studia Theologica* 45 (1991): 83–110.

8. For the way in which this point may be manifested syntactically, see Herbert Weir Smyth, *A Greek Grammar for Colleges* (New York: American Book Co., 1920), §1119–1124.

9. For this term, see James F. White, *Introduction to Christian Worship, Revised Edition* (Nashville: Abingdon, 1990). White builds especially on the work of Edward Schillebeeckx in *Christ the Sacrament of Encounter with God* (Sheed & Ward: Mission, Kans., 1963).

10. Such a tradition can be reconstructed from the various texts enumerated by John S. Kloppenborg, *Q Parallels* (Sonoma, Calif.: Polebridge Press, 1988), 42–45. Kloppenborg lists Matt. 7:15–20; Matt. 12:33–35; Luke 6:43–45; Did, 11:8; James 3:12; G. Thom. 43 and 45; Prov. 12:14 LXX. In my view, one is justified in reconstructing a form of this tradition that is independent of references to "the Lord" in Did. 11:8 and "the Jews" in G. Thom. 43, and it is such a form that I attend to here.

11. *The Interpretation of Cultures: Selected Essays* (New York: Basic Books, 1973), 126f.

12. As Schubert M. Ogden argues in ways that provide powerful corroboration of a systematic character to Marxsen's more historical investigations. See *The Point of Christology* (San Francisco: Harper & Row, 1982).

13. Nigel M. Watson seems to miss this point in "The Cause of Jesus Continues? An Investigation of the Intention of Willi Marxsen," *Australian Biblical Review* 25 (1977): 21–28.

14. On the former, see Marxsen's discussion in *"Christliche" und christliche Ethik im Neuen Testament* (Gütersloh: Gütersloher Verlagshaus Gerd Mohn, 1989), esp. 39–58.

1

JESUS HAS MANY NAMES*

Who is Jesus? To a Christian, this question seems superfluous, because the answer to it cannot really be in doubt. But the New Testament shows us that the answer we would probably give is at least not self-evident. This becomes clear as soon as we approach the first of the texts printed in our program:

> And Jesus went on with his disciples to the villages of Cae-
> sarea Philippi; and on the way he asked his disciples, "Who
> do the people say that I am?" And they told him, "You are
> John the Baptizer; and others say, you are Elijah; and others,
> that you are one of the prophets." And he asked them, "But
> you; who do you say that I am?" Peter answered him, "You
> are the Christ." (Mark 8:27-29)

Here we hear of a conversation on the road that Jesus has with his disciples in the vicinity of Caesarea Philippi. It concerns our question, "Who is Jesus?" Twice it is asked and twice answered, but the answers don't agree. First, "Who do *the people* say that I am?" and then, "Who do *you* say that I am?" The people say, "John the Baptizer or Elijah or one of the prophets." But the disciples say (through Peter's mouth) that Jesus is the Christ—and that means the Messiah.

*"Jesus hat viele Namen," *Der Exeget als Theologe* (Gütersloh: Gütersloher Verlagshaus Gerd Mohn, 1968), 214–25. (This was originally delivered at the twelfth Deutschen Evangelischen Kirchentag in Köln on July 30, 1965 and was first published in *Bibelkritik und Gemeindefrömmigkeit* (Gütersloh: Gütersloher Verlagshaus Gerd Mohn, 1966), 32–47.

Before discussing what the various answers mean, we want to make a few observations that are significant for our further reflections. The question who Jesus is is evidently necessary, because otherwise it would not have been asked. However, it is necessary because one could not immediately tell who Jesus was. To begin with, he was certainly (to stand in front of him and look at him) just a man; he had been "found in human form." It was not possible simply to read off this man Jesus of Nazareth who he was. However, since this could not be done, the question who he was could be answered in various ways, and indeed, this is just what happened.

Now people in our time obviously want to say that there are right and wrong answers here. But how are we to determine which answer is right and which is wrong (or at least insufficient)?

We need to pay attention to *who* gives the answers in any particular case. Some people say, "John the Baptizer, Elijah or one of the prophets." The people's way of characterizing Jesus speaks highly of him, not poorly. This has to be understood in the context of the ideas of the time. It was expected that at the end of time, immediately before the great day of God broke in, great figures of the past (in particular such as had not died, but had been carried off) would again come to earth. Their coming was supposed to be an indication that the end was at hand. One now had to prepare oneself for the coming of the day of God. By calling Jesus "Elijah," for example, people are saying, "It is the one who comes immediately before the end." Thus, he is something like the forerunner of the end— and therefore something like John the Baptizer. We see that the answer of the people holds Jesus in very high esteem.

Nevertheless, the second answer makes clear that this opinion on the part of the people is not entirely sufficient. Peter characterizes Jesus (in the name of the disciples) as the Christ. This is clearly supposed to say more, although (and this needs to be emphasized once again) what more can in no way be read off Jesus. If it could have been, then the others would also have been able to give the answer that the disciples give here. But they don't. What is the connection here?

We shall want to pursue this question presently. But first, we want to look around a bit further in the gospels. Thus far, we have established that, although very lofty names can be given to Jesus, Peter outdoes these by giving him an even higher one, "Christ."

Alongside these positive names for Jesus, however, we also hear of others in the gospels that are precisely negative. The mother and brothers of Jesus took him for crazy. Opponents said of him that he was a deceiver of the people. And even where Jesus did something that was apparently unambiguous, where he drove out demons, where all the bystanders could now see that someone who had been possessed had been healed, there it was said, "Here Beelzebub is driven out through Beelzebub," that is, "the devil is working through Jesus." Finally, one might be referred to Jesus' crucifixion. If it had been possible unambiguously to read off Jesus that he was more than just a human being, that he was the Messiah or (as is added in Peter's answer in the Gospel of Matthew-16:16) that he was the Son of God, then the Jews would scarcely have brought him to the cross. When they condemned him and delivered him up to Pilate, they were honestly of the opinion that they were doing away with a deceiver of the people and a blasphemer.

Therefore, we ought not to allow ourselves to be misled concerning our question by the presentations which our gospels (and particularly the Gospel of John) offer. They give us a completely different impression. There we see the Son of God striding in majesty over the earth. This is entirely obvious to every reader of the gospels. Nevertheless, we have to say that this was not the historical picture of Jesus.

When I speak here of the historical picture, I mean the picture that could be directly read off Jesus—that could be photographed, so to speak. Even this (historical) picture was ambiguous. However, the picture the gospels draw is not merely an historical report that remained ambiguous, but rather a picture of Jesus that has been seen with the eyes of faith. Unbelievers would have drawn the picture of Jesus completely differently. And yet in both cases we have to do with the representation of one and the same person, with the representation of one and the same happening. The merely historical picture is therefore open to various interpretations. And only because this is so, as we have said, were the questions possible, "Who do the people say that I am? Who do you say that I am?" If the picture of Jesus had been unambiguous, these questions would have been meaningless as questions.

But from all this it now follows that the answers that were given to these questions are not self-explanatory. For this reason, we must now consider how the different answers came to be given. In doing so, it is worth noticing that the answers are always indissolubly linked to the people who give them, be this the disciples, other people, or the opponents. Therefore, the question who Jesus is can by no means be answered merely by looking at Jesus. Rather, we simply have to include the people to whom the question is put and who now give *their* answer. I want to express this differently one more time. It is quite obviously the case that the question who Jesus is can by no means be answered unambiguously. The only question that can be answered is the question who Jesus is *for particular individuals*, for each of these is convinced of having given the correct answer. And now, once more: how did these different answers come to be given?

First, let us consider this more from a formal than from a material point of view. Various people stand face to face with Jesus. They hear him speak; they see him do something. This speaking and acting of Jesus quite obviously makes different impressions on the witnesses. Some are moved by it; others it leaves cold; still others are repulsed or angered by it. The same speaking and acting of Jesus has completely different effects on those who experience it. And now these people reflect; they consider. They experience Jesus speaking and acting, but it has different effects on them. Still, on the basis of these different effects, they reason back to the one from whom the effects proceed. And now they give Jesus different names: positive, neutral, or even negative.

Therefore, the names people give to Jesus are a result of a process of reflection. By no means will this always have been intentional. It may have occurred quite impulsively, for whoever was angered by the speaking and acting of Jesus would have said, "This Jesus of Nazareth is a great charlatan and deceiver. He is Beelzebub, the devil. He is a blasphemer and a deceiver of the people." On the other hand, anyone who was attentive to the speaking and acting of Jesus would have said, "He is indeed one of the forerunners of the kingdom of God." However, the person who was moved might have said, "He is the Messiah." So, this is the way it is with this business: the names, and to be sure *all* the names—the negative, the neutral, and the positive ones—were the result of a process of reflection people engaged in based on the experiences they had

4

with Jesus. And just as these experiences were different, so also people arrived at different names for Jesus.

Now in Jesus' manner, in his speaking and acting, there obviously lay an element that forced one to form an opinion. But this means that in his manner, in the speaking and acting of Jesus, there was an element that forced one to *criticize* him. (We ought not to understand the word "criticism" negatively, as is usually done.) Criticism has to do with separation and discrimination. Even the person who gives Jesus a positive name engages in criticism, since from among many possible names such a person critically selects one, decides critically on one of them.

(A great deal would be gained in our discussions if we would realize that criticism is in the first instance a neutral act which then, to be sure, leads to an appraisal. Even the person who calls Jesus the Christ therefore engages in criticism and makes a critical decision.)

I was saying: in the manner, speaking, and acting of Jesus there was evidently an element that forced one to engage in criticism and, in so doing, to form an opinion. Jesus therefore demanded criticism; that is, he challenged one to decision, for he came to the people with a claim that naturally assumed many different forms. He came forward with the claim to expound the old and familiar word of God in a new and binding manner. He spoke differently from the scribes and Pharisees. How was one now supposed to behave? Where was one supposed to get the standards for one's own critical decision? There was no test-case, by means of which one could first check to see whether Jesus was right, in order then (*after* such a test) to give oneself over to what one had heard. This could be checked out neither against Jesus himself, since he looked human, nor against his deeds, since they could have been done by the devil, as had been alleged. What we are generally accustomed to calling a miracle therefore *proves* nothing at all. So there was no possibility of testing the truth of Jesus' claim. One could only risk giving oneself to Jesus' words. And in fact, this is where the really critical question lies, the question that brings about the separation: Does one risk giving oneself over to Jesus, and that means believing him?

In the Gospel of John (7:16–17) this is expressed at one point in the following way. It concerns the question whether Jesus speaks the word of God or whether he speaks for himself. Here Jesus

5

claims, "My teaching is not mine, but his who sent me." But this claim is not testable. The only possibility of experiencing the truth of the claim comes into view in the continuation of the Johannine word of Jesus, "if anyone's will is to *do* his will, that person shall know whether the teaching is from God or whether I am speaking on my own authority." But this means that it is only possible to experience the words of Jesus as words of God if one *risks* doing so. But if one does risk this and in this act of risk does experience the words of Jesus as words of God, then (and only then) can one characterize Jesus perhaps as "the mouth of God." Anyone who did not risk this could not give him this name—and might then have said, "This is a swindler talking."

Jesus expected a great deal of the people—although he looked like other people and was unable to legitimize his claim in any way. He expected them to accept his exposition of the law, although the official Jewish exposition looked different. He expected the people to do what he said. He expected them to take up with him, to come to his table—where, however, even tax collectors and sinners had their place. He expected them to give up their care for the coming day and to rely trustingly on God's provision for them. He expected the sick and decrepit to allow themselves to be healed through encounter with his word. He expected people to allow God's judgment to be pronounced on them by him, "You are dear to God," and to let every care for the coming judgment be taken from them. In sum, he expected people to accept from his word and deed *what they actually could only expect from God.*

Now individuals might react in quite different ways to this expectation. One might dismiss it and then say, "Jesus is crazy." However, one might also—at a certain distance—confirm that not entirely ordinary things were happening here and then say, "He is John the Baptizer; he is Elijah; he is one of the prophets." Nevertheless, one might also give oneself over to him—thereby experiencing the truth of his claim—and then say, *"You are the Christ."*

And now we want to consider this last answer. The Latin name "Christus" goes back to the Greek name "Christos," and this is a translation of the Hebrew name "Messiah," that is, "the anointed one." First of all, we have to realize that this designation was by no means coined for Jesus. It had long been familiar in Judaism. At an earlier time, the anointed king had been designated "Messiah."

6

This was a way of expressing that God rules his people through the king. Later, especially after the time of the Babylonian captivity and in the time of the political powerlessness of the people, it was expected that God would again send a Messiah-king, who was to come from the house of David and who would then rule his people forever. It is clear that the conception connected with the Messiah bore decidedly political traits.

When people characterize Jesus as Messiah on the basis of their experience with him, they naturally do *not* take over *all* the conceptions that had *previously* been connected with the Messiah. It is not as if they lived with a definite messianic expectation, that they were waiting for the coming of this (always politically understood) Messiah, and now suddenly said, "With Jesus he is come." For *the one whom* they expected did *not* come, and he did *not* come *as* they expected him. On the contrary, it worked in just the opposite way. Since people experienced something in the encounter with Jesus that they really could only have expected from God, and since the one through whom God would act on earth at the end-time was expected as Messiah, on account of this they now gave Jesus the name "Messiah."

Thus, we need to pay attention precisely to the direction in which the statement "Jesus is the Messiah" came into being. It was not a matter of transferring all current messianic conceptions to Jesus, but rather of rediscovering (in the Messiah-concept) experiences one had had with Jesus. The name that Jesus receives therefore has to be filled with content from the experiences one had had with Jesus—not from the current messianic conceptions. Let me put this once more quite concisely, in order to make clear the direction of the attribution. One did not say, "The (expected) Messiah—that is Jesus." Rather, one said, "Jesus is the Messiah."

When we realize that this is the direction in which the transfer of names to Jesus took place (that is, from the experiences one had had with and alongside Jesus), then we also recognize just the contingency of precisely this title. What was taken over was a current title, one that was well known and that seemed to express to some extent just what one had experienced with regard to Jesus. However, this could also be expressed in completely different fashion and by means of completely different names. For example, one could characterize Jesus as "Son of David" or as "King of the Jews."

I said just now that the ruler of the end-time was expected to come from the house of David. Naturally, it could be said, "Jesus actually did come from the house of David." But then the designation "Son of David" would be nothing special at all for Jesus. In this sense, Joseph was also "Son of David," and so too were Joseph's ancestors and many contemporaries of Jesus besides. When Jesus is given the name "Son of David," what is meant is the king of the end-time. But naturally, the point was not to say that Jesus was a king. For that he most definitely was not. Yet, in the encounter with Jesus, people had experienced that he brought something that, among other things, the king of the end-time was supposed to bring. For this reason, they gave Jesus the name "king" and meant by it nothing else than if they had given him the name "Messiah."

And now I could show exactly the same thing for a wealth of further titles or names of Jesus. What is significant is always this. All the names that were given to Jesus already existed previously. Not a single name was coined expressly for Jesus. But in all the names there were certain traits that had been established long ago that could be adopted and made use of. Thus, Jesus was obviously never the High Priest. But since the High Priest had the task of presenting the offering and thereby of reconciling the people to God, and since people had experienced that Jesus brought reconciliation with God, they could call him "High Priest" as well, by virtue of this one function.

And I think this is now clear: We may not add up these names of Jesus and say that, only once we know the sum of the content of all the names can we state fully who Jesus was. Rather, it was like this: Since people who encountered Jesus had experiences which they really only expected from God, each independent title serves to make *the same* statement. For in all the titles what is aimed at is precisely that they identify a bearer who has a specific commission from God. On account of this, it makes absolutely no material difference whether one refers to Jesus as Messiah, as Son of David, as King, or as High Priest.

And this holds for the designation, "Son of God," as well. In Judaism, people did not yet mean by this (differently from the Greek context, as in Hellenism) a human being who was descended from God. Rather (long before Jesus) the king or even the people had been referred to as son of God. They had been called son of

God because they had been chosen at a certain point in time by God and had been appointed to sonship. The people *became* God's son when God authorized it as God's people. The king *became* this on behalf of all through his anointing. From then on, he served as the one who acted in God's name. The term "Son of God" therefore is very close to the title "Messiah." And if Jesus was given the name "Son of God," he was linked up with a designation that had been known for a long time, one that had in no way been coined especially for Jesus. Again, it is the same thing. Since people experienced that, when they surrendered themselves to Jesus' claim, they had of course to do with Jesus, but therein *at the same time* with God—for this reason, they now called him God's Son. And in the answer of Peter in Matthew, we even find the two placed together: "You are the Messiah, the Son of the living God" (Matt. 16:16).

Finally, it can come to be said quite directly, "Whoever has to do with Jesus, has to do with God." And then the formulation arises, "Jesus is God." But I should like once more to draw attention to the fact that this must be understood in *this* connection: "Jesus is God," but not "God is Jesus."

Let me now summarize what has been said. People meet Jesus. They encounter his claim. They give themselves over to this claim. In doing so, they experience that they have to do with more than only human words; that they are confronted with God. They reflect on their experience and then, on the basis of the experience they have had with Jesus, they express *who* it is with whom they had this experience.

Let us now go one step further and take a look at the development that follows. To begin with, I want to illustrate this with regard to one title. If, based on their experience with Jesus, people have made the judgment that he is the Messiah, and if they now go on to tell of their experience with Jesus and even to write it down, there are two possibilities. Either they now simply tell of an incident with Jesus of Nazareth, or else they take the name with which they have subsequently characterized Jesus right over into their account. But then they relate an incident about (for example) Jesus *Christ*, often even simply about Christ. At the beginning, this happens only seldom, but later it happens more and more frequently, and we all but take this for granted. We do this without reflecting at all on what we are saying.

I still remember well my first semester in theology, when my teacher, Professor Heinrich Rendtorff, once embarrassed me for a moment regarding this very point. I was speaking in a completely unreflective way about Christ healing the sick. Rendtorff immediately asked me, "*Who* did this?" I thought he had not understood me and said once more, "Christ." Then he corrected me and said, "No, Jesus!" In this instance, Rendtorff distinguished the two quite precisely and would not permit his students to speak imprecisely about this point. For if Christ often looks to us almost like a proper name, or at least like part of a proper name, we have overlooked the fact that it is a matter of a title. On this point we ought to have been quite precise, or at least to have known what we were saying.

In the case of narratives in the New Testament that tell of something Christ or Jesus Christ does or says, what Jesus brought, the experiences people had with him are presented twice—once unreflectively, insofar as what Jesus says or does is recounted, and the second time as reflected upon, and specifically in the title "Christ," that here is used for Jesus. But now that the title "Christ" stands at the beginning, there sets in a reversal of the direction (at first completely unnoticed) that I spoke of earlier. Originally, the experience arising from the encounter with Jesus was the first thing. The title was the response to the experience of the person who had been moved by the experience, and therefore the second thing. But now, when a story about Christ is told, the second thing is put first. How does this come about?

It is not difficult to answer this question if we consider the following. It was only possible to encounter Jesus, to have experiences with him up until Good Friday. After that, this was no longer possible. But since Easter, his community knows that he has not remained in death, that he is alive. And now it wants to introduce others to the encounter with Jesus. Naturally, it cannot do this by directly setting Jesus in front of people. However, it can do this by bringing Jesus near to these other people in his message. If faith came earlier from the encounter with Jesus, so now it comes (putting it in the well-known words of Paul) from the hearing of the preaching—therefore from the encounter with the word.

This word is now ambiguous in precisely the same way that the human appearance of Jesus had been. It encounters one as a word that people speak, and anyone who hears it can always avoid it by pointing to the people who deliver this word, by saying, for example (as the story of Pentecost has it), that they are filled with new wine (Acts 2:13). Thus, the same question confronts us now that confronted us earlier concerning Jesus, once again and changed only a little bit. Now the question is no longer, "Who is Jesus?" Instead, it is, "Whose word is it, that these people speak?"

When the apostles answer that it is the word of Jesus of Nazareth, then the counterquestion simply confronts them, "Can anything good come out of Nazareth?" For, Jesus of Nazareth—who is he supposed to be? And for this reason, the apostles more and more no longer simply say, "Jesus," but rather connect directly with Jesus the experience they have had with him, by directly introducing Jesus' title into the account and by now telling the stories as stories precisely of Jesus Christ or even as stories of Christ.

But how can the hearers of this apostolic message now be sure that it concerns not the message of just another person, not the message of somebody or other from Nazareth, but rather the message of the Messiah? This is not possible now any differently from the way it had been in the encounter with Jesus. The message comprises the same claim. Whoever surrenders to this claim, whoever does as he or she is told will perceive that the proclamation that encounters them in the form of a human word is more than a human word. And in doing this, they will also perceive that the one who brought this message was himself the messenger of God, the mouth of God, that he was himself the Christ.

Let me return once more to the issue of the directions in which this occurred. Originally, the encounter with Jesus was the first thing, and the title was then the answer and thus the second thing. During the course of the later proclamation, the order gets reversed. Christ is now spoken of first, and only then of what he brought. However, this is the case not only in the accounts in the gospels, but above all in the parts of the New Testament which actually relate nothing at all, or nearly nothing at all about the life of Jesus himself, that is, in the epistles. To this end, let us turn to our second text as another particularly characteristic example.

But when the time had been fulfilled, God sent his Son, born of a woman, placed under the law, in order to ransom those who stood under the law, in order that we might receive sonship. (Gal. 4:4-5)

11

We see that here, the reversal of direction of which I spoke has already taken place. It is no longer the case that who Jesus is is reflected in the encounter with him (such a meeting is indeed no longer possible after Good Friday). Here, what Jesus is is immediately presupposed. Paul immediately speaks of the Son of God who was with God in the beginning and who then came to this earth at the end of days. Paul emphasizes forcefully, to be sure, that this Son of God actually became a human being. He had been born of a woman. He had been placed under the law—and that means that he entered into all the realities of this world—into its ordinances, customs, and needs, subjected to hunger and thirst and so forth. He was a real human being.

But let us digress for a moment. Does Paul report this in order to instruct his readers about who Jesus was? Does he report this in order that they may be informed about the miraculous circumstances of Jesus' origin? No, by no means! For what could his readers have made of this? Then they would have been informed of a divine performance in the past. And they only would know this if they took Paul's word for it. But even if they had done this, what would this mean for *them*?

But the way he continues shows what Paul is actually aiming at. This sending of the Son of God—so he says—had the purpose of ransoming those who had stood under the law from their enslavement to the law and to this world, so that they might receive sonship.

The direction of the proclamation is therefore quite clear. It sets out from the Son of God and leads to what he has brought and now brings. The offer of being children of God now encounters the readers directly. But this means that something is expected of them. They are expected to live in this world, at a distance from God, in a foreign country, as children of God. They are told, "You have been ransomed from the enslavement of this world. You have been removed from servitude under the law. You are free. The coming of the Son of God has brought this about."

And now the readers stand before the question, "Is this message true?" Again, they have no possibility of checking this. They cannot *first* test whether God really has sent his Son and whether the sending of the Son really has effected the ransom, in order *then* (if this test proves affirmative) to surrender to the demand to live as

12

children of God. Rather, once again the matter is precisely reversed. If they make the demand that resides in this proclamation their own; if (simply "on the basis of the word itself") they risk accepting this offer, then (right then and only then) they will experience that what is presupposed really is true—that God really has brought about their ransom in the sending of his Son. Then they too can give Jesus the name "Son of God"; then they too can say that God has sent him for their liberation. But if they do not take the risk that resides in this offer, then they will never experience that Jesus is God's Son—even if Paul says it is so.

However, I now need to point to a further difference between this text and the examples mentioned earlier. The names of Jesus we encountered earlier were all simply titles. However, here in the letter to the Galatians we have to do with something that is not only a title, but rather (as I called it earlier) a "performance of God" that is related in connection with this title. Jesus is not merely the Son of God, but rather the Son of God *sent* at a specific time, and one who has accomplished a *task* on earth. Therefore, it is not only a title that stands in the background, but rather a complex of events. How is this difference to be explained?

The answer to this question is not entirely straightforward, since we have to do here with complicated problems of christological development—as the technical expression for this goes. I want to try to present this as simply as possible. Two things need to be pointed out.

First, as I have explained, various and distinct titles have been transferred to Jesus. Since each title originally had one and the same task, namely, that of characterizing Jesus as the "messenger" or "mouth" of God, various types of conceptions combined with the title. But now what happened is that a number of titles were also employed at the same time. We can observe this clearly in the answer of Peter.

According to Mark, Peter says only, "You are the Messiah" (Mark 8:29). However, according to Luke, who knew Mark's gospel and used it as a model, the answer runs, "You are the Messiah *of God*" (Luke 9:20). This makes scarcely any material difference, and yet, along with the title it is now said to whom this Messiah belongs. In Matthew, the answer is still more detailed. Matthew has also used Mark's gospel as a model. Therefore, we are dealing

13

with Matthew's addition when he now has Peter say, "You are the Messiah, *the Son of the living God*" (Matt. 16:16). The first title is now, so to speak, deepened. It is traced back to its origin. From whom this Messiah comes is now stated. By placing titles one after another, a certain movement comes to expression— in the case of Matthew, backward: from Jesus, over to the Messiah, then to God. However, if we now reverse this movement, we are already almost at the statement of Paul's.

But the difference between the individual titles and the picture employed by Paul of what God has performed is connected with yet something else. That Jesus was called precisely "Messiah" or "Son of David" depends on the fact that, in the Jewish milieu, people took as completely self-explanatory titles that were well known and familiar in the Jewish milieu. However, in the Greek-Hellenistic milieu, people actually did not know at all what a Messiah was, or what difference (specifically) Davidic sonship made. However, since the title of Messiah had evidently been connected with Jesus from early on, it was retained, even if people now regarded and employed it as a personal name. This can readily be seen in the Apostles' Creed. The second article begins not (as it really should) with the words, "I believe in Jesus, *the* Christ, the only-begotten son of God, our Lord," but rather, "I believe in Jesus Christ, the only-begotten Son of God, our Lord." Titles that have been consolidated hold on even in a foreign linguistic and conceptual milieu. Others, however, are no longer employed, since they are no longer understood. And at the same time, new ones arise.

It is a widespread notion in the Greek mystery religions that, through the descent to earth of a divinity, redemption takes place. I now need to say this again more precisely (that is, the other way around). Redemption takes place through the descent of a divinity to earth. Since the message is a message of the redemption of human beings, and this message is a message of the Son of God, conceptions from the environment get joined up with the Son of God—even his descent for the sake of redemption. To be sure, Paul says very clearly (and insofar differently from all mystery religions) that the Son who has descended really became a human being. But for all that he takes over conceptions that are known in the environment.

We should be neither surprised nor horrified at this development. It only shows that the message applies to all people and that

14

it can be expressed in every language. If Jesus is called the "head of the body" (or the "head of the community"), a Greek-Hellenistic conception has been transferred to him here as well. And the same thing applies to the title on which we rely so much, "savior," which is at home in the Greek world.

Now it must certainly be said that not all these titles were transferred to Jesus as the result of encounter with Jesus himself, but rather as the result of encounter with the message. People wanted to lend weight to the message by bestowing on him who brought this message to earth the highest title that stood at their disposal in any particular case. And then the fact that, in the way they are formulated, the creeds grow and change to some extent is connected with this. The Nicene Creed diverges not inconsiderably from the older Apostles' Creed. Does it proclaim or confess a different Jesus on this account? I think this could no longer be said on the basis of what has been worked out here. It is only that we are not to fall into the trap of turning these various names of Jesus into speculations. They are meant only to underscore that the one whose message we hear has a name that is above all names. But they do not mean to say who he is—*independent* of the message.

In discussions and agitated controversies it is sometimes asked today, "Is Jesus the Son of God or not?" "Is Jesus the Messiah—yes or no?" But in asking this one can easily miss the point completely. This question may not be answered today, either, independently of our actually surrendering ourselves to his message, our daring to live from his word, our daring to count on God in our lives contrary to appearances, our daring to give up our cares for the morrow, our daring to live in the freedom for which he has set us free.

But if we do dare to do this, then we can say who he is. Whether we then use the name "Son of God," "Christ," or some other name no longer matters. Over the course of this essay I have also introduced a few others. I have called him the "mouth of God," the "messenger of God." Perhaps there are still more. No, there are undoubtedly still more! I only mean that anyone who does risk surrendering to him and to his message will always use only the highest name one knows. And I *know* no higher name than when I say, "Jesus is God"—because in Jesus and through Jesus I have to do with God.

2

THE JESUS-BUSINESS: IN DEFENSE OF A CONCEPT*

The Jesus-business continues!

This is first of all an assertion, and a somewhat surprising one at that. It was made for the first time by people who had witnessed Jesus' failure on the cross. He had encountered them in Galilee. They had heard his call, given themselves over to him, and followed him. They had abandoned their daily routine and disassociated themselves from job and family because, in one way or another, they had experienced that this person offered and made possible something that was not to be had otherwise. What this was like in detail will be discussed later on. In any case, Jesus fulfilled hopes and, for this reason, himself became the hope of those who joined him as disciples.

In Jerusalem, this ended in catastrophe. Their leader was arrested. Although the city was swarming with people who had gathered there from all parts of the country to celebrate Passover, no one stood up for him. They themselves lost courage. And when they witnessed that Jesus suffered the horrible death of a criminal (or heard about it, because they did not themselves dare to be in the vicinity of what took place), they had reason to fear that they had been left in the lurch by one of the sundry preachers of salvation of that time and that they had been taken in by him. They fled and tried to save their own skins. And yet, only a short time afterward, they experienced in inexplicable fashion (later to be presented as appearances) that the Jesus who had died was living, that he was

---

*"Die Sache Jesu: Plädoyer für einen Begriff," *Die Sache Jesu geht weiter* (Gütersloh: Gütersloher Verlagshaus Gerd Mohn, 1976), 8–26.

the Lord precisely in his apparent defeat, and that they therefore had not the slightest cause for resignation. They now knew themselves to be sent on a mission, and they proclaimed and acted, not in their own name, but rather precisely in the name of Jesus, the crucified one. The Jesus-business continued.

I.

To be sure, the people of that time did not put this in these words. On the contrary, this way of putting it is quite new. I once used it in order to express in our own language what Jesus' resurrection means (*Die Auferstehung Jesu als historisches und als theologisches Problem* [1964]: 25f.). What happened to this linguistic attempt is what often happens to such attempts. Some people find them helpful and gladly appropriate and make further use of them, since they make it possible to understand what is often very much more difficult to make sense of otherwise. Nevertheless, other people reject them, because they doubt that the formulations convey in a suitable way what they are actually meant to express. They then regard such phrases either as inappropriate or as simplistic and superficial.

However, in this instance, something else also happened that does not occur in every new formulation (something which, when I employed it, I had not thought of at all). The "Jesus-business" which continues became a slogan that got out of control and took on a life of its own, utterly separated from the context in which this phrase had arisen. But here, as I readily admit, I have not always been happy with my own "child" and have gotten into a peculiar situation because of it. On the one hand, unless I am prepared to retract the phrase (which, as things have gone, is scarcely possible), I have to argue in my own defense and further justify why I chose the formulation I did at that time—why, despite all the polemic, I cannot concede that it is simplistic or superficial. On the other hand, I also have to oppose the misuse of this formulation and ask myself whether I occasioned this myself and how I can guard against its further misuse (if this is possible at all).

Perhaps it would be helpful if, to begin with, I once again remind both of the parties to this discussion of its context. As I said, I intended to express what Jesus' resurrection means in our own language. However, in that connection, I proposed not just this one phrase, but two, stated them right alongside each other and tried to make it clear that they are to be understood in relation to each other. The one phrase was precisely "The Jesus-business continues." The other is, "He still comes today."

It is a matter of great concern to me that both sentences be kept connected. If they are torn apart and only the former is used, this formulation can in fact easily be understood as an oversimplification of what is meant by the claim of Jesus' resurrection. For, if it were only a case of carrying on a "cause" that Jesus of Nazareth had once introduced, then there would be no reason to speak of his resurrection at all. Then, rather than serving to *interpret* the confession of Jesus' resurrection, the phrase "the Jesus-business continues" would indicate that this confession was at least unnecessary, if not even false (because misleading) and so would only serve to *eliminate* it. However, I might point out that this is just what I have not done. The context shows quite clearly that I understood this phrase as indissolubly joined to the other one, that is to say, to the phrase, "He still comes today." Thereby, I meant to express that I regard the cause of great people of the past continuing and the Jesus-business continuing as completely different things, for I would precisely not say that these great people of the past still come today.

Thus, treating the disputed phrase in an isolated way is precisely an oversimplification of what I presented. For this reason, I must ask both parties to the discussion whether, in their polemic against this formulation, or in a hasty (and *then*, in fact, often in oversimplified) fashion, they have paid sufficient attention to the context. In this respect, my question is naturally directed more pointedly to those who have engaged in critical discussion with the phrase since, in their case, one might have had the right to assume such attention to context. In contrast, the person who becomes acquainted with the phrase once it has already become a slogan normally does not even know where it comes from and how it was meant to be understood in its original context.

To begin with the latter group. One can finally only ask them whether what they understand and pass off as the Jesus-*business* is really the *Jesus*-business. People who continue to make use of the slogan also reasonably have to be expected to be open to this question if they claim to be taken seriously as parties to the discussion. For one might still suppose that they don't mean to pass off just anything as the Jesus-business (that is to say, what "the general public" today would take to be specifically Christian), and that they are accountable for the content of what they portray as the Jesus-business, which is to say, what is presented as the *Jesus*-business in (and behind) the New Testament. In any case, I fear that the requisite care has not always been taken in deciding these issues. But then, this was bound to have discredited the whole phrase.

Let me give just one example of this. In so-called political theology, what has sometimes been called "social pietism" is presented as the Jesus-business. The Jesus-business is then understood as standing up for the oppressed, the poor, those who have it hard, the socially underprivileged. That one finds all of this in the gospels is not to be disputed. But is this presented there in such a way that one may speak, as it were, of a "program" on Jesus' part, to the fulfillment of which he committed himself and to which he summoned others? How all this is connected with God's rule that Jesus announced as *now* breaking in ought first to have been examined more closely, especially since there is at present a broad consensus that this is where we have to do with the center of the proclamation and the activity of Jesus. To be sure, the view is also widespread that this "imminent expectation" is to be characterized as a "mistake" on Jesus' part. We shall go into this later. However, eliminating the *entire* topic of the "inbreaking of God's rule" on the basis of this "mistake" was hasty in any case, for this is precisely where we have to do with a "proprium" of Jesus. Certainly, Jesus was concerned with "altering conditions." And it was just as certain to him that this was to happen through people. However, he never understood this as being a matter of a program, the fulfillment of which lies within the framework of human possibilities, because human beings are simply not in a position to bring God's rule—even though they naturally are in a position to alter conditions. *This* remains a human possibility through and through. However, if this is passed off as the Jesus-business, it is no longer the *Jesus*-business. By being declared to be "something that can be accomplished," it has been robbed of what for it is indispensable.

Hand in hand with eliminating the inbreaking of God's rule from the Jesus-business went the loss of christology. Naturally, this is a somewhat different matter. Christology was not eliminated, since in the Jesus-business *there is no* christology *of an explicit sort*. Still, only if the Jesus-business is understood as the inbreaking of God's rule is there a recognition that the Jesus-business at least *implies* a christology. Even if many christological claims (preexistence, divine sonship, messiahship, etc.) appear alien to us today and therefore stand in need of interpretation, they are still by no means inappropriate on this account. This may not be the easiest thing to see, especially since one also has to resist a trend (clearly recognizable at least since the Enlightenment) that can be characterized as an aversion against any christology. Jesus as human being, as example, as teacher, perhaps even as revolutionary—these one could imagine. However, christology seemed just too much. A "Jesus-business," as this was now understood (namely, without reference to the inbreaking of God's rule), seemed to present a solution, for now a christology appeared on the scene that one did not know what to make of anyway and that was not required for *this* business. It could, therefore, finally be given up. Taking one's bearings from the Jesus-business could now be understood in the sense of relating to a cause, a program, a platform that had been called for by the historical Jesus.

This is precisely what those people feared who were doubtful about interpreting the claim of Jesus' resurrection by means of the phrase that his "business" continues. This fear was evidently fully justified. However, they should not have directed this reproach at me, because I do not feel it applies to me. I can scarcely be held responsible for consequences that follow from an oversimplification of what I not only meant, but even explicitly said. Far from suppressing the fact that Jesus still comes today, I had linked the two phrases together (even in rather explicit fashion). And now it was argued repeatedly that what was at issue is a person, not a "cause." But this argument does not apply to me.

In the course of such polemic, it was precisely christology that was again vigorously brought into play. It was emphasized that there is an indissoluble connection between this person and his fate, the death on the cross and the resurrection of the crucified one. This frequently led not only to everything being directed to the exalted Lord, but also to placing weight on the "event" of his exaltation, since by doing this one could draw a clean line of demarcation from the earthly Jesus.

Now, I feel that the set of alternatives, "person, not cause," is a most unhappy one. It is simply distorted and, for this reason, can only provoke a dangerous misunderstanding—indeed, it has repeatedly done so already. Let me demonstrate this.

There is widespread agreement on the point that (the historical) Jesus did not characterize himself as Messiah or Son of God (in a christological sense). The post-Easter community first did this. That is where (explicit) christology began. With this, a date gets assigned. However, this goes beyond merely indicating a *terminus a quo* for when christology becomes explicit. This date is also taken to have extraordinary material importance. One often speaks in this regard of the turn of the aeons that took place at Easter, of the new era that broke in at that point. In so doing, the earthly Jesus gets left behind. As is emphasized again and again, he was still looking forward to God's rule. It was a matter of the future for him. This very future is then supposed to have become present with Easter, with the result that, after Easter, it was possible to look back on the rule of God that had broken in. With this, a second set of alternatives is now added to the first ("person, not cause"). It is said that we have to do not with the cause of Jesus, but rather with the resurrected, exalted Christ.

However, this poses the fundamental question of the relation of this (exalted) Christ to the earthly Jesus. Naturally, one asserts their identity. But what is the value of asserting the identity of persons, if one cannot show this of the persons themselves? Jesus of Nazareth and (the exalted) Christ are in no way to be compared to each other. However, if it is Christ that is supposed to be of decisive importance, then Jesus somehow stands under a "deficit" and of course, along with him, his "cause" as well—hence, what he was concerned with, why he mattered. It is then supposed that this minus-sign is only removed through Jesus' exaltation, because at that point a "not yet" became an "already." However, this widespread conception not only introduces a serious difficulty that is virtually intractable, but also shows itself to be its own particular sort of oversimplification.

The difficulty consists in it now no longer being possible to explain how the synoptic gospels arose at all, for what they are concerned with is without any doubt always in one way or another the *Jesus*-business. These works arose after the date of Easter. However, is it then not necessary to ask whether they had not already been fundamentally superseded by virtue of Easter, by virtue of the exaltation of Jesus? They constitute a christological anachronism by still portraying (decades later!) the situation of the "not yet," at any rate in the bulk of the traditions they present. How is this to be explained?

As hard as people have tried, no one has yet found an answer to this question. But perhaps it is actually a false question, since the presupposition for asking it has not been clarified. For instance, if to the claim that Easter means that the Jesus-business continues, it is objected that what is important is not Jesus and his cause, but rather the exalted one, this can very easily lead to an oversimplification that is the exact opposite of what the phrase "the Jesus-business" was reproached for. For, is it not all too easy to forget that we are to concern ourselves, not in a virtually isolated fashion with an exalted Christ, but always with his "coming" as well? Is it not problematic (to express this by means of two other concepts) to speak of a savior, if one does not *at the same time* speak of the salvation that he offers and brings? The only person who can call a savior *the* savior is one who knows something about his salvation. To me it makes no sense to offer up merely a *person* as a savior. This is exactly why I also find the contrast "person, not cause" distorted as an expression of alternatives. Indeed, the question is how one relates the two terms, whether this needs to be done, and how it can be done.

This still needs to be gone into. But before doing this, something else can be clarified. I said that the identity of the earthly and the exalted one is indeed asserted, but that this does not constitute a comparison of these "persons" with each other. However, if one's bearings are taken from the "person" of the exalted one, not in an isolated way, but looking to the salvation that he brings and that is experienced through him, then comparison really is possible. For in that case, it can be asked how this salvation (of the exalted one) is related to the Jesus- business. That there is a *christological* difference between the earthly Jesus and the exalted one who is raised is not to be disputed. However, if one insists on this alone and proceeds in a one-sided fashion on such a basis, a *soteriological* difference quickly opens up. If a "not yet" applies to Jesus, then his cause stands under this "not yet" as well. If the resurrection brought the turn of the aeons and, with it, the dawning of the "already," then at this point (but only at this point) the salvation brought by the risen one does have the character of the "already." If we proceed on the basis of the "christological difference," both these conclusions just follow logically.

In contrast, the situation is different if the comparison is developed with regard to soteriology. Then it is at least conceivable that there is no difference. If this is the case, it would in fact be possible to speak of the identity of the earthly and the exalted one. This claim, which has always been recognized, could then be shown to make sense. Inasmuch as one was concerned with the same salvation, one could identify the bearers of salvation. At the same time, the "christological difference" would not need to be levelled out. The task of explaining it would remain, but we would not make ourselves dependent upon it from the outset.

The (since Bultmann) customary distinction between implicit and explicit christology could then be explained rather easily. And not only that! It could be shown that it is not as if explicit christology only represents a stage of development that is to be explained with reference to the conditions and conceptions of that time, but that can be dispensed with today. Rather, it could be recognized that this christology is a way of making the business itself explicit, and that this, in turn, is not to be left out of the picture, at least so long as we continue to take our bearings from the Jesus-business and are not prepared to oversimplify this.

I said that it makes no sense to me to offer a savior in an isolated way, without at the same time saying something of his salvation. In contrast, I do not find it senseless in the least to offer salvation without *explicitly* naming the savior. If at some point in the past, Jesus merely set a cause in motion by means of his proclamation, or if he pointed to a salvation that was (perhaps shortly) to come, then he himself stands outside it. To be sure, it can then be known at some later point that this cause once started out from him, but at that point what matters is no longer Jesus, but only his cause. He himself might be understood as at best an illustration of how this cause is lived, but a christology would be unnecessary ballast. However, this could not be said of the salvation that the exalted one offers, for if this salvation is experienced as God's salvation, then explicit christology is an appropriate expression of it. But did the Jesus-business have this same character?

Bultmann speaks of the *proclamation* of Jesus implying a christology. I regard this as a narrowing-down that then leads to oversimplification. I mean that Jesus' proclamation is not to be separated from his deeds and his conduct. For this reason, I understand his activity as a whole as an expression of his business. The question now is how this activity was experienced. Was it something by means of which Jesus made a start that could now be read off it and carried on, with the result that one would, like Jesus, be on the way to a salvation that was to come? In this case, such activity would scarcely imply a christology. However, if Jesus' business (and this now means precisely Jesus himself in his proclaiming, actions, and conduct) was experienced as God's salvation, then this certainly *did not have to* become explicit in a christology, but explicit christology was nonetheless an appropriate expression of this salvation. In this case, to say that the Jesus-business continues is at the same time to say that he still comes today.

Let us now test this out.

II.

To begin with, let me take my bearings from the closely connected conceptions of the turn of the aeons and the coming of the kingdom of God, since time and again it is claimed that this is where the decisive difference between Jesus and the early community enters into the picture most clearly.

Jesus, so it is said, announced the imminence of the kingdom. He looked ahead to its coming; he expected it in the near future. In this regard, reference is made to Mark 1:15, "The time is fulfilled, and the kingdom of God has come near. Repent (turn about) and believe in the gospel!" To be sure, there is widespread agreement that we do not have to do with the verbatim transmission of a saying of Jesus in this verse, but rather with an appropriate summary of his proclamation. Jesus' activity is then seen from the point of view of expectation.

It is supposed to have been completely different in the case of the early community. In this regard, reference is made above all to Paul, and 2 Cor. 5:17 is eagerly cited. "If anyone is in Christ, that person is a new creation. The old has passed away, behold, the new has come." According to these (and similar) words of Paul, one can now give oneself over to (the exalted) Christ and, thereby, the new reality can come to exist in the life of Christians, for at this point they are a new creation. Christology and soteriology are connected to each other. However, the reason why "the new" is now a possibility is that the turn of the aeons, to which Jesus was still looking ahead, has occurred in the meantime; thus, expectation has turned into fulfillment. What for Jesus was still (and only) future is now behind one.

If this were so, there would in fact be a profound difference between the Jesus-business and the salvation of Christ.

However, this whole approach is simply a schematic misrepresentation. At least with regard to Paul, this can be readily shown. Of course, it is not to be disputed that Paul and the early community speak of an "already" when they look back to something that has taken place in the past, on the basis of which they recognize that God has acted decisively there. A "new" did in fact begin at that point, out of which they were now able to live. Expectations were fulfilled. It is just that the early community realized, as Paul in particular must have experienced in several of his communities, that this "new" which had broken in could be dangerously misunderstood. This occurred especially in the case of (gnostic) enthusiasts, fanatics, and perfectionists who, on the strength of the "new" that had broken in, imagined that they were already at the goal, claimed to possess the Spirit, thought they had achieved perfection—and fell into the power of a libertinistic ethic. Everything, so they believed, was permitted to them (1 Cor. 5:12; 10:23), and the situation of the community in Corinth clearly shows that this principle was taken dangerously in earnest.

Paul opposes this, and the way he does so is significant. He in no way disputes the "already." Nevertheless, he opposes the perfectionistic misunderstanding of it by means of the so-called eschatological proviso, by counteracting the "already" (which he, too, continually asserts) with the help of a "not yet." So, for example, he says that believers do already have the Spirit, but in this world that is passing away, they always have it only as "first fruits" (Rom. 8:23), that is, as a "down payment" (2 Cor. 1:22; 5:5). Its actual possession in full remains a promise for the future. Christians have an immeasurable treasure, and yet they have it in earthen vessels (2 Cor. 4:7). Paul portrays himself as one whom Jesus Christ has laid hold of and, in the same context, he emphasizes that he has not yet been made perfect, that he does not regard himself as though he had already obtained everything (Phil. 3:12). Examples of this sort abound in Paul.

However, it is then quite problematic to say that Paul already has the turn of the aeons behind him, at least if this claim is not immediately safeguarded against the misunderstanding that it refers to something like a state of affairs. Whether, in contrast to a mere expectation on the part of Jesus, we may speak in Paul's case of a fulfillment that has intervened in the meantime, must still be investigated. However, it is one-sided to speak of fulfillment in Paul's case if, at the same time, we do not say that this fulfillment always exists only in the form of expectation. Even the Christian ever lives only in this old aeon that is passing away and always has the end of this aeon in front of him. Paul never employs the concept "the turn of the aeons," and it was unfortunate that it was introduced in this context, particularly since the apostle can explicitly say that the kingdom of God is a future inheritance (1 Cor. 6:9). If the turn of the aeons initiates the kingdom of God, this is for Paul specifically *also* a future reality. What the apostle has behind him is a real, but nevertheless a fractured fulfillment of expectation which, because it is fractured, remains even as fulfillment a matter of expectation. So, Christians really already are children of the (coming) light and of the (coming) day (1 Thess. 5:5). However, they are this always as the sort of people who still live in the darkness and in the night of this world; who still have the "day" before them (1 Thess. 5:1). They *are* redeemed, to be sure, but in *hope* (Rom. 8:24).

Therefore, if one may by no means speak unqualifiedly of fulfillment in Paul's case, since the element of expectation is not to be eliminated, it should now be asked whether one must speak unqualifiedly of expectation on the part of Jesus, or whether the element of fulfillment is not perhaps to be related in some way to that of expectation here.

At this point, however, I must first briefly go into a problem concerning method. Since we do not possess a single line from Jesus' own hand, we may not, at least directly, speak of Jesus' attitude toward God's coming kingdom. We must rather, as it were, put everything in parentheses. We learn only how Jesus was understood. This qualification is not to be taken as a form of historical skepticism. It merely follows from an understanding of the character of our sources. These come not from neutral observers, but from believers, which is to say, from people who gave themselves to Jesus, who allowed themselves to be moved in encounter with him, and who then formulated these pieces of tradition for the sake of summoning others to this same encounter. To put this in technical, theological language, we have to do with kerygma. This does not imply any judgment regarding the value of the contents of these traditions for historical purposes, insofar as they narrate matters of the past. It has to do rather with a judgment about literary type. They are witnesses of faith in a twofold sense: They are formulated by believers and, insofar, are an expression of their faith. Moreover, they are intended as a summons to faith. Thus, our precise question needs to be, "How was Jesus' announcement of God's rule understood and received by those who were moved by him?"

In order to identify what is distinctive of Jesus, we have to know how the kingdom, which is to say, the rule of God, was spoken of in Judaism at the time he lived. The concepts that were employed overlap in part. Since this also holds true of usage within the New Testament, some uncertainties result from taking our bearings simply from terminology. Nevertheless, this problem can be mitigated by examining the terms in their contexts. We can identify two aspects that need to be distinguished—a present and a future one. It may be helpful to speak of the *rule* of God in regard to the present aspect and of the *kingdom* of God in regard to the future aspect (independently of the terms that are employed in particular contexts). This produces the following distinction. One can take the *rule* of God upon oneself now. In the Jewish view, one does this when one fulfills the commands of God in detail. Seen in this way, the decision to permit the rule of God to come rests with the individual. However, this is not true of the future aspect (or is so only in a qualified way), for the *kingdom* of God is the coming aeon, which God himself will inaugurate. The individual has at most the possibility of hastening the coming of the kingdom by means of "repentance." Nevertheless, at the same time, this itself always remains God's work. The individual is passive with regard to it. One can only await, receive, inherit the kingdom. This will happen after the turn of the aeons, when God will redeem the present evil aeon by way of the decisive coming one. Sometimes signs are looked for that announce the end of this present age. There is also the idea that the turn of the aeons will be accompanied by catastrophes (earthquakes, famines) and wars. In the coming aeon, in the kingdom of God, salvation is expected in the form of a state of affairs for Israel or for the righteous of the whole world. It is the kingdom of peace, of a perpetual fellowship with God that is frequently represented as table fellowship. The anxious question for people in this old aeon is always when this kingdom is coming and whether one will have a share in it oneself.

However, it is just this question that for all practical purposes Jesus relativizes. In any case, this is how his followers understood him. He refers to the idea of the coming aeon, that is, to the "kingdom." However, he modifies it by way of the other concept of the "rule." This is precisely what has led to the question discussed over and over in the scholarship, whether for Jesus the kingdom of God (that is, God's rule) is a future reality that he perhaps expected as imminent, but which as such nevertheless also remained future, or whether it has to do with something present. If the former option is accepted, we do indeed have to speak of expectation on Jesus' part. However, if the second possibility is included, we can no longer speak of expectation alone, for then the element of fulfillment somehow also has to be related to that of expectation.

There can scarcely be any doubt that Jesus and those around him knew of the idea of the coming kingdom and, as children of their time, counted on the coming of the kingdom in the future. In all probability, they thought of this future as very near, and about this they were mistaken. However, does this justify speaking of an error *on Jesus' part*? I do not understand why this is always insisted on and this question about a particular date is made into a special problem in his case, for didn't Paul make the exact same mistake (cf. 1 Thess. 4:15; 1 Cor. 15:51)? Quite apart from the question of a date, must we not say that the whole conceptuality is largely mistaken? The people of that time were "mistaken" in their worldview in many respects. Nevertheless, people today do not go about manufacturing problems from these "mistakes." Why treat the part of the problem having to do with the question of a date any differently? We cannot be about the business of taking over ancient worldviews today. All the same, it is worth asking where we are to locate the particular matter at issue within the framework of that conceptuality. Let us try to bring this into focus.

If we start out from the (overall) conception of the expectation of the "kingdom," two sorts of things are striking. On the one hand, there is a (even if only cautious) modification of the content of what is expected. For instance, criticism can be levelled at all-too-human conceptions of the coming aeon (cf. Matt. 22:30). On the other hand, the favorite question of the signs of the time (Luke 12:54) can be unmasked as an evasion in the face of being moved in the present (v. 57!). All calculation of dates is renounced. Naturally, *within the framework of this conceptuality* of the coming kingdom, all this does not do away with its futurity.

However, alongside this, we also find a very strong emphasis on the present. What in principle is expected only of the new aeon is already taking place (Matt. 11:4-6). Demons are now "coming out" (Mark 1:26). An "already-having-come" can be spoken of (Matt. 12:28), as well as the presence of the kingdom "in the midst of" the hearers (Luke 17:21). This presence of the coming kingdom is evidently not a state of affairs. To this extent (if we stay with our terminology), one may not speak of the presence of the "kingdom" of God (that is, of the new aeon). Nonetheless, an anticipation of the future is lived out and experienced. At least to this extent, it actually is a matter of fulfillment of expectation.

Perhaps we may express the particular matter at issue in this way. The "kingdom" breaks into this world as "rule." This brings two modifications along with it. First, in the Jewish understanding, the individual could take God's rule upon himself by observing the law; its coming was therefore in one's own hands. In contrast, the bringing of the new aeon was strictly God's work. Precisely this motif now enters into the conception of the rule of God. Now the individual can only take this upon himself or herself by permitting it to occur of itself. The second modification is directly connected with this. The content of God's rule is defined differently. It comes not through the doing of the law, but rather through allowing the fellowship with God that belongs to the end-time (which was originally only expected in the new aeon) to occur now and of itself.

Thus, law has become gospel, and this is the context for the exegesis of Mark 1:15. Faith in the gospel means giving oneself over to God's rule that is now breaking in, risking the fellowship with God that is offered. However, where this happens, the consequence can only be this: immediate turnabout. This is decisive for the order of events. This turnabout is not a condition for the coming of God's rule, but its consequence. In this turnabout, God's inbreaking rule reaches its goal.

If this is an accurate account of the particular point at issue, it should be clear that it is misleading to speak of a "mistake" on Jesus' part with regard to his expectation that the new aeon was imminent. It probably cannot be disputed that he shared this conception (just as this conception also still stays with the early community for some time, now in the form of the expectation of the imminent return of Jesus, as Son of Man or as judge). However, it would be false to say (as it often is said) that Jesus proclaimed the inbreaking of the "kingdom" of God as something that was soon to occur. He may have expected this, as others did, too. However, this misses what is characteristic of him. He declares the conception, which he perhaps shared with his contemporaries, to be unimportant. Adhering to this conception is dangerous, because it puts the individual under the illusion of still having time for oneself before encountering God. Emphasizing this conception keeps God at arm's length. To the contrary, Jesus announces that there is no time left.

The person who risks a turnabout experiences that one does not need to fear the encounter with God in allowing God's rule to come, and that it is actually gospel, good news, that is announced here. The king comes as a father. God's rule brings love, peace, salvation, safety. Whoever gives oneself to it need no longer fear a coming judgment, for the judgment that one (properly) only expects at the end is already being pronounced now (Luke 12:8; Mark 8:38).

All this people experienced with regard to Jesus, his deeds and his conduct. This becomes especially apparent as he holds table fellowship (of the end-time!), as he associates with sinners, those marginalized by society, the despised, common people. Jesus' conduct in its entirety is fundamentally misunderstood if one sees in it the expression of social conscience and passes *this* off as the Jesus-business. Understood in this way, the Jesus-business would be nothing more than law. God's rule would once more simply correspond to what the Jews wanted to take into their own hands. At the same time, the law would merely have undergone minor alterations on Jesus' part. It would, however, still have remained law. He might perhaps have helped to make the world a bit better place. And anyone who clings to a hope for utopia counts on human efforts (spurred on by Jesus) changing things in such a way that a perfect state of affairs will be brought about.

However, such a hope for utopia cannot appeal to Jesus, and anyone who passes this program off as the Jesus-business has misunderstood Jesus precisely at the decisive point, for, according to him, the new world comes only through God. As a result, the human being is always a recipient. Nevertheless, this does not mean that people are to adopt that attitude of expectation in which there is nothing to be done but to long for the coming of the kingdom, to leave its coming to the future, and to live at a distance from it. No, the kingdom both means to and can break in now, as rule, yet as a rule that never achieves its goal except through the turnabout of the individual. Here we would need to speak of a passive activity on the part of the human being. Where this tension is broken, the Jesus-business is perverted.

I fear that this has often not been seen. But then it is quite understandable that controversy developed over the concept, "the Jesus-business." The very same people who took up the slogan and felt spurred on to action overlooked the fact that what is at issue is a passive activity. Those who emphasized christology in a polemic against the Jesus-business so understood recognized this quite clearly. It is just that a one-sided emphasis on christology is itself in danger of breaking the tension that constitutes passive activity. Here doing *follows* receiving. However, although this is the (logically) correct order, it is not to be turned into a temporal sequence, as would happen by supposing that one could have the gift other than in the doing, for God's rule comes in the turnabout of the individual and never in any other way.

However, since the turnabout is not a matter of bringing about a state of affairs, it always has to be risked anew. One cannot stay put in God's rule, but can only be on the move in it. Therefore, the Jesus-business consists in letting God's rule come in one's own turnabout. Insofar, it is always expectation and also expectation ever anew. Where turnabout is risked, however, expectation becomes fulfillment.

People experienced such fulfillments in the company of Jesus. On the one hand, Jesus' deeds and conduct were experienced as the dawning of God's rule. On the other hand, by way of Jesus' activity and proclamation, people gave themselves over to God's rule, by letting this happen in and through themselves. This is just what the Jesus-traditions show us in their character as kerygma. They are formulated not only to evoke faith (as Jesus' conduct, activity, and proclamation had been to evoke faith), but also on the basis of faith (as Jesus' activity and conduct had been experienced as being moved by God). Therefore, this Jesus-kerygma permits one to see that the people who passed it on knew the inbreaking of God's rule to be behind them. It is only that they do not have it behind them as a *turn of the aeons* that had taken place once and for all, and yet, as we have seen, neither is this the case for Paul. However, they experienced God's rule as having once broken in (in relation to Jesus and through Jesus in relation to themselves) in such a way that, *as* it broke in once in Jesus, it opened up the one time for all times.

This is how the Jesus-business continues. To be sure, it only continues as the *Jesus*-business if it continues *in this way.*

III.

In conclusion, I want to consider briefly the connection between the Jesus-business and christology.

Our starting point will have to be somewhat broader than is usually the case. I regard it as too narrow merely to look to the proclamation of Jesus and then to regard him as a proclaimer. This approach leads (in connection with Bultmann) to the familiar phrases, "Jesus' proclamation implies a christology," and "The proclaimer became (after and through Easter) the proclaimed."

I think one may certainly say that the Jesus-business implies a christology. To be sure, it is not to be concluded from this that making christology explicit is the presupposition of the Jesus-business continuing. Nor may one draw the different conclusion that the process of being made explicit leads to the mere bestowing of qualifications on the person of Jesus, in the sense of transferring titles of sovereignty to him. Without exception, these titles are functional in character. But this character is easily forgotten if christology loses itself in speculation about the person. I have already said that speaking about the savior only makes sense if at the same time one speaks about the salvation he brings.

THE JESUS-BUSINESS: IN DEFENSE OF A CONCEPT

However, if the Jesus-business is understood as at once a claim of experienced salvation and the invitation to a new experience of salvation, then christology consists in making the character of this salvation explicit. Concretely, this means making explicit the inbreaking of God's rule that has been experienced and that, for this reason, is announced as something that can be experienced. This is just what happens in the oldest traditions in a variety of ways. All the same, essentially two different approaches may be distinguished.

Within the synoptic tradition, the functional moment stands in the foreground. One draws a picture of Jesus in action and at the same time portrays the effect his action creates in a heightened way. Miracle stories are transferred to him, even to the point of nature-miracles and raising the dead. What is actually only expected at the end (and is expected of the new aeon) is claimed already to have dawned in Jesus' activity. By giving oneself over to Jesus, one gives oneself over to God's inbreaking rule. This becomes especially clear in the Son of Man traditions, as we have mentioned. In the encounter with Jesus, the judgment is now already issued that in principle was expected only in the future (Luke 12:8; Mark 8:38). And then it naturally lies close to hand to understand Jesus himself as the Son of Man, since he exercises the very same functions that the Son of Man does. That this transfer of the title to Jesus only occurred after (the date of) Easter is scarcely to be disputed. However, that this took place through Easter is certainly to be disputed. This was not occasioned by an "Easter-experience," but rather through the experience of the Jesus-business. If this was concerned with the inbreaking of God's rule, then it was just Jesus who permitted it to break in and it was through him that this inbreaking had been experienced. In the same way that experiencing salvation led to his being claimed as savior, the making of a "Son of Man judgment" led to his being claimed as Son of Man. It is even significant that the attribution of the title "Son of Man" is restricted to the gospels and is not found in the Christ-kerygma of the New Testament letters that is determined by Easter. Jesus' *activity* was understood as eschatological event, and the Jesus-business is then the offer of an eschatological event. To the more inclusive understanding of this eschatological occurrence at a later time, corresponds the more inclusive presentation of this eschatological occurrence when Jesus was alive in the

33

past. However, this is precisely the means whereby Jesus' activity continues into the present and, with his activity, he himself. For this reason, it is he who comes today.

In contrast to the emphasis in the synoptic tradition on the functional moment of the coming of Jesus in the business regarding him, the accent in the Christ-kerygma lies in an emphasis on the person. The starting point for this tradition is the cross of Jesus. It confronted those who were directly touched by it with the radical question whether Jesus and his business had failed. Could *the cross* be the consequence of allowing God's rule to come? Impossible! But then, who really was this one whose life ended in catastrophe, in spite of the unheard of claim made for him? Jesus had refused to legitimate himself to his contemporaries and to furnish the proof of his own character by fulfilling the demands for signs. For this reason, it was always a risk for those around him to give themselves to the rule of God that he declared was breaking in. At the same time, they had witnessed that he himself openly took this risk. But in this case, didn't his death on the cross itself refute him? At this point, the question about his business was transformed with inevitable trenchancy into the question about his person.

The Easter-experiences answered this question. I do not want to go into the problem now of what happened at that time; I have done this explicitly elsewhere. In any case, the confession of the resurrection of Jesus meant the overcoming of the shock that his fate called forth. However this confession was occasioned, it always means this: in spite of his death, he still comes today. But it is precisely this that is a "yes" to his "business," for it is the selfsameness of this business that justifies identifying the risen with the earthly one.

This "personal" christology was developed further to the point of adopting divine predicates. If the Jesus-business is understood as the breaking in of *God's* rule, this is not only understandable but even fitting, for who else but God can bring God's rule?

This, then, clarifies one last point. In the phrase "the Jesus-business" the ancient christological confession of the *vere homo-vere deus* (true human being-true God) is as it were "joined together." This is not to be treated in isolation as a statement about the character of the person. Doing this leads to speculations about how to imagine divinity in the human being Jesus and how to imagine the humanity of him who, as the exalted one, sits on the throne of God. Through a human being (who was a human being, really human and nothing but human), there breaks in the rule of God that only God can bring. And as the one who brings God's rule, this human being is experienced really and entirely as God.

When one understands this, one also understands that human speech can be experienced as God's word today. And the *Jesus*-business continues only where, in *passive* activity in *their own* dealings, people permit *God* to act.

3

JESUS—BEARER
OR CONTENT
OF THE GOSPEL?*

By assigning me this topic, you have asked me a question that is actually seldom put in these terms today. But of course, you also meant to evoke associations with the past. This is how I will approach it.

I.

You are quite obviously alluding to my phrase, "the Jesus-business continues." If we connect this phrase to the question that forms our title, we have the surmise (or, if you like, even the suspicion) that I should have to answer it in the same way Harnack did around the turn of the century in Berlin in his famous series of lectures, "What Is Christianity?" What has probably become the best known sentence from these reads, "The gospel, as Jesus proclaimed it, has to do with the Father, and not with the Son."

With this, the following seems clear: for Harnack, Jesus was not the content of the gospel. To be sure, precisely in view of the sentence cited, this ought not to be asserted too quickly in so general a way. People have frequently overlooked the words, "as Jesus proclaimed it." In doing so, they have consciously or (probably) unconsciously changed the meaning of at least this sentence. This remains to be considered. In any case, Harnack's overall slant in the way he represented the essence of Christianity was to repress christology for the sake of emphatically expounding "discipleship." The gospel

---

*"Jesus—Bringer oder Inhalt des Evangeliums?" *Die Sache Jesu geht weiter* (Gütersloh: Gütersloher Verlagshaus Gerd Mohn, 1976), 45–62.

of Jesus is the reference point. For this reason, the point cannot be to believe *in* Jesus. Rather, what counts is to believe *as* Jesus. He brought the gospel. He only became its content later.

However, when I speak of the "Jesus-business" that continues, I evidently place myself on the side of Harnack. If my phrase is understood as a description of the essence of Christianity (to express this as Harnack does), then this essence is apparently also described in a way that, so to speak, bypasses christology. After all, have I not basically only replaced the word "gospel" with another, namely, "Jesus-business"? We would then be meant to understand Jesus as bearer of this business, but nevertheless not as its content and certainly not as the "business" itself. The phrase "the Jesus-business continues" would just be a way of freshening up the old liberal position of Harnack. This would generally be considered a relapse into a conception that had been overcome in the meantime.

Nonetheless, this "business" does not seem to me quite so simple. I do not now want to investigate whether Harnack has been understood perfectly accurately if he is squeezed into the set of alternatives in which our topic is formulated. It is probably undeniable that he has been understood in these terms. This interpretation suggests itself, since if Harnack thought that Jesus was (at least originally) not the content of the gospel, then he was precisely— *merely*—its bearer. This is correct. Nevertheless, please take note of the fact that I have now added the little word "merely." But then the question in our title should no longer read, "Jesus—Bearer or Content of the Gospel?" but rather, "Jesus—*Merely* Bearer of the Gospel, or *Also* Its Content?" But this not only makes the question more precise; it transforms it. Whether Jesus was the bearer of the gospel is certainly not a matter of dispute. At least for Harnack, there was no doubt about this. People are not always so certain about this today, as we shall see. Now there are genuine as well as false sets of alternatives. In heated controversies, people all too quickly succumb to the temptation to pose false alternatives. Others are unwittingly taken in by these and then they become subject to the demagoguery that nearly always lurks in false sets of alternatives.

The situation is similar in the case of another set of alternatives I have already pointed to, namely, faith *in* Jesus or faith *as* Jesus. In precisely the earliest phase of the discussion of the historical

Jesus, the spirits often divide at this point. However, do we divide them correctly if we divide them *in this way*? Does faith *in* Jesus rule out that, *in* this faith, one's faith is *like* that of Jesus? In truth, the difference lies somewhere else entirely. The question is whether a faith like that of Jesus *must* become faith in Jesus, as it can and did, for, just as little as one would deny that he bore a gospel would one deny that Jesus had faith. In these discussions, close attention has to be paid to where the point at issue actually lies. If this is not done, false battle lines are set up all too quickly. However, anyone who is attacked in one's position, as I am, has to be on guard against accepting a false set of alternatives.

Therefore, I cannot accept the question of our title as it stands, even if I can accept the intention behind it. And since the way it is formulated is indebted to an older discussion, I want to begin by bringing one or two things from this discussion to mind.

II.

Harnack did not stand alone in his view. He was a representative of so-called liberal theology, the value of which he in particular had effectively shown. For this very reason, the controversy flared up around him more than around many others. It was a controversy with so-called conservative theology, which set great store by the statement that Jesus is the content of the gospel, while for the liberals he was "only" a bearer.

We need to see that, in this controversy, two planes of thinking were fused, the dogmatic and the historical. For instance, symptomatic of this is the fact we have already mentioned, that the most frequently cited sentence from Harnack's lectures was nearly always cited in a shortened form, and that this presumably happened completely unconsciously. The historical finding that Harnack's statement makes about the gospel "*as Jesus proclaimed it*," got turned into the dogmatic proposition, "The gospel has to do with the Father only, and not with the Son." In the framework of Christian theology, these two planes, the historical and the dogmatic, can certainly not be cleanly separated, since they are connected with each other. The dogmatic one is invariably made to depend on the historical one in some way or other, and the historical one invariably leads into the dogmatic one. Nevertheless, they have to be distinguished, and this distinction has to be maintained as carefully as possible, lest one end up with short-circuits. All the same, this has happened time and again, and it is a fair question whether the problem has a definitive solution at all. Perhaps it is a function of the issue itself that all answers entail new questions all over again, since the "en route" character of faith and theology displays itself in this structure of question-answer-new question. On the one hand, this gives us the freedom to criticize earlier answers. On the other hand, it keeps us modest and prevents us from thinking that we have found the definitively correct answer.

The *real* controversy at that time was a *dogmatic* one. It concerned the confession of faith. To take one's bearings from its central formulation, "I believe in Jesus Christ," is evidently to concede that Jesus is the content of the gospel. The call, "believe in the gospel," with which Jesus began his public activity (Mark 1:15), and the contemporary confession of faith in him are then identical. On the other hand, if Jesus is removed from the gospel, if he is understood "merely" as its bearer, then it becomes a different gospel. This seems clear, and on *this* plane, we can understand the passion with which the exchanges were pursued.

In spite of this, this controversy was settled principally on the *historical* plane, because this is the one from which the arguments were drawn. People sought to answer the dogmatic question, the one that takes its bearings from the present (Who *is* Jesus?), by means of an historical finding (What *did* Jesus *bear*?). On this plane, the opinions then diverged. To be sure, it was never seriously disputed that he bore a gospel. But, in so doing, did he bear "something" (however one determined its content), or did he bear—and perhaps even primarily—himself? In this exchange, something most peculiar can be observed. In the controversy as a whole, the fact was overlooked that there was agreement on a decisive point and that, precisely on this point, a mistake had been made. Specifically, across all their differences, the participants had shared an assumption in common and yet had neglected to examine whether this assumption was sound. This task was neglected on both sides. For the sake of carrying the discussion forward today, nearly everything depends on accurately identifying this point on which everyone was agreed. It can be specified quite readily. They supposed that the results of historical research could be introduced directly into dogmatics. If (the historical) Jesus did not himself belong to the gospel he bore, then, so it was concluded, neither could he rightly be designated as the content of the gospel today. However, if historical research did succeed in showing that he belonged to the content of the gospel from the beginning, then he had to belong to it today as well—but also, only on this condition.

To see this connection is immediately to understand the passion of the *historical* exchange. Its results (as *both* sides believed) impinge directly upon faith. This is the conviction that so tended to rob the process of historical inquiry of that impartiality which may not be renounced if things are to be seen as they were, rather than as one might like them to have been. The liberal theologians in particular reproached their conservative colleagues with the claim that they were pursuing their historical investigations with a dogmatic prejudice and, in doing so, were already corrupting the entire historical task from the outset. For their own part, in contrast, the liberals claimed to be undogmatic. They arrived at unconventional results that naturally were bound to shock anyone who considered historical results to be dogmatically binding and was now confronted by the liberal theologians with results that could not be brought into harmony with the confession of faith.

When we today look back at the historical scholarship of that time, we would have to judge that the results achieved by liberal theology have won very widespread acceptance. The same thing cannot be claimed for the historical results of the conservative theologians. Obviously, there were also scholars on the liberal side who (not infrequently because of a certain allergy to the church's dogma) overshot the mark in their historical criticism. This sort of thing proved irritating, but it can probably never be completely avoided. On the whole, however, the judgment can be made that there is hardly anyone today that does not have to respect the frank honesty of those liberal theologians. These scholars were prepared publicly to defend their (often also to themselves) surprising and, for this reason, by no means always comfortable results—and then to draw dogmatic conclusions from them as well. At the same time, they accepted the fact that, frequently enough, this earned them the charge of being "unfaithful."

To be sure, it also needs to be stated that these liberal theologians succumbed to a self-deception when they supposed that the reproach of being dogmatically prejudiced touched only their opponents, and when they imagined that they themselves were free from *every* dogmatic bias. This proved to be true only of their historical work. There they actually were undogmatic, to the extent that they did not allow themselves to be controlled by confessions of faith. This resulted in their historical findings having even greater aftereffects. Nevertheless, they, too, were prejudiced by a dogmatic conception, one that merely lay elsewhere and that, for this reason, also took on a different appearance. It was not the confessions of faith that controlled their historical work (and in general, this is the only sort of dependence we are accustomed to calling "dogmatic"). In spite of this, they allowed themselves to be controlled by an uncritical trust in the capacity of their historical findings to produce *dogmatic* results. Only what was historically reliable could and should be binding for faith. Once more, in relation to our specific problem, Jesus could only count as the content of the gospel today if he had been the content of the gospel that he bore. This was the assumption that was no longer examined. However, assumptions that are not examined are dogmatic.

It would certainly be unjust, because too cheap, to reproach the liberal theologians at so great a distance for not having seen *their* dogmatic bias. Even people who check over their own assumptions very critically will never identify them all. Someone else often sees them more clearly, and later generations nearly always better. Nevertheless, what is peculiar about the case before us is precisely that the liberal theologians *shared* the relevant bias with their conservative colleagues, namely, that they, too, had a burning interest in grounding the confessions of faith historically. With regard to *this* dogmatic assumption, both sides were in agreement. The difference between them consisted merely in the fact that the conservative group meant to ground the contemporary confession of faith historically, while the liberal one explained that this was not possible.

It is a peculiar thing about labels. It is difficult to define what "conservative" and what "liberal" mean. In general, such labels concern particular conclusions. If a conclusion agrees with the confession of faith, it is conservative; if not, it is liberal. But this way of classifying things is not unproblematic, because it attends only to conclusions. However, "liberal" can also designate an approach. In that case, if we say that what characterizes liberal *theology* is that it takes historical conclusions to be (all but unqualifiedly) theologically relevant, then there is every good reason to characterize the so-called conservatives as *theologically* liberal, too. For they themselves made use of precisely this *approach*.

Therefore, what has remained undecided in this discussion is actually not a disagreement over conclusions. To be sure, this is always what is most striking. And yet, to direct attention to this is to see only what is in the foreground. What ultimately remains undecided is rather the methodological question of the proper relation between historical study and the confession of faith. Is this really as direct as it was taken to be on both sides? *If* one were to enter into this, one could only succeed in doing so by pursuing the *historical* question in a genuinely "liberal" way. If dogma did need to be grounded by way of historical study and, thus, to be tested according to the criterion of historical findings, then such a process of testing could only have a point to it if the criterion itself were worked out historically to begin with, irrespective of the confession of faith. For this reason, the liberal theologians doubtless had the better position with regard to their *historical* work.

However, the difficulty with this position becomes apparent here at the same time. Such a criterion can only accomplish the task intended for it if its content can be clearly defined. This was only possible in turn if clear and secure results could be obtained. But the liberal theologians did not manage to do this. The insight also gradually dawned that this would presumably never be possible. Scholarly results are always subject to change. If a consensus does emerge here and there with respect to particular issues (I might mention here the two-source theory, by means of which the synoptic problem was solved), even this did not remain uncontested. Added to this was the fact that at that time the extensive introduction of the (discovery) and evaluation of sources from the history of religions constantly introduced new uncertainties into historical judgments. But then, how were such results to be introduced into dogmatics?

The answer that was finally felt to have been found to this question sounds downright astonishing, even fantastic when you first hear it. And that is, "not at all." The relevance for dogmatics of—invariably insecure—historical results was denied altogether. Was this not a way of making a virtue of necessity?

III.

One might certainly get this impression, and it would be an attractive way to depict the whole development that is supposed to have led to the victory over liberal theology. I cannot treat all of this here, since to do so I would have to lay out the history of scholarship (and its influence on the church) that began immediately after the First World War and that came to a certain conclusion in the fifties. I can only hint at this and do so by taking my bearings from the issue that lies behind the question in our title. During this period of the theology inaugurated by Bultmann (at the time under the influence of Barth) and then later called "kerygma theology," a widespread consensus was achieved that can be conveyed by means of the oft-quoted sentence, "The proclaimer became the proclaimed."

This sentence might convey the impression that the discussion had not yet gotten beyond Harnack. Jesus was the proclaimer (that is, the bearer of the gospel); subsequently, he became the proclaimed (therefore, the content of the gospel). Had Harnack said anything different? And again, people often spoke of the "old liberal solution" (which, as I have said, is also often suspected behind my phrase, "the Jesus-business continues").

Nevertheless, this impression is deceptive, as can be shown first with regard to kerygma theology. There is no doubt that there is (at least widespread) agreement between the liberals and kerygma theology about the *historical* findings. However, their *dogmatic* positions are diametrically opposed. For liberal theology, the statement that the proclaimer of the gospel became its content means a distancing from the original gospel. When christology was introduced into this original gospel, it was fatefully altered. However, since the gospel today has to correspond to the original content, it became necessary to undo these alterations. Now to be sure, kerygma theology is also concerned that today's confession of faith take its bearings from the original gospel, except that for kerygma theology, the gospel as gospel begins only at the point at which the proclaimer became the proclaimed, and for it, this means with cross and resurrection. Although Jesus was "merely" the proclaimer (and this is an *historical* observation), it is nonetheless legitimate to proclaim him as the content of the gospel and to declare him as what is believed in today's confession of faith (and these are *dogmatic* claims).

We will still have to ask how this way of construing things could arise and what consequences grew out of it. But first, let us pause for just a moment and compare this way of construing things with the one we find around the turn of the century. What took place at that time in scarcely two generations has often been recounted, but has still not begun to work its way into the general consciousness. This has been very much to the detriment of many discussions, even—and especially—the public ones. The prevailing view is that kerygma theology has inherited the legacy of liberal theology. As an example, it is only necessary to point to Bultmann, who is descended from the liberal school. (His *History of the Synoptic Tradition*, the first edition of which appeared in 1921, is the work of a liberal theologian.) However, this label all too quickly leads to overlooking what is essential, in particular the influence of dialectical theology (and later of Heidegger) that was soon to make itself felt on the (still) liberal Bultmann. Now, it is bound to be unsettling to learn that kerygma theology comes to the same conclusion that the old conservatives came to *with respect to dogmatics*. Both agree that, for today's confession of faith, what counts is what is proclaimed. It is not at all a matter of believing *as* Jesus; Christian faith is by definition faith *in* Jesus Christ. But this is precisely what Harnack never could have said, and none of the old liberal theologians would have agreed with this. One would therefore have to suppose that those who carried on the old conservative traditions must have felt themselves confirmed. Even if they might have been of a different opinion from the point of view of historical study, they were once more ultimately in agreement with respect to the (contemporary) confession of faith. The angry doctrinal controversies of the turn of the century, which had also on occasion led to disciplinary proceedings over doctrine in the churches of the Reformation, could be settled.

We know that this is the very thing that did not happen. How could it have? A singular "exchange of positions" took place (Käsemann). The conservative side was willing to recognize the confession of faith on the part of kerygma theology only on the condition that kerygma theology *also* justify it historically. This kerygma theology could not do. In its historical scholarship, kerygma theology remained liberal. Not only did it come by its historical results uninfluenced by the confession of faith; it also conducted the discussion (within its own ranks as well) of differing historical results without any tie to the confession of faith. The *historical* discussion was actually set free, because the confession of faith was not touched by its results.

It is precisely this for which the conservative side reproached kerygma theology. It was often said by way of a warning that there could not be "unlimited freedom" in theology—even in historical scholarship within theology. But, why not, if one kept strictly to the historical approach? Well, just because history and the confession of faith are to be related to each other. Only if Jesus had been the content of his gospel originally, could he be the content of the gospel in the confession of faith today. But this means nothing less than that the conservative side held fast to the liberal *way of conceiving the issue*. For this is the very logic that had informed the older liberal theology, as it engaged in its criticism of dogma on the basis of just this way of conceiving the issue.

So it can in fact be asked who is properly to be called "liberal" and who "conservative." Should we take our bearings in this matter from the results, or is it the fundamental way of conceiving the issue that should be decisive here? The answer is once more made difficult by the fact that these terms are by no means always used in a neutral way. Not everyone is prepared to be called a liberal theologian. Although it may be something of a simplification, we can at least contribute to clarity by making a distinction. Kerygma theology had abandoned the liberal way of conceiving the issue. In its dogmatic statements, it was conservative; in its historical work and in its historical results, it remained liberal. The traditionally conservative side, in contrast, preserved not only the dogma (on which they now might have been able to agree with kerygma theology), but also the old liberal way of conceiving the issue, the specifically liberal character of which for the most part they did not grasp. In historical work, liberal tendencies came to prevail in time, in varying ways among individual scholars. With respect to historical results, however, a propensity for the conservative continued throughout.

Naturally, such a classification may only be employed with caution, since it makes schematizing unavoidable. For all this, it can clarify trends. Both sides struggle to get away from liberal theology. They want to overcome it, and yet this can only happen by making contact with it. All the same, where one needs to stay in contact and where one needs to go on ahead remain a matter of dispute; nor is one always aware of when one has in fact taken along the old that one meant to overcome.

IV.

It was undoubtedly kerygma theology that broke most sharply from liberal theology. It alone radically called into question the old *assumption* and then disputed its validity. Let me return to the question of our title in order to make this clear. Harnack was still of the opinion that Jesus was the bearer of a gospel which not only can be proclaimed with the same content today, but which also should be proclaimed only with this content. Strictly speaking, according to him, a gospel that had Jesus himself for its content was a different gospel. With the sentence, "The proclaimer becomes the proclaimed," the kerygma theology endorses Harnack's *historical* conclusion. From a *dogmatic* standpoint, in contrast, it claims (and this now precisely versus Harnack) that Christian faith is to be defined as faith *in* Jesus Christ, that it therefore has the proclaimer as its content. If the historical conclusion is combined with the dogmatic claim, it follows that only *since* the proclaimer became the proclaimed has there been Christian faith.

The difference emerges even more sharply if we attempt to compare the different terminology employed by each position. Let me do this by expressing the statement of kerygma theology in the terms employed by Harnack. If Christian faith, which has the proclaimer as its content, is equated with the gospel, then this is the way we would have to put it: Jesus did indeed proclaim, but what he proclaimed was not yet the gospel. This did not yet exist at the time of Jesus. What for Harnack is *the* gospel (namely, the content of the proclamation of Jesus) is not *yet* for kerygma theology "gospel" at all. Conversely, what to Harnack appears to be a different gospel, namely, the christologizing of the proclamation through and after Easter, is in the kerygma theology really *the* gospel for the first time.

I think it is now unmistakably clear that something like a complete misunderstanding of the position of kerygma theology occurs if its sentence about the proclaimer who became the proclaimed is understood as a repetition of the old liberal view of Harnack's. We ought rather to say that this has been stood on its head, for, in the liberal way of conceiving the issue, the historical judgment implies a dogmatic one. In contrast, in kerygma theology, the dogmatic judgment now implies precisely (at least indirectly) an historical judgment. Since Christian faith (and, therewith, gospel) begins only once there is faith in the proclaimer, the Jesus who proclaims *cannot* yet have borne a gospel.

Of course, at this point one instinctively asks whether this can be so. Did Jesus really not bear a gospel? Is conceding this the price that has to be paid in order to overcome liberal theology? For a long time, this was in fact the view of kerygma theology, but this is not so everywhere today. Still, before we criticize what follows from this way of conceiving things, let us briefly ask how it came about and what assumptions were involved. After all, insights emerged in the polemic against liberal theology that I believe we may still not give up today, even if we may not take over the consequences of this polemic as they stand. For here too, there is a legacy to protect, just as kerygma theology for its part properly remained indebted to the legacy of the historical work of liberal theology. To be sure, I can only give some hints here as well. Let me approach the various motifs in such a way as to take my bearings from the historical and dogmatic aspects, the relation between which forms the background to our problem. Let us consider them in turn.

Historical scholarship within theology had occupied itself since the Enlightenment with the (so-called) historical Jesus, basically with a dogmatic interest from the outset. Albert Schweitzer's history of scholarship on the life of Jesus presents a vivid picture of this, but at the same time shows why this research was bound to fail if it kept to the Enlightenment's way of posing the question. No generation succeeded in presenting Jesus as he was historically. Each generation sketched its own portrait. Martin Kähler called the quest for the historical Jesus (shortly before Schweitzer) a false trail. These efforts were then taken up and carried on immediately after the First World War by so-called form criticism. It came to the conclusion that the texts we have simply do not permit us to accomplish what we had previously expected from them. The very texts that took up and formulated the individual traditions and that later made their way into the synoptic gospels were not interested in painting an historically and biographically accurate portrait of the life of Jesus. Rather, they meant to make use of their own texts in order to proclaim. They intended by way of their proclamations to call people to faith, to maintain them in faith, to help shape faith as people lived their lives, and so forth. To be sure, the texts had the past as their content, but they presented the past so as to address the present by means of it. This present-oriented character of the texts was called "kerygma." However, if we have to do with kerygma in these texts, it follows from this that they cannot (at least not directly) be consulted for historical accuracy. To do this is to consult them in violation of the intention of their authors. Precisely because they pursued a kerygmatic interest, these authors could deal "carelessly" with the presentation of the past, with which historical accuracy is concerned. They could do this all the more readily, since the modern way of posing the historical question was still entirely unknown to them. But then it is not at all surprising that the attempt to achieve exact historical results today with the aid of these texts is extraordinarily difficult. For here we have to bear in mind that historical results are always uncertain and subject to change in the course of scholarship, and this is aggravated by the fact that the texts themselves are not intended to provide what is expected from them in consulting them historically. They are for the sake of faith, not historical information. If an historian now approaches the texts, (at least) the first result that is obtained is not the history of Jesus; rather, the historian encounters kerygma and is able to discern in this kerygma the picture that the early community drew of Jesus, but that it did so for the sake of proclaiming in its own present.

This exegetical insight then (already at the beginning of the twenties) ran into dialectical theology, with its dogmatic interest. Here in particular the concept of the word of God played a role, and this concept was transferred to the kerygma. As word of God, it confronts people with decision. It makes an immediate demand of obedience and, on account of this, permits of no guarantee. Anyone who still wants historical security first when faced with the summons that has been issued to him refuses faith.

This makes clear that faith has the character of risk. We now recognize that the liberal attempt to insure the content of the confession of faith by way of historical investigation detracts from the risk of faith. However, this corrupts faith completely; it is no longer faith at all. Kerygma theology undoubtedly saw this correctly. For this reason, it was able to set historical scholarship free, since the results of historical scholarship no longer possessed any theological relevance.

Naturally, there remained the possibility of examining the kerygma historically. One Jesus-saying could be explained as historically authentic and another as the creation of the community. The deeds of Jesus could be similarly assessed. Here, too, altogether differing conclusions might result. These were not important theologically, because historical judgments do not affect the claim of the kerygma. This was (whether its content was historically genuine or not) for the sake of faith. It demanded the risk of giving oneself over to it.

In the wake of this development, Bultmann was only being consistent when he began his *Theology of the New Testament* with the sentence, "The proclamation of Jesus belongs to the presuppositions of the theology of the New Testament and is not a part of that theology itself." Christian faith begins only with the kerygma. But the kerygma begins only with Easter.

This "dismissal" of the historical Jesus from theology is no longer uncontested, even among Bultmann's students, ever since Käsemann's famous essay of 1953 ("The Problem of the Historical Jesus," in *Essays on New Testament Themes* SBT 41 [London: SCM, 1964]: 15–47. Reprinted Philadelphia: Fortress, 1982). The discussion that has attached itself to this in the last twenty years is, of course, extraordinarily involved, and a consensus is not yet in sight. Nevertheless, I will not go into this at any further length here.

V.

Instead, let me once again take my bearings from the intention behind the question of our title and with this in mind turn to two ideas of the kerygma theology—one that should not have been given up, and another that needs to be modified somewhat.

The idea that ought not to have been given up is that faith has the character of risk and therefore is corrupted if one expects to guarantee it historically before being prepared to embark on it. In contrast, what needs to be modified is the proposition that the proclaimer became the proclaimed.

All the same, it needs to be emphasized immediately that this proposition is without a doubt historically correct. The historical Jesus did proclaim, but he did not turn himself into the subject-matter of his proclamation and did not call for faith in himself. To this extent, there is a break between his proclamation and the proc-lamation of the earliest community. However, I regard it as a one-sided simplification when this break is always linked up temporally and materially with Easter. Again, it is correct in this regard that only since Easter has there been faith in Jesus Christ. The "Christ-kerygma" was formulated out of such faith, and its aim is to sum-mon people into this faith.

However, it is most peculiar that, throughout the synoptic source material, that is, in the individual traditions that then made their way into the first three gospels, never once is there faith in Jesus Christ, nor even is this the case in the gospels themselves (except for Matt. 18:6; 27:42). Nevertheless, in this branch of tra-dition, as form criticism and redaction criticism have taught us, the concern is not with historical reports, but with individual instances of proclamation, that is, with kerygma. I should like to speak here of "Jesus-kerygma," in order to express the fact that the earliest Christian kerygmata have differing contents and, in particular, dif-fering structures. Jesus or Jesus Christ is in each case the respective content of the kerygmata. In the case of the Christ-kerygma, he is this as the one who is proclaimed and believed in. In that of the Jesus-kerygma, however, he is this (still) as one who proclaims or acts, as the case may be, and as the one who summons to faith.

It is quite clear that we can discern no material influence due to Easter not only in the oldest Jesus-kerygma, but in the bulk of the Jesus-kerygma in general as well (apart from very few later excep-tions). This is not to make any judgment about when this kerygma was formulated. In many cases, it will have arisen in the form in which we have it (or in which we can reconstruct it) only after the death of Jesus. However, if the break that ensues with Easter is characterized in such a way that the (historical) Jesus, who sum-moned to faith, has now become the one in whom people had faith, then *this* break was not achieved by the Jesus-kerygma. *Insofar*, it could be said that the Jesus-kerygma forms a "pre-Easter" stage of tradition, even if it was formulated after the date of Easter and if

Jesus (though as proclaimer and as one who acts) is the content of the kerygma and therefore the proclaimer.

At the same time, it must also be said that there is no basis for the supposition that Jesus-kerygma first arose only after Easter. At all events, the beginnings go back to the period of the earthly Jesus. The question then faces us whether this period must be viewed as operating under what might be called a "deficit," as a "not yet" that was only superseded by an "already" that took place through and with Easter. Yet this is evidently the view of kerygma theology when it emphasizes that only with the resurrection of Jesus did the early community believe that it had behind it the turn of the aeons, to which (the earthly) Jesus still looked forward.

Nevertheless, I regard talk of the turn of the aeons that took place at Easter as dangerously misleading. That Jesus looked forward to this (as did many of his contemporaries) is not to be disputed. However, that Paul, let us say, looked back on it (which he himself never asserts), can only be said by someone who employs this apocalyptic concept in a completely different sense. After all, it means the replacement of this cosmic era that is passing away by the new world of God. However, this is still a matter of the future even for Paul. Thus, if we take our bearings from the conception of the turn of the aeons, we may not speak of a "deficit" in the case of Jesus. In this regard, Jesus and Paul still live in the time of expectation.

To be sure, it must immediately be added that, for both, the expectation is counteracted in a peculiar way. Jesus announces the present breaking in of the kingly rule of God (thought of as in principle something that is coming) (Mark 1:15). Paul says that, amidst the night that still persists, the Christians live as children of the coming day (1 Thess. 5:5). Thus, both say that what counts is to accept God and God's salvation now, in the midst of this world that is passing away. This is always a risk, because appearances speak against it. Yet this is precisely what faith is. It was not Paul who first summoned people into this faith; Jesus had already done so.

This is just what the Jesus-kerygma shows. At the same time, we still have to pay attention to the fact that the Jesus-kerygma not only is for the sake of faith, but also is formulated by believers, that is, by people who have given themselves to Jesus' summons. However, by doing so, they gave themselves not only and simply to his proclamation, but at the same time to him, since they experienced him as someone who lived God's inbreaking kingly rule himself. The Jesus-kerygma that has as its content Jesus' deeds and conduct makes this clear. With regard to the question of the gospel Jesus bore, it was precisely a mistake of liberal theology to have thought one-sidedly about his proclamation, which can be investigated historically and which can thereby be detached from him. However, if it is seen that the Jesus-kerygma was formulated by believers who also incorporated Jesus' conduct and deeds into their own summons, then we simply have to state that Jesus was the content of the kerygma from the start. To put it too succinctly: Jesus brought himself.

Naturally, this is not meant in the sense that Jesus called for faith *in* himself. We may not simply equate the one statement, that the proclaimer became the proclaimed, with the other, that he who summoned to faith became the one in whom one had faith. Only the former statement holds for the Jesus-kerygma, and it may not be narrowed down to apply only to the proclamation, but must rather include his activity as a whole. Jesus is proclaimed as one who acts, and he is proclaimed as having expected people to believe *him* to be the present inbreaking of God's kingly rule, as he lived it in these people's midst. It is precisely this that I take to be the "Jesus-business." It is *his* life of the inbreaking kingly rule of God, *his* giving himself over to God's present salvation. In the Jesus-kerygma, this is announced to others by believers—and lived by them personally. In this way, they bear Jesus to others. For this reason, it holds true that he still comes today, that the Jesus-business continues. The history of the synoptic tradition is the literary witness to this continuation.

With this, the question of our title (or at least the intention that stands behind the question) permits of an answer—and yet one that is considerably different from Harnack's. The old liberal question about the historical Jesus overlooked the kerygmatic character of our traditions. It would be fairer to say that they had not yet recognized this. So they isolated Jesus and did not see that what is at issue is always a being moved that is occasioned by Jesus. Those who believe Jesus are a constitutive component of the kerygma which, for its part, now expects others to risk the same faith.

VI.

In conclusion, one short word more about faith *in* Jesus Christ. After what has been said, this much should be clear: I cannot understand why people are willing to speak of Christian faith only once Jesus Christ is the one believed in. To be consistent, the synoptic gospels could not then be termed Christian witnesses of faith. As a matter of fact, kerygma theology has considerable difficulty explaining why the synoptic gospels arose so late, if Easter is understood as the sharp break in which the one who calls to faith became the one believed in. The gospels would then be a relapse into a stage that had been overcome with Jesus' resurrection.

In my view, the mistake lies in thinking of the early community as growing out of a single root, namely, that of the Easter faith. In fact, we have to reckon with two roots. The one is represented by the Jesus-kerygma of the synoptic tradition, the other by the Christ-kerygma of the pre-Pauline and Pauline theology, the epistolary literature of the New Testament as a whole, and the Gospel of John. Obviously, the Christ-kerygma found a much wider circulation than did the Jesus-kerygma. We may only be able to conceive this coexistence with difficulty, and I admit that there are many unresolved questions here. Yet people quite unwittingly assume that there must have been connections. No matter how close these may have ever been, the fact is that neither branch influenced the other in its use of language for a very long time. The language is always either of believingly giving oneself to Jesus or of faith in Jesus Christ. A mutual penetration occurs only very late.

The Christ-kerygma quite certainly has its origin with the cross and Easter. Jesus' death must have been understood at first as his failure and must have led to the question, "Is it possible for someone who gives himself over to the presence of God as he does to perish in such a way?" The question about the Jesus-business now became a question about Jesus himself. This question confronted those who witnessed Jesus' death. (In Galilee, where the Jesus-kerygma was presumably at home, this question did not pose itself in this way.)

The Easter-experiences (whatever they were like) gave the witnesses the answer: God has raised Jesus. In this context, it then came to be a matter of faith in the risen one, a faith that also found expression in this language and was elaborated by means of explicit christology. To be sure, we must immediately note that the risen one was none other than the earthly one. For this reason, giving oneself to the risen one still means giving oneself to the same business that the earthly one had offered and demanded. A new "stage of salvation history" is not reached with Easter, even if this is the way it has often been viewed subsequently. All the same, the real point is this: is faith in Jesus to risk believing Jesus and, for his sake, to live ever again and ever anew as a child of the coming day in this world that is passing away—with all the risk this faith implies.

4

JESUS
OF NAZARETH:
AN EVENT*

The phrase "the Jesus-business that continues" turned into a
ready slogan shortly after it came into use. It was also subjected to
the fire of criticism from the start. Where this took place, the
polemic against this phrase usually created a forced choice between
two alternatives. Christian faith, the objection went, is concerned
with the person of Jesus, not with a (that is, with his) "cause." In
the meantime, I have tried to show that this is a false opposition.
What was intended by the "Jesus-business" had obviously been
misunderstood. However, I would prefer not to pursue this here.

Instead, I want to approach the real issue from as it were the
other side of this purported set of alternatives. Therefore, I will
proceed from the person and speak about Jesus of Nazareth. Nevertheless, even in the title of this essay, I characterize just this person as an event. Perhaps this will take some people by surprise. In
what way is a person an event? As I reflect on the discussion up to
this point, two possible objections come to mind.

The first objection concerns the fact that I do not speak simply
of Jesus, thereby at least leaving undecided whether it is the earthly
Jesus or the risen one that is meant. And yet, it is said, the two may
not be separated. However, if what we are concerned with is Jesus
of Nazareth, then the whole subject of Easter is left out of account.
As the discussion is currently being conducted, such an approach
is liable to be suspected of being a massive oversimplification.

---

*"Jesus von Nazareth—ein Ereignis," *Christologie—praktisch* (Gütersloh: Gütersloher
Verlagshaus Gerd Mohn, 1978), 36–57.

JESUS OF NAZARETH: AN EVENT

The second possible objection concerns the more specific characterization of the person Jesus as event. For that is scarcely what was intended in the original demand that Christian faith take its bearings from the person, instead of from the cause. In this case, one would presumably speak not of an oversimplification, but rather of a softening. By "person," what is invariably meant is above all the "character" of this person—Jesus the Son of God, the Messiah, the Christ, not "merely" an event. Does not speaking of Jesus as an "event" create once more the impression of skirting the decisive point, what is at stake in Christian faith?

In an effort to head off from the outset the sort of false anxieties that might lead many of you to listen only skeptically and with hesitation, I would like to offer a different formulation of the topic: In Jesus of Nazareth, God became incarnate. Strictly speaking, becoming incarnate is, as a matter of fact, an occurrence, an event. At the same time, I want to emphasize immediately that I am not playing some kind of trick, as if (so to say, in order to set your mind at ease) I were offering a formulation, only to modify it or even completely to take it back later on. On the contrary, this assertion will still be left standing at the end of this essay. In Jesus of Nazareth, God became incarnate. However, this means for me not that Jesus was "merely" the Messiah, the Christ, the Son of God (or what the "weakened" predicates that were later attributed to him express), but rather, that Jesus was God. To formulate this even more pointedly, I should even venture the claim, "Jesus of Nazareth was the God who raises the dead." In saying this, the most exalted predicate known to the Judaism of his time is attributed to Jesus. Indeed, it is probably even the most exalted claim we can formulate today. The predicate "God" was first transferred to Jesus very late on in the course of the development of christological claims. But I want to employ it already for Jesus of Nazareth.

In what way then do we have to do with an event?

I do not want to approach this theoretically or by means of arguments from systematic theology. Rather, I simply want to start from texts. In order to do this, I need to identify three presuppositions that I will not justify more fully, because there is, or at least there should be a consensus regarding them among us today.

The first presupposition is generally accepted and is so self-evident to everyone who deals with the synoptic gospels that I just want to acknowledge it once more. The Jesus-traditions are first found as independent traditions that were only later put together into collections and that we finally have in the form of three gospels. (That this is not simply a *literary* issue, but one that involves matters of substance at the deepest level, will become clear later on.) We call these independent traditions the material of the synoptic tradition. When we look at this material, we readily see that it has gone through a history. Not every piece of tradition is original, and not every one is in its original form in the form in which we have it now. We can clearly recognize alterations in many a double- and triple-tradition. How these are to be explained is sometimes disputed from case to case, and the point in time at which a piece of tradition was formulated and when alterations were made are on occasion similarly disputed. But this uncertainty in individual cases does not negate the secure insight that we have to do with originally independent traditions and that these have gone through a history. This is my first presupposition.

While *the second presupposition* is not so widely acknowledged as the first, still, in my view, there cannot be the least doubt concerning it. It is that the beginnings of these traditions go back to the period before Easter. It is often said that the community that passed on the Jesus-traditions believed in the risen one and then presented the words and deeds of the earthly one *together with* this faith in the risen one. Therefore, it is said that Easter must be presupposed even in the case of the individual traditions that have what happened before Easter as their content. I do not want to contest this in any fundamental way, even if I take the view that this is much more seldom the case than is usually supposed. However, I can let this be. In spite of this, I believe there is not a single good reason for the assumption that people first began to pass on and then also to create Jesus-traditions after Easter. The beginnings must lie in the period of the earthly Jesus. This is what I am concerned with here, and this is precisely why I speak deliberately of Jesus of Nazareth. It is he that I want to try to reach.

Then we can mention *the third presupposition*, concerning which there can again be no doubt. We cannot reach Jesus directly. We do not have a single line from his own hand. Therefore, we can only ever ascertain how people understood Jesus, how they experienced him, how they heard him. By this I in no way mean that what these people narrate is "unhistorical," as we usually put this today. However, I do mean to say that there is no method for leaping over these people in what they say. Even on a photographic plate, all that is recorded is what it is technically equipped to record. What it is not equipped for is not recorded on the plate, even if it is "objectively" there. In the case of these people, what this means is that they did not pass on what did not interest them about Jesus. Conversely, it follows that what these people did pass on, they passed on as people who were interested in Jesus. This interest on these people's part that is reflected in the traditions blocks access to (what people call) an objective-historical Jesus. At the same time, it should also be clear that this is not a regrettable loss. For what sort of interest could we have in a Jesus who sparked no interest in the people around him? If Jesus intended to spark interest, and if the traditions formulated on the basis of such interest show that Jesus succeeded in what he intended, then we would be frustrating this "success" on Jesus' part if we were to eliminate this interest from the traditions. The quest for the so-called historical Jesus from the Enlightenment through liberal theology (in which Jesus was taken "objectively," that is, Jesus without and before any interpretation) therefore proves fruitless for reasons of method. Moreover, and much more important, an effort to reach *this* Jesus is extremely dubious on material grounds. This effort is identical with renouncing precisely what is decisive. I called this in a general way the "interest in Jesus." With regard to this, I might also say that it would be a renunciation of faith. But this can only be clarified later on.

Therefore, we need to insist that, when Jesus of Nazareth is asked about, the question has to be asked with precision. How was Jesus understood? How was he heard? How did people who talked about him experience him?

It is just this question that I want to address to several texts. So that I do not proceed arbitrarily, let me begin with a passage that has a summarizing character and that, for this reason, very probably does not belong to the oldest stratum of materials, namely, Matt. 11:2–6. This deals (as does Luke 7:18–23) with the inquiry of John the Baptizer, who hears of the works of the Christ while in prison and now wants to know by way of messengers whether Jesus is the one who is to come, or whether they are to wait for another. Jesus' answer is evasively ambiguous. The messengers are to go to

58

John and tell him—precisely not (as they had inquired) *whether* Jesus is the one who is to come, but rather—what they see and hear, namely, "the blind are given sight, the lame walk, lepers are cleansed, the deaf hear, the dead rise, and salvation is proclaimed to the poor." The question arises immediately whether this is an answer or not. If this remark is taken as referring to actions that would decide the question at issue, one might conclude that these "miracles" are advanced as proof of the messiahship of Jesus, for the question is who *he* is. Matthew and Luke very probably understood this in this or some similar way. (This can be shown by the way they arrange their material and by the insertions they make.) However, for our purposes, I am concerned not with interpreting the views of the gospel writers, who incorporated the prior tradition (from the so-called sayings-source) in their work, but rather with the original traditional material itself. It is striking in this regard that these actions on Jesus' part are of the sort that were only expected to occur at the end-time, after the turn of the aeons. It was expected that God would do all these things at that time. But this is where we find what is distinctive. Through Jesus, miracles occur. At least when each is considered for its own sake, these are miracles that were attributed to other miracle-workers of that time as well. Therefore, the action of Jesus "proves" that he is—a miracle-worker, nothing more. However, whether he is the one who is to come (and that was the question) can precisely not be perceived in the miracles *as such*. This is why Jesus' answer concludes with the words, "And blessed is the person who takes no offense at me!"

I said that here we have to do with a composition that is not original (from a literary point of view, one would call it a summary). It conveys the impression that people got from the activity of Jesus. He engaged in observable and verifiable *actions*. Nonetheless, this activity was by no means unambiguous. Precisely for this reason, it also ultimately proves nothing at all. An extraordinary miracle-worker might be at work here. However, it might also be the case that Jesus is already doing now what is expected of God in the future; he makes all things well. Naturally, there is no doubt at all about the view of those who formulated this piece of tradition. They had given themselves to Jesus and were sure of their ground. But at the same time, it was clear to them that it was not as if they could directly refute the other view. Therefore, this is the situation in this piece of tradition: To the question about who Jesus is, there is no answer. Instead, there is a reference to actions that really do take place, to be sure, but that are not unambiguous.

Luke 11:14–23 (and parallels) reveals a corresponding ambiguity in the *activity* of Jesus. Since what is narrated is the healing of someone who is possessed, we are dealing with an event that is subject to verification. All the same, the reproach is heard that Beelzebub is at work here. In contrast, we have Jesus' assertion that he is driving out the evil spirits by the finger of God and that, therefore, God's rule is now occurring right here before people's eyes. Again, there is of course no doubt about the view of the people who formulated this piece of tradition, namely, that wherever Jesus acts, God's finger is at work. And they assert this, however clear it may be to them that they cannot offer a "proof" for the presence of God's rule, no matter how powerful and extraordinary what occurs there may be. Unusual things happen in this world all the time, and what still seems unusual today might somehow be explained as completely "natural" tomorrow.

So it is also obviously pointless to demand a sign of Jesus to legitimate *him*. Accordingly, it is frequently said that Jesus repudiated signs. Conversely, this naturally means that "miracles" that take place are never to be misused as proofs of the "character" of Jesus (as we already find in the time of the New Testament and as people try to do time and again today). To do this misses the decisive point. What is decisive is not the fact in itself, but how the fact was understood—that is to say, its interpretation. However, this cannot be read directly off the fact. Rather, it always has to be *risked*.

The people who formulated these traditions risked this interpretation. In this regard, I want to point out once more *what* they interpreted: It is not the *person* (as the Baptizer and as those who demanded signs wanted them to do). What they interpret is rather what Jesus *does*, that is to say, an *occurrence*. Thus, Jesus is in view only insofar as the occurrence proceeds from *him*. However, what he makes happen is an occurrence, of which at the same time it is said, known, believed, that it is *God* who initiates it. Let me express this somewhat formulaically. What is confessed is, "Jesus enacts an act of God." This now needs to be made more precise.

In this regard, let me take my bearings from a catchword that was actually used, the "rule of God." This very catchword is found in a summary at the beginning of the Gospel of Mark. I think it can constitute the key for understanding Jesus as the one who brings salvation. Jesus appears in Galilee, proclaims the gospel of God, and cries, "The time of this world has become full. The rule of God has drawn near. Turn about and believe in this gospel" (Mark 1:14f.).

You probably know that these verses contain a wealth of exegetical and historical problems, all of which I cannot possibly clarify in passing. Scholarly opinion is unanimous that we have to do here not with the *ipsissima vox* of Jesus (that is, with an historically exact, verbatim repetition of his speech), but rather with a summary that conveys an overall impression of Jesus' activity. Because of this, I can take my bearings from the texts considered previously and bring what we learned there to bear here. Then, in conclusion, I shall, so to speak, pursue this experiment by refering to additional texts, in order to see whether I have understood this verse correctly.

In the case of the healing of the possessed person, the claim was that Jesus drives out demons by the finger of God and that, therefore, the rule of God became present. With this, we face the problem of how the words "has drawn near" in Mark 1:15 are to be understood and, therefore, the problem of the so-called imminent expectation of the kingdom on Jesus' part.

We run into the following claim time and again in this regard: Jesus counted on the inbreaking of the kingdom of God in the immediate future. In Jesus' view, this inbreaking was utterly imminent, and yet it remained (even precisely as imminent) a future occurrence. It is then further claimed that this expectation on Jesus' part became a matter of fulfillment in the understanding of the earliest community. This is supposed to be connected with the events of Easter. Paul is usually named as the chief witness for this opinion, which is formulated in this way: What Jesus still looks forward to, Paul now looks back on, namely, the inbreaking of the new aeon by way of the kingdom of God. To this way of conceiving things is then linked the view that the earthly Jesus has no significance for the theology of the New Testament. According to Rudolf Bultmann (and a large part of his school), the proclamation of Jesus belongs to the presuppositions of the New Testament, but not to the New Testament itself. The actual "beginning" is the point at which the inbreaking of the kingdom, only anticipated by Jesus, actually occurred. However, this was the case (according to this way of conceiving things) only after Jesus, if still before Paul.

I have considerable misgivings about this view of things. In particular, I fear that several things have gotten mixed up here. I would like to demonstrate this at two points.

a) If we assume for a moment that Jesus really was waiting for the imminent inbreaking of the kingdom of God, then (according to the way of conceiving things at that time) he was waiting for God to establish a new *state of affairs*. The new aeon that arrives with the kingdom of God removes the old aeon, replaces it, and then continues to exist. Now this undoubtedly did not happen. If one so desires, one may speak of Jesus' having been mistaken on this score. It is just that one now needs to see this: If *Jesus* expected a new *state of affairs*, then it may not be claimed that Paul looks back on this state of affairs having come about in the meantime. Paul is also still waiting for the new heaven and the new earth. At the least, it will have to be said that, if Jesus and Paul are seen according to the scheme of "expectation-fulfillment," what was expected is not at all in accord with what is alleged to have been fulfilled. But then this whole scheme (if it is informed by the turn of the aeons and the kingdom of God) becomes meaningless.

b) This way of construing things does not take seriously the fact that in Mark 1:14 we have to do with a summary formulated in the early community. Therefore, this (at least indirectly) conveys the impression Jesus made. We learn only how people understood Jesus. It always remains possible that they did take Jesus merely to have expected the kingdom of God to break in, for, since people were waiting for this themselves (specifically, at the parousia of Jesus), this could still be presented as an expectation on Jesus' part. Therefore, we must be dealing with a very early saying here, because after the expectation of an imminent parousia had been abandoned, this saying could hardly have been formulated any longer. However, the earliest community may not be said to have understood the turn of the aeons to have occurred any more than Paul may be said to have done so. In that case, the summary would still express the expectation (shared by the earliest community) that the kingdom was soon to break in.

If we now look once more at how these things are connected with each other, a question arises. How does a kingdom of God that Jesus was only expecting to break in fit with the statement that, where the finger of God is at work, the rule of God has become present? I see only one way to relieve this tension. In order to indicate this as simply as possible, let me introduce a conceptual distinction precisely between the kingdom and the rule of God.

By *kingdom of God*, I mean the apocalyptic way of conceiving things. At the end of time (after the turn of the aeons), God will establish a new state of affairs, at the beginning of which the dead will be raised and the living and (raised) dead will be judged. Those who make it through the judgment enter into the everlasting kingdom (characterized in quite earthly terms) where, for example, they will sit at God's table.

I regard it as quite possible that the historical Jesus shared this conception. It was widespread at the time, and even an imminent expectation was by no means something that was specific to Jesus. And yet, if this is what is supposed to have been distinctive about the message of Jesus, it was nothing distinctive at all.

However, the early community evidently saw what was distinctive elsewhere. What (in the framework of this way of conceiving things) was expected only of the future takes place *now*. Blind people see, the lame walk, lepers are cleansed, and so forth. The finger of God is at work now. Here I should like to speak of the *rule of God*. The decisive difference is this: The kingdom of God is the new state of affairs. However, it belongs to the essence of the rule of God not to be a state of affairs, but rather to break in again and again. Putting it this way takes nothing away from the *reality* of the inbreaking. Nor is anything taken away from the reality of the activity *of God*. It is just that the rule does not last. Rather, just as it has really come, so, too, it is always immediately coming again. It is expectation.

I believe that this distinction opens up the way for understanding the summary of Mark 1:14f. What we have here is an announcement regarding time. The time of this old aeon has run out. For this reason, there is now no time left, because God is offering to break in with his rule right now.

We need to make clear what it is that is surprising about this offer. It consists in the fact that God means to overcome the distance between himself and human beings. You might say that God comes right up to you. People are deeply fearful of this, because they would like to get ready for the encounter with God first (if they really desire this at all). The other surprise consists in the fact that all the intermediate events, particularly the judgment, are virtually deleted. God means to come with God's rule now. But to this coming no conditions at all are attached.

If this is true, then there is only one possible consequence for the individual: an immediate turnabout; *metanoieite*; repent; about-face! Now, it needs to be clearly noted that such a turnabout is a consequence. In the case of the Baptizer, so far as we can still determine, things were different. He summoned to a turnabout, and this was a condition of the individual's escaping the coming judgment. In the gospel of Jesus, however, the turnabout is a consequence. Whoever believes in this gospel (which is no intellectual process and which, for this reason, is more accurately conveyed by the words, "whoever gives oneself over to this joyful news"), such a person actualizes this involvement in her or his turnabout.

This is how the early community understood the activity of Jesus in retrospect. Whoever gave himself or herself to Jesus' offer already had to do with the well-being of salvation right then and there and waited for whatever else might come along—with which they, too, still struggled. However, by having to do with the well-being of salvation (and only thereby), their own being-saved became a reality. In their own turnabout, their own becoming-well, the salvation of the end-time came to them.

However, it goes without saying that this becoming-well did not transport these people into any new state of affairs. This turnabout did not bestow upon them any *character indelibilis* (a "quality" that cannot be lost). Rather, even for those who had been saved, becoming-well remained ever anew a matter of the future. In this sense, it might be said that the imminent expectation is a continuing state. But this is a misleading formulation. What it means to say is that, from now on, one continually had becoming-well as a possibility in front of oneself that both was meant to and also really did actualize itself anew again and again.

I want to show how this works for several additional texts, but first, I would like to return to a remark I made earlier but did not pursue at that point. I said that the Jesus-tradition originally comprises independent traditions that were only subsequently combined, until they worked their way into our gospels. However, as I said, this fact constitutes a set of problems that, far from being merely literary, is of the most profoundly substantive character. It is just these that we are now in a position to identify. The rule of God does not break in as a state of affairs; rather, even once it has broken in, it means to break in again and again. It is this very invitation which each independent tradition voices anew, and each independent tradition can be seen as exemplifying what this inbreaking looks like.

I believe that the insights of form criticism need to be taken much more seriously than they often are. The independent traditions are kerygmatic in character. However, this does not mean merely, as is usually claimed, that the independent traditions are intended to proclaim, rather than to inform historically. It means a good deal more than this! It means that these independent traditions come from an *experience* that was repeated again and again and ever anew, and that they are for the sake of an *experience* that is to be repeated again and again and ever anew. But the experience is precisely the inbreaking of the rule of God.

Once this feature of the "again and again" is recognized, we can also recognize how problematic it is to link these independent traditions together in additive fashion into a sequence of events. Doing this is bound to give the impression that what was a "from time to time" became a permanent state of affairs. However, once this sort of impression arises, consequences immediately follow. These have more to do with Jesus himself than they do with the people around him. In any number of ways, it is stated that these people fell away from the faith they had once attained and had to risk it ever anew. In the case of Jesus, however, there is a shift of interest—away from ever new actions of occasioning the inbreaking of God's rule, through a permanent activity of occasioning God's rule, and over into a characterization of the person who is able to occasion God's rule. At that point, a statement as problematic as that of the sinlessness of Jesus can arise (Heb. 4:15). What was originally experienced as an ever new occurrence is now transferred to the "nature" of him who initiated the experiences. Soteriology has turned into explicit christology. In the independent traditions (at least in the early ones), however, this either does not yet exist or is implicit to the highest degree. It is implicit insofar as the experience of *saving well-being* remains inseparably and exclusively bound to *Jesus. Only he* offers saving well-being in his gospel.

To be sure, more needs to be said than that Jesus offered this gospel (which I shall say a bit more about shortly). What seems to me decisive is this: People around Jesus experienced that he himself gave himself over to his announcement concerning time. He risked living the rule of God again and again in the midst of the old aeon.

Perhaps this becomes most vivid in regard to the conception that those who have passed through resurrection and judgment will sit at God's table in the kingdom of God. There, shalom (peace) rules. There, there are no distinctions. God serves all those who take part in the meal. The separation between God and human beings is overcome just as much as is that of people from one another. This salvation can be depicted further, and this can and should be depicted in thoroughly human terms. Yet only that person can speak meaningfully of the well-being of salvation who knows and suffers from the evil that corresponds to it as its opposite. The evil from which people suffer, however, is always quite concrete evil in this world and is describable in human terms. Naturally, one may be convinced that the saving well-being of the beyond exceeds what is *conceivable* in human terms. And this thought is evidently suggested in the Jesus-traditions as well, as when we read in Mark 12:25 that those who are raised neither marry nor are given in marriage, but are like the angels in heaven. And we might well want to emphasize still more strongly than was possible and even necessary in the ancient world-picture the *totaliter aliter*, the complete otherness of what is to come. Nevertheless, if salvation is not to remain an utterly bloodless notion, a mere cipher that is no good to anyone, one needs to try to visualize it, and to do so precisely as the antitype of vivid and concrete evil.

So, too, the saving well-being that Jesus dares to live and that people experience in Jesus' life in his deeds and conduct is very concrete. Jesus holds table fellowship with sinners and tax collectors, that is, with those who were universally regarded as outcasts. Sinners were shunned because they were cultically impure, tax collectors because they exploited their own people. To be sure, those who exploit always did (and do) have power, but at the same time, to the extent that others have the power to do so, they fight against them. People around Jesus experience that he turns toward the unwanted, toward those who otherwise do not count for anything. I do not need to elaborate these features. They are well known.

However, it is important to see how people understood this action and conduct on Jesus' part. We have already seen that Jesus' activity could be misunderstood. Whether the finger of God or Beelzebub was at work could not be read off what Jesus did. The same thing applies to the attempt to interpret Jesus' conduct in summary fashion. Putting it in modern terms, it is quite possible to say that Jesus was about changing society, creating just conditions, and so forth. And then he is understood as an example to be emulated.

If this interpretation were correct, it would have to be stated at once that Jesus failed in his purpose. This could well be true. It would then follow that what one means to do today is finally to complete (indeed, to improve upon) what Jesus unfortunately did not manage to achieve.

Nevertheless (as might again be easily shown by means of a literary approach), this way of construing things overlooks the fact that the Jesus-tradition originally arose as independent units. No incremental program can be constructed from these units. Rather, *each* independent tradition contains the *whole*, even if from a differing perspective in each case. In this way, each tradition both expresses and invites one into the experience of the whole.

Where God's kingdom does happen (even if it occurs from time to time), it happens whole and does not admit of increase. Where God is at work, God is at work right now and fully. That God is at work fully finds expression in the saying that God makes his sun to rise over the evil and the good and sends rain on the righteous and the unrighteous (Matt. 5:45)—quite expressly, not only on the good and righteous, but rather on the evil and unrighteous as well.

Jesus enacts just this "conduct of God." This is why the christological title of "bridegroom" is applied to him. In his presence, there is no fasting (Mark 2:18f.). Why not? Well, because those who sit at table with him are guests at a wedding. It is quite clear that here we have to do with a picture of the fellowship at the end-time after the turn of the aeons. This fellowship *occurs* through Jesus. At the same time, the image shatters, because the bridegroom is not really the master of the house at the wedding banquet. But this shattering of the image is necessary in order to make clear both the identity and, at the same time, the difference between the activity of Jesus and the activity of God. Naturally, the point is always Jesus of Nazareth and so, in reality, a human being. However, he is already now acting as God is expected to act at the end. Thus, it is precisely the incarnation of God that takes place. It really does take place, and it takes place visibly. One ought to be cautious about speaking of a "hidden" activity of God here, to be followed by a "manifest" activity after the turn of the aeons. I think the point is a different one. In what Jesus does, the activity of God occurs not in a way that is hidden, but in a way that is visible. What remains hidden is only that this is an activity *of God*. So, too, in the incarnation of God, the rule of God breaks in not in a way that is hidden, but in a way that is visible, even graphically so. And yet, that it is *God's* rule—this cannot be directly read off.

To be sure—and here I come back to the thought that was put to one side earlier—this actual incarnation of God in what Jesus does cannot be held on to. This already gave people trouble early on. An example of this is the story of the transfiguration (Mark 9:2–8). At the sight of the transfigured Jesus, Peter wants to build a booth for him, as well as for the figures of the end-time, Moses and Elijah. That is, he wants to lend permanence to the moment; he wants to hold on to it. But the cloud comes, and the curtain, which had been opened for a moment, is drawn again.

Is Jesus' conduct understood as a pattern here? I believe this question can be answered with a confident "Yes," at least on one condition: that this pattern is not to be treated simplistically. And yet, such a simplification is what results from the desire to imitate the conduct *as such*. All the same, this conduct is a *consequence*, and it is the consequence of the fact that Jesus gave himself over (and I need to emphasize once more: ever again and ever anew) to the inbreaking of God's rule. For this reason, his concern is not to change the world. His concern is not to bring about a *kingdom* of God one day by a gradual process on the basis of the *rule* of God. It is not a matter of a process at all. When it does come, the rule of God always comes whole. Still, when and where Jesus does enact the rule of God, *this* obviously cannot remain without consequences for the world.

It is therefore quite fitting that the feature of changing the world should play an important role in the contemporary discussion. It is just that one needs to pay close attention to the place this feature occupies in the structure of Christian claims. Since we are concerned here with a *consequence*, this aspect may not be regarded as a Christian *proprium*. This Christian *proprium*, which people experienced in encounter with Jesus, finds expression in Matt. 6:33: "Seek *first* the rule of God; then the rest will be given to you." "The rest" certainly also includes changing the world and society. All the same, even if nothing of this "rest" becomes at all visible in the world around them, *this* is not something Christians will have to strive for. However, they will have to ask themselves whether they really have given themselves over to the coming of the rule of God.

Jesus' living out the rule of God toward people around him implied the invitation to them to give themselves over to it. To be sure, two other reactions were also possible. One was being glad that this was happening, since this meant that finally, one had to do with a good person for a change. Jesus is then understood simply and merely as someone who does good things. This misunderstanding is illustrated in the story of the ten lepers. Nine enjoy their cure; only one turns back (Luke 17:11–19). This story also shows that it makes no sense to distinguish people's well-being (here, their health) and their salvation. It is quite evident (at least today) that restricting the meaning of the well-being of salvation (perhaps to the "inner" life) is fundamentally dehumanizing. But it would be just as false to tear this unity apart by supposing that human well-being were to be achieved *first*, so that people might *then* become capable of receiving salvation. That would also be a way of understanding the well-being of salvation as something merely inward. This might also lead to people imagining that they *themselves* were able to and responsible for creating the conditions—then and only then—for *God* to be able to break in with his rule. No, the bestowal of the rule of God is always aimed at the whole person, and it implies the impertinence on people's part of understanding the bread they pray for as God's own invitation to repentance. Is this always actually and adequately kept in mind when *Christians* become involved in development aid or charity?

Alongside this reaction simply to be glad to have Jesus do what he did stands the other of objecting to Jesus, to the point of opposing him and getting rid of him. I do not want to pursue this here, because I would have to speak in too much detail about Jesus' suffering, about his passion, and about how this has been understood. This would be a topic in its own right (and a very broad one). All that needs to be mentioned is this: Giving oneself over again and again to God's rule makes the person who risks this, as it were, unpredictable. So, for example, such a person can no longer join in thinking about friends and enemies in the usual way. And it needs to be realized that precisely this was very widespread in the Judaism of Jesus' time. The Judaism of Jesus' time was by no means as uniform as it might too readily seem in retrospect, especially since we almost always look to the traditions from the period after 70 C.E. This (at least relative) uniformity arose only after the destruction of Jerusalem. By contrast, during the time of Jesus there was an abundance of groups that understood themselves as exclusive communities of salvation. Whoever did not belong to the group was an enemy. However, such a person was not only an enemy but, at the same time, an enemy of God. One could oppose such a person and be convinced that one was acting according to God's will. To be sure, it does not say in the Old Testament that one is to (love one's neighbor and) hate one's enemy (as Matt. 5:43 would have one suppose). But this was religious practice. Whoever lives out God's rule in a situation like this risks getting caught between all fronts.

Thus, people in the earliest community witnessed both of these possible reactions to the activity of Jesus (and in the case of the latter reaction, this was not all that surprising). Nevertheless, our traditions show that the people who formulated these traditions reacted differently. They gave themselves over to Jesus' invitation to see God's action in his action, the inbreaking of the rule of God, and in so doing, they took upon themselves the risk of a turnabout. That is to say, they believed in the gospel, as Mark 1:15 puts it.

However, if faith is giving oneself over, it is clear that faith is an occurrence that becomes concrete in this about-face. Quite obviously, Jesus offered pointers for what this occurrence might look like. These traditions generally take the form of the imperative. Thus, we are dealing with concrete life-situations. It is just that these imperatives may never be disconnected from what Jesus *does*, from his enacting God's rule. If the imperatives are isolated from what Jesus does, then one gets the impression that Jesus preached law. This has occasionally been claimed, by Rudolf Bultmann, among others, who even cites a sentence of Luther's in support.

Connected with this is also the fact that no rightful place is found for Jesus of Nazareth in theology. However, I do not want to pursue this broad topic in detail here, so let me restrict myself instead to what is usually called the ethics of Jesus.

There is a certain inconsistency in the way this matter is viewed. On the one hand, it is said (and this is often the prevailing opinion), that Jesus made the law stricter. One needs only to refer to the antitheses of the Sermon on the Mount in this regard. Not only the person who kills shall be liable to judgment, but even whoever is angry. It is not only the husband who has an affair with another woman that commits adultery, but even the one who looks at her lustfully, and so forth. But what is peculiar is that, alongside the increased strictness people claim to find in the ethics of Jesus, an astonishing laxness can be noted, which becomes evident particularly in the case of sabbath observance. People have occasionally pretended to resolve this inconsistency (between making the law more strict and making it more lax) by saying that it is true that Jesus did make the moral commandments stricter, but that, in contrast, he also repealed the ones regarding the cult. However, such a distinction is completely misleading. To be sure, we have no proof for the claim that Jesus kept the sabbath. But how could we? What goes without saying does not get said. There cannot be any doubt at all that Jesus understood the commandments as God's commandments, including the sabbath commandment. But then how is his criticism of the commandments to be understood? For Jesus engages in criticism in both cases, whether we understand it as making the commandments stricter or as making them more lax. And yet, the criticism grows out of a common root in both cases, namely, the will of God.

Even if God did give the law, and therefore human beings now, so to speak, "have" the law, this does not dispense them from asking for God *in* the law, and this means asking for the purpose God is pursuing by means of the law. However, since God has a good purpose for human beings, God's will occurs in the observance of the law only when this good purpose is given a chance. In other words, Jesus radicalizes the law. This is not meant in the sense of making the law stricter. Rather, he traces it back to its root. But then surprising things can come from it and, in fact, written law is no longer needed at all.

For, anyone who gives herself or himself over to God's inbreaking rule already has an idea of what that life at the table of God will look like, to which one has now already been called in the present. And so, such a person simply lives life at the table of God. This is possible because this person shares in the well-being of salvation without deserving it. That there is no killing at the table of God is obvious. But even the idea of having to forbid anger at the table of God is quite superfluous. Anger does not need to be forbidden, because there is no anger at the table of God. It would be just as absurd to imagine that the truth of what one said would have to be vouched for by an oath. Yes means yes there, and no means no. At God's table there is no lustful glance, and it is self-evident that no enemies are there. And, since an eternal sabbath reigns at the table of God, of course the sabbath there is made for human beings (cf. Mark 2:27). Naturally, the ethics of Jesus finds expression largely in the imperative. However, this is misunderstood if it is regarded as instructions to be obeyed. What looks like instruction is in truth a consequence. Anyone who actually lets himself or herself now be granted God's rule simply lives this. The grammatical form of the imperative is merely an expression of the fact that even being turned about, whether it happens once or more than once, still always remains a matter of the future.

So what happens in the kingdom of God (and what can happen now in giving oneself over to the rule of God) is at first surprising, to be sure. However, upon reflection, it makes basic sense, or at least it is insightful and persuasive. The ninety-nine sheep are at home. So it is the one who is lost that is a matter of concern (Matt. 18:12–14). It is certainly an impertinence for one's neighbor to knock on the door during the night demanding bread. But he needs it, and so he gets it (Luke 11:5–8). And one could go through the parables and exemplary stories with this in mind. However, the most surprising thing remains the fact that, in the way he acted toward them, the people around Jesus experienced that all this happened to them without their having any qualifications for it and without their having to expend any special effort on it. It happened. And in allowing it to happen of its own accord, they had allowed themselves to be turned upside down—and they allowed the same thing to go on happening.

Paul will later express this in this way: "If anyone is in Christ, that person is a new creation. The old has passed away; behold, the new has come" (2 Cor. 5:17). Time and again, one hears that this statement was not yet possible at the time of the earthly Jesus, because it presupposes Easter and the post-Easter Christ-kerygma. Formally, this is of course correct. "Being in Christ" is a later way of putting things. But materially, this Pauline statement holds true already of the period of the earthly Jesus.

After all that has been presented here, what still needs to be understood is this: Whoever gives oneself over to Jesus of Nazareth gives oneself along with him to the inbreaking of God's rule and then lives "a new creation." For this person (again and again, in each such act), the "old" that has surrounded him or her has "passed away." It is no longer determinative. Therefore, the "new" has actually come.

However, one has to understand the reality of this "new" in an accurate way and not weaken it. For the person who really does live out the "new" (that is, who now lives as if this were the first time it had ever occurred to one), it is exactly the way it is expressed in John. "Whoever believes has passed across from death to life" (John 5:24). And now I think it will be completely clear to you why, at the beginning of this essay, I could use the words, "Jesus of Nazareth was experienced as the God who raises the dead." Anyone who does not live God's rule *is* dead. But whoever does live it has been raised from death.

I would like to give an explicit warning against spiritualizing this resurrection and, thereby, no longer taking it seriously. We are all in danger of doing this. When we speak of resurrection of the dead, we generally think of something that happens following physical death. This is how materialism thinks. For it, there is only resurrection of the dead (if there is any at all) after physical death. But precisely this is a dangerous way of thinking, because it means no longer taking seriously the reality of God's inbreaking rule.

I have already shared my misgivings about saying that God is at work only in a hidden way in God's rule that is breaking into this world, for the occurrence of God's rule is not hidden. It is visible; it is concrete. What is hidden is simply that *God* is at work. If one still wants to draw a distinction between a "now" and a "then," one only does so in a misleading fashion by means of the terms "hidden" and "manifest." For *how* God's *rule* that is working in the present will perhaps one day take shape in the *kingdom* of God escapes our knowledge. Of this we have absolutely no adequate notion.

By saying this, I certainly do not want to encourage the misunderstanding that a final *state of affairs* is brought about by means of the *real* inbreaking of God's rule into people's lives and, thereby, their *real* resurrection from the dead. If a distinction between the "now" and the "then" is wanted, perhaps the formulation, "now-broken, then-unbroken," would be suitable. However, if the word "broken" is to be used, there is to be no thought of surreptitiously retracting or of weakening either the reality of the inbreaking of God's rule or, as its result, the reality of the resurrection of the dead that occurs in the event of the turnabout. Even if this reality does not last in the midst of this old world, it still really does happen, and it really happens ever anew. However, as soon as it does happen, it has to be expected anew.

The memory of a person's past experience can be a decisive aid to this expecting anew. It is to just such experience that we owe the Jesus-kerygma. It declares that Jesus occasioned something to which people gave themselves, because they experienced how Jesus gave himself to God's inbreaking rule in their behalf. This is later expressed in the words, "He gave himself up for their sake." Thus, for these people Jesus of Nazareth was an event. Naturally, this is an abbreviated formulation, as indeed very many theological statements are shortened forms for a more complex state of affairs. "Jesus of Nazareth: An Event." This is meant to say that what was decisive for these people who encountered him was their experience: he enacts God *for us*. However, since he has enacted *God* for us, therefore we now invite others to have the same experience along with him.

I have no misgivings about saying that, with regard to all this, we have to do with a utopia. Now, utopia means "no place." And the saving well-being of God's rule has no place in this world. People yearn for utopia to be actualized one day. Dreamers believe that, through effort and exertion, step by step, it can be obtained in this world by force. Jesus leaps over such human effort by giving himself over to what has no place here, in order time and again and ever anew to make room for it and to allow it to become *actual*.

Martin Luther once spoke the bold word that it is the dignity of the Christian to be Christ to the neighbor. That was probably still not bold enough, for, since it was the dignity of Jesus of Nazareth to act in *God's* place toward human beings, what is now the case is that anyone who gives herself or himself over to Jesus of Nazareth receives God's inbreaking rule as a gift. However, endowed with this, *this person* then personally acts in *God's* place toward his or her neighbor. But then one finally understands this as well: The person who has received this gift is able, again and again, to be perfect (not, however, gradually to become, but really again and again to be perfect)—perfect as one's father in heaven is perfect.

5

WHEN DID
CHRISTIAN FAITH
BEGIN?*

Rudolf Bultmann has given a clear answer to this question. "Christian faith first exists once there is a Christian kerygma, i.e., a kerygma that proclaims Jesus Christ as God's eschatological act of salvation, and specifically Jesus Christ the crucified and risen one" (*Theologie des Neuen Testaments*, 2). In this context, the little word "first" is meant to make unmistakably clear that Christian faith did not yet exist during the time of the earthly Jesus. But is this true?

When you assigned me this question, you attached to it the expectation that I come to terms with this claim of Bultmann's, particularly since you suspected that I would not be able to agree with it as it stands. This is in fact the case, and I will try to explain why.

The issue before us concerns one aspect of the larger subject generally characterized as the question of the historical Jesus and of his theological significance. In the last twenty years, the discussion of these questions has taken on such a scope that no one, not even the specialist, can claim to survey it in its entirety. For this reason, there would be little point in my trying to introduce you to it, especially since the views that are represented within it are often bewildering in their unclarity. Therefore, let me choose a different approach which, I hope, will prove helpful. I shall take my bearings neither from the current discussion nor directly from the sentence cited from Bultmann. Rather, let me begin by briefly calling to mind how Bultmann arrived at this claim.

---

*"Seit wann gibt es christlichen Glauben?" *Die Sache Jesu geht weiter* (Gütersloh: Gütersloher Verlagshaus Gerd Mohn, 1976), 27–44.

I.

Permit me to start off with several reflections on the concept of kerygma. In the understanding of it that is current today, this concept arose in connection with form critical research, with which the old life-of-Jesus research came to an end. Once the two-source theory was worked out around the final third of the previous century, people occasionally still held the optimistic view that it was possible to recognize the course of the life of Jesus in broad outline in the Gospel of Mark ("perhaps reduced in detail," as H. J. Holtzmann put it). This confidence was shattered by the writings of Martin Kähler, William Wrede, and Albert Schweitzer. They corroborated in their way Adolf Harnack's dissertation of 1874, *Vita Jesu scribi nequit* ("a *life* of Jesus cannot be written"). At the same time, literary criticism had shown that the synoptic gospels contained collected material and that, therefore, the Jesus-tradition began as a tradition of independent stories. People worked at reconstructing these. At the same time, they continued to think that (if no longer the composite works, then still) the individual traditions could be employed as historical sources.

However, this is just what form criticism called into question. It showed that the *immediate* interest of the community that passed on the traditions was precisely not an historical one. On the contrary, as Günther Bornkamm later strikingly formulated it, this community meant to say not who Jesus was, but rather who Jesus *is*. To be sure, the community did this with recourse to the past. Nevertheless, this did not happen for the sake of this past itself; rather, a story from the past was told in order to say something to one's own present. They were not interested in what we today call "historical accuracy." This problem, rather familiar to us, simply did not lie within the writers' field of vision. The intention was not to report, but to proclaim. Accordingly, the independent traditions have a kerygmatic, rather than an historical character. As the result of this insight, around the beginning of the twenties one began to speak of "kerygma." However, in New Testament scholarship (insofar as it had anything to do with form criticism), this meant the end of liberal theology. If the agenda of liberal theology was to guarantee the proclamation historically by appealing to the historical Jesus to authorize contemporary proclamation, it became clear precisely on the basis of the kerygma that this approach was inappropriate. The kerygma is address; as such, it demands faith in an immediate way. This all seems in principle conclusive and, in my judgment, it is. Moreover, as I see it, there ought not to have been any retreat to the situation that preceded this *fundamental* insight. Nevertheless, it needs to be carefully noted that certain inaccuracies crept in at several points, inaccuracies which were not—perhaps even could not be—seen directly in connection with this work.

From the independent materials, the insight had been won that the material from which the tradition had been constructed was kerygma. However, this insight was hastily applied to the gospels and became the slogan, "The *gospels* are proclamation, not historical report." That this was by and large correct (if, to be sure, also with some modifications), redaction critical work was of course later to show, since the extent to which the gospels as complete works are to be called kerygma remained quite unclear until into the fifties. However, that the slogan should have arisen is understandable. It was aimed at combatting the old liberal way of posing the question, which remained interested in the historical Jesus (and often still in the life of Jesus). At the same time, this was in harmony with dialectical theology, which in its own way also meant to overcome liberal theology. Its understanding of the word of God, which confronts the individual, to which one is to respond (without asking any questions), fits in exactly with the understanding of kerygma. It is only that, as has been said, the inaccurate transfer of this understanding of kerygma to the gospels as complete works immediately created a momentous short-circuit. From the incontrovertible fact that the gospels were composed after Easter, it was now concluded that the gospel writers therefore presuppose Easter. This is how kerygma *eo ipso* came to be understood as Easter-kerygma. However, it was then also taken for granted that what arose after Easter is also influenced by Easter and, therefore, is determined in its content by Easter. This claim (which at best can be derived from the gospels as complete works) was also presupposed for the individual materials. It would still be possible to start out from the (at least high) probability that these traditions were first fixed in writing after Easter, and some independent traditions (one might think of the transfiguration stories) could also be seen to have been substantively influenced by Easter. However, this remains an exception and in no way justifies the assumption that such a thing holds true for all pieces of tradition. This would have to be investigated much more carefully than has usually been done.

For our purposes, it might prove helpful to make a distinction in the way the phrase "after Easter" is to be used. While, on the one hand, "after Easter" can stand for the mere assignment of a date, on the other hand, it can be used to make a substantive claim. How broadly this distinction applies is something we shall have to ask. That it is a fundamentally legitimate one, however, is not to be disputed. For, if a tradition is characterized as "after Easter" because it was written down or, indeed, even first arose after (let us say) 33 C.E., this does not immediately also have to mean that, because of this, its substance was determined by Easter (in saying which, however, I do not want to go into the problem of Easter as such in this context). Therefore, if one makes this distinction, it remains at least conceivable that traditions which emerge *chronologically* after Easter were formulated without being influenced by the "business" of Easter.

This may sound strange at first, but that is only because it is assumed that the early community was a homogeneous entity, at least to the extent that it stemmed from *one* root. To be sure, this is the picture that Acts draws. The conviction is widespread today that this will not withstand historical criticism. But will it withstand "theological criticism"? This is scarcely ever investigated. Thus, for instance, precisely in Bultmann's *Theology of the New Testament*, the talk is always of *the* early community in the beginning. As an entity that is taken to have had its start chronologically after Easter, it is taken as an established fact that it is also substantively determined by Easter. Do the texts give us the right to identify these two things?

In connection with this, one further point deserves attention. Early on, in the twenties, the concept of kerygma played a role almost exclusively in New Testament scholarship (as well as in the systematic theology influenced by it). After what has been said, it is readily understandable that kerygma was always taken to mean Easter-kerygma. However, in the meantime, the concept of kerygma had (quite rightly!) been taken up by Old Testament scholarship as well. But this can help us become more aware of at least one insight that had been securely won at the beginning of form criticism, but that had not always been thought out precisely enough. Kerygma is the name of a literary form (or genre) and, as such, has nothing at all to do with Easter. Yet, this concept was introduced and employed as a way of drawing a line of demarcation over against the "genre" of historical report. Therefore, kerygma was meant to be defined as a literary form intended to address, to move its audience in the present.

If the presynoptic individual materials are to be called "kerygma" in this sense, then kerygma needs to be understood as a term that refers strictly to genre. Whether there are substantive relations to Easter will have to be investigated, if the origin of this material (in part) is to be dated to a time after Easter. Thus, it is today generally conceded that the sayings-source, for instance, contains neither the cross-kerygma nor the resurrection-kerygma. All the same, their traditions must be called kerygma *in a literary sense*. And what holds true for the sayings-source holds true equally for a wealth of other individual traditions which made their way into the synoptic gospels at a later time. Whoever takes the results of form criticism seriously cannot dispute this *literary* judgment. At the same time, one must guard against immediately making this into a substantive judgment and understanding kerygma as Easter-kerygma. The influence of Easter will have to be demonstrated with reference to the individual texts in each case. In no case will an argument suffice that consists in a mere reference to the date of Easter.

Therefore, I want to repeat an earlier suggestion, since I think it can help us avoid misunderstandings. If the term "kerygma" is employed in a strict sense only to designate a literary genre, one also needs to specify the content of any given text. Then it would be possible to distinguish within the New Testament between the Christ-kerygma that is determined by Easter and a Jesus-kerygma, in which a substantive influence of Easter is at least not discernible.

II.

After this brief sketch and these few critical questions, we can return once more to the sentence of Bultmann. "Christian faith first exists once there is a Christian kerygma, that is, a kerygma that proclaims Jesus Christ as God's eschatological act of salvation, and specifically Jesus Christ the crucified and risen one." Now what we need to take note of becomes clear immediately. Here, the act of designating the content of the kerygma (the crucified and risen one) at once designates the *terminus a quo* of this kerygma and the *terminus a quo* of Christian faith as such. However, it is only the Christ-kerygma that is under consideration. Bultmann contrasts this (and, indeed, precisely in reference to the sentence cited) with the proclamation of the earthly Jesus, from which it then follows that Christian faith can be spoken of "for the first time in the kerygma of the early community, but not in the proclamation of the historical Jesus." But is this really correct?

If we mean to understand kerygma as an address that is aimed directly at moving people, we must allow this to remain a formal statement to begin with and not bring specific contents into play too quickly. But then it is probably neither possible nor even desirable to dispute that the proclamation of Jesus was kerygma. Bultmann himself repeatedly characterizes it as a "call to decision." We can leave it completely undecided whether this call is to be reconstructed as *ipsissima vox* (the historically genuine words of Jesus). Historians can work at finding the historical Jesus and will continue to do so. For them it remains a meaningful task, even as they will concede that various scholars arrive at different results. The uncertainty of the results is inevitable.

Meanwhile, we can leave this aspect of the problem of the historical Jesus alone and focus on form criticism, since it remains undisputed (and indisputable!) that in the independent traditions it is not Jesus who speaks, but always people of the early community. This remains the case even if they repeat verbatim what they have heard from Jesus. However, if it is true that they have preserved the proclamation of the historical Jesus not out of historical interest, but rather with the intention of saying something to their own present, then these traditions should be referred to as kerygma in each instance.

In this case, however, another feature comes into view, one which is almost completely ignored by Bultmann, namely, Jesus' conduct and Jesus' activity. Here again, we are not asking about historicity. I want neither to assert nor to dispute this. For our purposes, the following statement will suffice: Recounting (possibly accurately) the conduct and activity of Jesus also serves not simply to inform, but to address those who hear it, so that they will give themselves to Jesus and recognize who it is, to whom they have given themselves. The content of this kerygma is then, in the broadest sense, Jesus—not merely his proclamation. This is precisely why I entitle it "Jesus-*kerygma.*" The question is whether one may call this kerygma "Christian," or whether it is not yet this and, more specifically, what conditions would have to be met for a kerygma to be referred to as Christian kerygma.

One might get the impression that this is merely a question of definition. At first, it is hard to see why it should be denied that such a Jesus-kerygma is Christian kerygma. No one (including Bultmann) will want to claim that a sermon on a piece of tradition from the synoptic gospels that has been worked out in literary-critical fashion and form critically interpreted is (still) not a Christian sermon. In this case, however, we would have to call such a Jesus-kerygma Christian kerygma, too, even if Easter were not explicit in it. If we followed Bultmann's lead and added to it the considerations that have been presented here, we would have to say something like this: Christian faith begins once there is a Christian kerygma, and that means a Jesus-kerygma in which Jesus is the content of the proclamation. This was not yet the case in the proclamation of Jesus himself. But then the question arises of the significance of Easter for the emergence of the Christian kerygma.

It seems to me worth observing that Bultmann never understood the resurrection of Jesus as an event which would have added anything to the proclamation of Jesus that was not already there before. The change from before to after Easter consists, according to Bultmann, not in a deficit that had existed previously now being removed, but rather in something (Bultmann refers to christology) that had already been present throughout in implicit fashion now becoming explicit. That this did occur by way of the "Easter-experiences" is indisputable. However, were these "Easter-experiences" necessary *in every instance*, so that the Christian kerygma first arose only with the Easter faith of the disciples? Even if this were not the case, one could still argue that this is what actually did occur. To be sure, this assertion is made over and over. But is it correct? It still has to be verified for the Jesus-kerygma *with respect to its content.* Yet this is just what one cannot succeed in doing in virtually every case.

Of course, the question of date now comes back into play. We explicitly prescinded from asking about the historical Jesus and meant to go back only to the point at which people in the early community made Jesus (that is, his speaking, conduct, and activity) the content of their proclamation. Insofar, there remains a "break" between the historical Jesus and (now) the Jesus-kerygma of the early community. But is the beginning of the early community to be dated at Easter?

Nearly all scholarship proceeds on the basis of this assumption, not just Bultmann. One reckons with *one* early community that owes its origin to the Easter-experiences. Of course, one then confronts the difficulty of assuming that the content of the earliest Christian kerygmata was shaped by Easter even where, at least in the traditions themselves, this cannot be discerned. In spite of this indisputable finding, it is asserted that "all the documents of the New Testament proceed from a preunderstanding given by Easter." This might still be accepted so far as the extant written texts are concerned, but the claim continues with the assertion, "This holds good in principle for all stages of the New Testament tradition" (J. Ernst, *Anfänge der Christologie*, Stuttgarter Bibelstudien 57 [1972]: 76f.). Naturally, one can make reference to the fact that Easter did not *have to* become explicit in each individual case. This may be conceded at once. However, if Easter does not become explicit in such a large number of traditions, and if a "preunderstanding given by Easter" is claimed for them in spite of this, then this holds good only on the assumption that *the earliest* community owes its origin to the Easter-experiences, and to this extent we have to do with *one original* community. Then Christian faith is always "Easter faith."

To be sure, one also frequently encounters the above-mentioned claim in formulations that are much more circumspect, such as, "The statements concerning the pre-Easter history of Jesus are imbedded in the New Testament in the testimony of faith of the community" (F. Hahn, *Die Frage nach dem historischen Jesus*, Trierer Theologische Zeitschrift 82 [1973]: 196). Here the talk is precisely not of Easter faith. And yet, time and again this assertion is understood in that way. For, after citing it, W. G. Kümmel can go on to say that it expresses "the unanimous view of the overwhelming majority of all critically engaged theologians," that "the oral Jesus-tradition, as well as the way this has been assembled in the gospels have been passed on or shaped by people who believed in the resurrection of the crucified Jesus and who spoke as believers of Jesus" (*Jesu Antwort an Johannes den Täufer. Sitzungsberichte der wissenschaftlichen Gesellschaft an der Johann-Wolfgang-Goethe-Universität Frankfurt/Main* XI, 4, Wiesbaden [1974]: 138).

Yet this is exactly where the problem arises. Faith in the resurrection of the crucified Jesus is immediately equated with faith in Jesus. It may indeed be said that the Christ-kerygma presupposes Easter faith. It may definitely be said that the Jesus-kerygma presupposes faith through Jesus. But are these the same thing from the outset? That *all traditions* have been shaped by faith is not to be disputed. But that in *every* instance, faith is always and forthwith Easter faith seems to me a short-circuit. At the very least, this is a claim—one that is quite understandable on the assumption of *one* original community, but that has by no means yet been proven. And I believe that the burden of proof lies with those who make this claim.

Must we then reckon with "two types of faith" in the early community and *insofar* with two early communities? Anyone who means to travel this (today still) unconventional road needs to be aware of the problem it entails. One engages in an *argumentum e silentio*, as it were. Since no influence on the part of Easter is discernible in the majority of the traditions of the Jesus-kerygma, one reckons that there was none. Naturally, the possibility of an implicit influence may not be ruled out. Indeed, at first, an influence of this sort seems like a self-evident assumption, for where is one to imagine the early community that knew nothing of the Easter-experiences in which others perhaps took part? As we usually picture the early community, this sounds rather improbable. Quite considerable arguments will have to be advanced if, with the aid of this *argumentum e silentio*, one is to infer the existence of two early communities: one that owes its origin to the Easter-experiences, and another that at least at first was not influenced by these.

III.

As I now mean to try to show why I do reckon with two such early communities and to indicate how these are to be characterized, I want to preclude from the outset a misunderstanding that might possibly creep in. I am not thinking of two early communities that lived in tension. This thought readily suggests itself if one looks at the controversies that did in fact occur in early Christianity, for instance, those between Jewish Christianity and gentile Christianity or between orthodoxy and heresy. The two early communities of which we shall be speaking here rather embody "two types of faith," though again not in the way that Martin Buber has presented the difference between Christian and Jewish faith in terms of an opposition. I mean rather that these two Christian types of faith (of which one to be sure is very similar to Jewish faith) are in no way mutually exclusive. However, they do indeed accent and formulate their faith differently at times.

In the New Testament writings, two separate branches of tradition can be readily discerned. For the one, what is distinctive is its faith *expressis verbis in* Jesus (Christ). This is the case in the entire epistolary literature, in Revelation, and in the Gospel of John. To be distinguished from this is the other branch of tradition, to which the synoptic gospels and the traditional material that precedes them belong. Here there is never talk of faith in Jesus (Christ). (The only two exceptions are Matt. 18:6 and 27:42. However, comparison with their source material, Mark 9:42; 15:32, shows that here we have to do with a very late and isolated assimilation to the linguistic usage of the other branch of tradition.) What is striking here is the extraordinary consistency with which each of the two branches of tradition maintains its linguistic usage. By no means is this to be explained as an accident.

Now, following Bultmann and in the framework of so-called kerygma theology, it was emphasized time and again that, "Through the Easter events and the certainty of the resurrection of Jesus Christ from the dead, the proclaimer became . . . the proclaimed, the one who summoned to faith became the content of faith" (G. Bornkamm, *Jesus von Nazareth* [1956]: 172). If this were so, then one thing that we observe is extremely curious. In the synoptic gospels, written since about 70 C.E., Jesus is still never he *in* whom one believes. Therefore, if the one who summoned to faith became the one believed in through the Easter events in the early community, and if we really can start from *one* early community, then it is scarcely possible to explain why the synoptics have remained uninfluenced by this. For by speaking in this way, they fall back into a "pre-Easter" stage. Against this background, one can very well understand that a gospel like that of John now arose. Here, the kerygma that knows of belief in Jesus Christ is presupposed, and together with this, traditions from the life of Jesus are taken up. However, these are shaped in such a way that Jesus now calls for faith in himself. But the emergence so late of the synoptic gospels remains puzzling—if the Easter-kerygma is presupposed. People have tried to solve this puzzle. So far, no one has succeeded convincingly in doing so, not to mention there being any sort of consensus in this regard. The effort continues to be made in spite of this. I fear that success will not attend it.

In fact, what is at issue is not only the question of how the synoptic gospels could still have arisen at this point (that is, after 70). By locating the problem in these works, one all too easily overlooks the fact that they grew out of a completely autonomous tradition in which, while there was no gospel at all before Mark, there certainly were a variety of ongoing developments within the traditions and also some incipient collections. Therefore, the question ought not to be directed toward the gospels, but should rather be, "How is it that a branch of tradition was able to maintain itself for so long in which, long after the date of Easter, Jesus was still not presented as he *in* whom one was to have faith? On the other hand, however, it is then also striking that the branch of tradition which, *expressis verbis*, takes its bearings from faith in (Jesus) Christ, for all practical purposes completely ignores the Jesus-traditions. I cannot explain this to myself in any other way than that we do, in fact, have to take account of two relatively separated early communities, self-sufficient and independent of each other. Against this, it will not do to argue that this is hard to imagine, on the grounds that there must have been contacts between these two communities and that, therefore, they must also have been aware of each other. This is entirely possible. Nevertheless, it is indisputable that even such contact as may have existed between the communities did not bring either of them to the point of taking over the way the other group formulated its faith in stating its own. There are no mixed forms at all. But this can scarcely be an accident. One needs to find an explanation for this. The explanation closest to hand (and plainly demanded by the fundamental insights of form criticism) remains that of supposing that there were two early communities.

IV.

To begin with, we shall have to direct our interest to the community in which the Jesus-kerygma was formulated and handed down. In this regard, I can refer to reflections that W. Schmithals has recently engaged in and that (at least at the outset) exhibit a strong similarity to what has just been laid out. Schmithals reckons with the existence of "Jesus communities. . . that [took] no notice of the Easter occurrence and of the confessional development resulting from it." He suspects these in Galilee, and a good deal speaks in favor of this, because we evidently have to do with communities that owe their existence to the activity of the earthly Jesus. Since the Easter-kerygma played no role in these communities, however, Schmithals speaks here of a "Jesus sect" (*Jesus Christus in der Verkündigung der Kirche* [1972]: 72). It is clear that Schmithals is referring to Bultmann's way of conceiving the matter, but that he has now modified this by making it more precise. If, in Bultmann's view, the proclamation of the earthly Jesus does not yet summon one to Christian faith, according to Schmithals, neither does this take place even after (the date of) Easter in cases where Jesus-traditions are indeed preserved, but where the Easter-experiences have not been materially incorporated into them. It is precisely on this account that one must speak of a sect here.

However, if this were correct, we would also have to follow up on it in a way that is consistent. What I assumed in an earlier context as self-evident must now precisely be called into question. If, by means of literary criticism, one reconstructs from the synoptic gospels a piece of tradition that derives from these Jesus-communities, then form critical exegesis would have to show that it is the Jesus sect, and not yet a Christian community, that is speaking here. But in that case, a Christian community could not appeal to it today, and such a piece of tradition would not be suitable as a text for a Christian sermon. For it will not do simply to replace the name "Jesus" in such a piece of tradition with the term "the risen one." The *content* of the piece of tradition would not yet become Christian merely by doing this, for what is said does not become different just because someone different says it.

Now I obviously do not want to fall into the error of "refuting" a view by treating its untoward consequences as an argument against it. To be sure, this is an approach that is taken often enough and that is made use of with particular gusto when the results of theological scholarship are an irritant to church practice. However, what finds expression here is the unwillingness of practice to submit itself to theological examination. All the same, things are not right just because they have always been that way. Anyhow, noting a consequence such as this can get our attention and then cause us to reexamine how this view was arrived at.

What is striking is that Schmithals is at pains to avoid describing the Jesus-traditions as kerygma. This caution makes sense if one starts out from the assumption that kerygma first came into being at and through Easter, that the New Testament kerygma is therefore invariably Christ-kerygma. However, avoiding the term "kerygma" for the Jesus-traditions does not make sense if the insights of form critical research are taken into consideration. Form criticism concerned itself precisely with these presynoptic traditions, and it taught us to understand these very traditions as kerygma, and not as historical report. It remains true that this kerygma does not call for faith *in* Jesus Christ. Here, at least at the start, no confession of Jesus is present. Nonetheless, it remains just as true that this kerygma was formulated by believers. Even if one thinks one has to disqualify the bearers of this tradition by referring to them by the term "sect," one still should not in this way at the same time deny them the faith in and from which they formulated and passed on this tradition as kerygma. The question is only what sort of faith we have to do with here.

It is absolutely certain that it was not, *expressis verbis*, faith in Jesus Christ. Nevertheless, it has to do in each case with a faith that was initiated by Jesus. Do these two faiths have anything to do with each other? Probably no one will want to claim that they differ completely. How they are related to each other can perhaps better be shown by replacing the term "faith" with another that unites both formulations of faith in itself. In both cases, one is concerned with an event of being moved. The Christ-kerygma does not simply mean to provide information about Jesus' resurrection and the risen one, from which then (in a second step) being moved can follow. To the contrary, only within this event itself does it make sense to speak of the risen one. It is a matter not of isolated conceptions, but rather of being engaged in the present on the basis of conceptions. The christology that is developed in the course of time in the Christ-kerygma is misunderstood if it is viewed as a thought-experiment engaged in at a writing table, as speculation about the origin and the manner of being of the risen one, and specifically, the exalted Christ. That this very thing later happened is not to be disputed. At first, however, it was a question of how this more inclusive understanding of a person's being moved came to expression in the ongoing development of christology.

Nevertheless, in the Jesus-kerygma christology is entirely lacking in the beginning. All the same, this Jesus-kerygma was formulated by people who allowed themselves to be summoned by Jesus to this event of being moved. Sometimes (not always) they expressed this being moved as a being moved by God. Today there is unanimous agreement that the written traditions were preceded by an oral one. And it would probably also be agreed that this oral tradition at least began during the lifetime of the earthly Jesus, since there is utterly no reason to think that such activity began to occur only after the death of Jesus, much less that it first became possible then. The Jesus-kerygma therefore does not presuppose the death of Jesus. However, one might say that it presupposes his absence. For, in the Jesus-kerygma, people moved by Jesus convey what they have experienced with regard to and through Jesus, in order, by doing so, to call others to this same event. In the beginning, their kerygma did not reflect the one who initiated this event at all. In this respect, they stood in the line of the proclamation of Jesus. Moreover, he had not made himself the object of his proclamation, nor had he called for faith in his person in the first place, thereby creating a precondition for people's giving themselves to what he expected of them. His authority became concrete in his speech, in his conduct, in what he did. Through this, people allowed themselves to be moved by him, and in this being moved, they believed *him*, without formulating this as belief *in* him. But should one not be permitted to call this Christian faith?

V.

In accord with what has preceded (with regard to the sentence of Bultmann's that was cited at the beginning), we would now have to say this: There has been Christian faith since there has been a

Christian kerygma. And since, in its origin, the Jesus-kerygma is certainly older than the Christ-kerygma, Christian faith began with the Jesus-kerygma. To declare that Easter is the *terminus a quo* for Christian faith must appear arbitrary, so long as it cannot be shown that the "Easter-experiences" made possible a being moved that is qualitatively distinct from that to which the earthly Jesus led people. However, I am convinced that this has not yet successfully been shown to be the case.

It is misleading to make this issue hang on christology and then to be willing to speak of Christian faith only once there is an explicitly christological confession, for this brings only one aspect of the complex phenomenon of faith into the picture. It overemphasizes the one who initiates the event of being moved and threatens to isolate him. And then it is no longer sufficiently clear that he initiates the event of *being moved*.

Therefore, if we want to compare the faith into which one is summoned by the Christ-kerygma to the faith into which one is summoned by the Jesus-kerygma, we get off on the wrong foot by comparing the kerygmas with each other. Rather, we need to compare the two events of being moved. If they are in accord, it makes no difference which of the two kerygmas occasions them. If, in the Christ-kerygma, one *confesses* that one knows oneself moved by the exalted one, and if the very same event of being moved takes place through the Jesus-kerygma, since one *trusts* Jesus by giving oneself to him, it may *then* be said that the earthly one and the exalted one are identical. However, this (dogmatically correct) proposition only makes sense if it is actually taken seriously, and not if it is only the exalted one that first gets credit for something that the earthly one was *as yet* utterly unable to accomplish. In order to escape from a *theologia gloriae*, which a theology of the resurrection all too readily brings along with it, we simply have to insist that even the exalted one is still the earthly one and that "imitating" the exalted one is always an imitation on the way of the cross. The resurrection of Jesus does not make this way glorious, but rather *shows* that it is the way of glory. In any case, this is how those who participated in the Easter-experiences saw it. It is Paul who makes this point most clearly, when he "proclaims not so much the crucified one as the one who is risen, but rather the risen one as the one who is crucified" (E. Jüngel, *Unterwegs zur Sache* [1972]: 143).

Of course, we should draw attention to a danger that can crop up in the branch of the tradition that takes its bearings from the Jesus-kerygma. When the event of being moved is passed on without explicitly characterizing the one who initiates it, its eschatological character can easily be overlooked. There are many examples of this. So, for instance, the parables of the kingdom of heaven, which were originally intended to address people directly, are misunderstood as information about heaven (and about God). Or one attempts to garner ethical instructions from them. The conduct that the kerygma expects of someone or even that it represents is then read off the kerygma, precisely because it is itself so concrete. This can lead to the view that what is important is an imitation, in which Christians, at least, are supposed to engage. But then the kerygma no longer has to do with an eschatological occurrence, and such imitation rather becomes a human possibility. This sort of thing can then be further transformed, so that now only when someone resolutely decides for this possibility does God's will occur. What was intended as eschatological existence has now been turned into law. This law may now be more strenuous and the ethic therefore "better" than people used to and presumably typically still do find it to be. But it is by means of striving that this law is to be fulfilled. Once it is realized how much striving this takes (of course only later, upon reflection), an ethic develops with two standards, only a small circle is expected to keep the whole law, and this is now demanded of them alone.

This development can be fully illustrated in the tradition of the Jesus-kerygma. We should also not fail to acknowledge that this sort of danger is present in a virulent way today, for if someone wants to give himself or herself to "the Jesus-business" today as a way of escaping christology, such a person is likely to succumb to this misunderstanding. All the same, the "Jesus-business" means being moved through the Jesus-kerygma. And the Jesus-kerygma, for its part, implies a christology. If this is overlooked, being moved loses its eschatological character. To be sure, in the "Jesus-business," properly understood, it is not necessary that christology be made explicit. However, if the Jesus-business is no longer understood as eschatological event, it is no longer the business of Jesus.

It is exactly because the danger of a "slippage" of this sort was sensed during the course of development of the synoptic tradition that pains were taken even here to make christology explicit. However, it may not be said that it was through this christologizing (carried through in various ways) that a faith first arose that may properly be called Christian faith. Its purpose was rather to keep the event of being moved that was initiated by Jesus an eschatological event—one that, to be sure, had once been experienced in the encounter with Jesus, but that had been precisely *an experienced* event and that therefore could not be "produced," but only ever awaited anew. This is also the meaning of the so much discussed "imminent expectation of the parousia" in early Christianity. This served to counter the misunderstanding of wanting and of trying to live out this eschatological event of being moved as if it were a permanent condition. It is well known that this led to new problems as soon as the next generation. The imminent expectation was misunderstood as the specifying of a fixed date. In the present context, however, I have to forgo pursuing these issues any further.

VI.

Nevertheless, I do want to go into one point in closing. The statement that Christian faith began with the Jesus-kerygma still needs to be made a bit more precise. Strictly speaking, this statement only designates that point in time at which Christian faith can be identified as such. This is possible only from the point of the oldest Jesus-kerygma we can gain access to, which is to say, that we can reconstruct. However, there is of course no reason why every event of being moved by Jesus should have been recorded as kerygma. For this reason, the beginning should now be defined more precisely in this way: Christian faith began with the event of being moved by Jesus.

This consideration may seem so simple that it is scarcely worth mentioning. However, it leads us back a step further, since the question now comes into view of the relation in which Jesus himself stands to Christian faith. A formulation of J. Wellhausen's that Bultmann subsequently took over has given a great deal of offense, namely, that Jesus was a Jew, not a Christian. I do not at this point want to pursue whether this set of alternatives is a genuine one. In any event, this statement is understandable on the assumption that Christian faith has been defined as faith in Jesus Christ. For in that case, Jesus could indeed only be called a Christian if his faith included a confession of himself. Such a thought is naturally absurd.

However, we have already seen that it is problematic to speak of Christian faith only in cases in which it is articulated as confession of Jesus Christ. Rather, we also have Christian faith in cases in which it finds expression as being moved by Jesus, which is to say, where the element of trust is articulated. Only such a trusting giving of oneself to Jesus can, even if it does not have to lead to this explicit confession of him. If we bear this in mind, our question takes on a different aspect, for now events of being moved can be compared with each other.

In this case, the old (liberal) historical question must once more immediately be put to one side. It is absolutely impossible to say anything *directly* about being moved by the historical Jesus. Just as little do we know how he understood himself, because we do not possess a single line from his own hand. In the Jesus-kerygma, we only ever experience how people who encountered him and who experienced being moved by him went on to speak of what they experienced.

And yet what is significant is this. Being moved by Jesus (that is to say, faith), out of which these people fashioned their kerygma and into which they meant to call others, is something they testify to as a being moved, of which Jesus was the center. As a result, it is clear immediately what a dangerous narrowing down it is to restrict inquiry about Jesus to his proclamation and to identify this alone with the kerygma. Of course, the kerygma itself is proclamation. However, its content is not only Jesus' proclamation, but rather, and to precisely the same degree, his action and his conduct. In fact, often it even turns out that these "three contents" cannot be clearly separated from one another at all. What can be distinguished in many pieces of tradition are only distinct aspects of *one* event of being moved. However, this is that very event out of which the Jesus-kerygma was formulated and into which it means to summon people. This event, cast in its various forms in the kerygma, is presented as occasioned by Jesus. But at the same time, the kerygma expresses being moved by Jesus as being moved by God. So, when people give themselves to the kerygma, this means that they thereby give themselves to Jesus and that they thereby give themselves to God.

WHEN DID CHRISTIAN FAITH BEGIN?

In Christian dogmatics we have to a large extent become accustomed to speaking first of God, then of Christ, and then of salvation. This makes perfectly good sense on the basis of certain presuppositions. It is just that we need to recognize that a systematic reversal has taken place here. In Christian "experience," it is quite a different matter. The kerygma presents the expectation to give oneself over to Jesus. The person who experiences the event of being moved that results from this as salvation can make soteriological statements. By reflecting upon the one who has initiated this salvation, such a person can make christological statements and then develop these into theological statements. As has been said, this order can be reversed. However, if it does not remain unmistakably clear that we have to do with a reversal here, the impossibility arises of wanting to make statements about God in the absence of the event of being moved. However, these are then not statements about God at all (and therefore also are not theological statements), but rather are statements about conceptions of God (and therefore statements that belong to religious scholarship). Anyone who is engaged in Christian religious scholarship is mistaken to think that, insofar, he or she is already engaged in Christian theology. It seems to me that this set of issues needs to be thought through very carefully. If it were, the word "theological" would not be used as casually as it often is today in the Christian sphere.

However, let me now return to the statement that was put to one side earlier. I said that when people give themselves to the kerygma, this means that they thereby give themselves to Jesus, and that they thereby give themselves to God. Bultmann frequently employed the formulation that preaching (today!) is an eschatological event. Perhaps it ought to have been said somewhat more precisely, that preaching is meant to initiate the eschatological event (among those who hear it). It means to do this, because it summons to the same event of being moved into which the Jesus-kerygma meant to summon people. The Jesus-kerygma owes its origin to the experience of a certain being moved that people had in regard to Jesus. However, if it is a matter of the very same event of being moved in the case of these people and of Jesus, then there is no longer any point in disputing whether Jesus ought to be called a Christian or not. He is "the pioneer of faith" (Heb. 12:2). For this reason, he precedes all Christian faith. However, he precedes it in such a way that, as "pioneer" of the very same event of being moved, he also always belongs to this faith, so that one may venture with Luther the daring formulation, that it is the honor and task of the Christian to become Christ to the neighbor.

But in this case, one can also venture the claim that Jesus was the first Christian.

6

CHRISTIAN FAITH AS RESURRECTION OF THE DEAD*

The title of this essay is formulated as an assertion. Yet this very assertion doesn't seem to make any sense at all at first hearing. Therefore, let us clarify what the problem is at once.

I.

Two topics are touched on in the title: Christian faith and the resurrection of the dead. No one will dispute that each has to do with the other. In any case, this is the common view, not only among Christians, but more generally as well. If one speaks of Christian faith, one expects that somehow the theme of resurrection of the dead will *also* be discussed. Therefore, it would not be at all surprising if this lecture were entitled, "Christian Faith *and* (the Hope for) the Resurrection of the Dead." This title might still be troubling enough because, especially today, it is anything but clear what place the claim of the resurrection of the dead occupies in the structure of Christian faith. Non-Christians shake their heads; many Christians are uncertain. Does this concept still fit into our modern scientific worldview? This is not infrequently disputed, and then the question can even come up of whether anything at all is left of Christian faith, if one must and then also does give up the hope in the resurrection of the dead. When a Christian theologian says "Christian Faith *and* Resurrection of the Dead" in this situation, the normal expectation is that he or she is about to mount a defense of this concept. At this juncture, Christians want to feel

---

*"Christlicher Glaube als Auferweckung von den Toten," *Christologie—praktisch* (Gütersloh: Gütersloher Verlagshaus Gerd Mohn, 1978), 58–80.

96

more certain about a point on which they are perhaps uncertain. Non-Christians, on the other hand, will listen more critically and try to figure out what is shaky about the argument. But in that case, there is plenty of material for discussion.

It is precisely because this subject is (or at least seems to be) so problematic today that the way the title of this essay is formulated needs to be surprising; otherwise, what I want to ask about would be brushed right aside. The resurrection of the dead ought not to be treated as one possible topic among many that belong to Christian faith. To the contrary, the two are meant to be equated here. Christian faith *as* resurrection of the dead means then nothing less than this: Wherever someone believes in a Christian way, there (and by that fact) resurrection from the dead *occurs*. But this is just what doesn't seem to make sense.

Non-Christians might call such an assertion an act of desperation or suspect some kind of trick. By the same token, it might make Christians anxious. The usual way of presenting the matter is as follows: Christian faith is a concern of the present. People do or should believe in a Christian way today. But resurrection of the dead has to do with the future; whoever believes today expects it. Faith bases its hope on it. However, if what one hopes for is declared to be already present, this not only seems like a rather ridiculous utopianism in view of the reality around us, but also at once signals a danger: Is there anything at all that one can hope for as a Christian? If what is hoped for is asserted to be present, but present reality contradicts what one hopes for (resurrection of the dead hasn't happened yet!), then the result can all too easily be hopelessness. What should and can a person still hope for in this case? It is precisely for the sake of hope that one wants to maintain that the resurrection of the dead is a matter of the future. Only then, it seems, is there anything to hope for at all.

Now it is not as if this objection to the assertion contained in our title were one that has only been made by Christians today. This objection already occurs in the New Testament. So let us take a look around there for a moment.

II.

In the third Christian generation, there were people who asserted that the resurrection was a present reality. These people are strongly opposed as heretics in the Second Letter to Timothy (written at the beginning of the second century). There we read,

> Don't get mixed up with this godless, empty chatter, for by it people only fall ever deeper into godlessness. And their doctrine spreads like a cancerous ulcer. Hymenaeus and Philetus belong to them. They have deviated from the course of the truth by saying, "The resurrection has already occurred." Thereby, they destroy many people's faith. (2 Tim. 2: 14–18)

So you see, whoever supports the assertion of our title at least runs the danger of being reckoned among the heretics who were opposed at that time. So, if a New Testament scholar were to agree with this very assertion, wouldn't he be refuted by his own documents?

Now of course, the scholar knows this text, too (even if it is commonly little known). But alongside it, he knows others, especially from the Gospel of John, that he could advance precisely in support of the legitimacy of his assertion. Of many, let me cite only one. The Johannine Christ says, " 'Truly, truly, I say to you, whoever hears my word and believes in him who sent me *has* eternal life and does not come into judgment, but rather already *has* behind him the step from death over into life' " (5:24). However, this cannot be understood in any other way than that, where there is faith, resurrection of the dead occurs. This is just the view that is taken in the Gospel of John. Was its author then ultimately himself a heretic? Does he belong among the people that are opposed in 2 Timothy?

Seldom as one encounters it, this suspicion is not utterly farfetched. In the early church, the Gospel of John was in fact contested in many places, and it was suspected of heresy because of this and similar passages. Now, if we read the whole Gospel, we may state that there are also passages in which the resurrection is spoken of as expected in the future. Since it is only with difficulty that these two views can be made to agree, it is frequently supposed that the Gospel of John has undergone a so-called ecclesiastical redaction. Originally, it spoke only of salvation in the present (in technical terminology, it advocated a "present eschatology"). However, because this was felt to be intolerably one-sided, passages

98

were later added in various places that have as their content the future character of salvation (that is to say, "future eschatology"). This is the form in which we have the Fourth Gospel today.

I regard this literary judgment (that is, the supposition of an "ecclesisatical redaction") as well established but, nevertheless, I do not want to insist on it, since I do not want to burden my remarks with hypotheses. Even without this hypothesis, that our problem as such occurs in the Gospel of John can be clearly enough read off the text. Statements stand alongside each other which, on the one hand, represent the resurrection as present and, on the other hand, represent it as future. And I could now demonstrate with a wealth of further texts from the New Testament that differing opinions concerning just this problem were evidently voiced in the early church (for example, in the case of the question whether the parousia of Jesus was to come soon or only after some time, or whether it had somehow already taken place). I cannot go into this in any more detail here. The only thing that is important to me for the moment is to have shown that the view widely shared today, that resurrection of the dead is only to be expected in the future, was by no means as unanimous a matter as it is often assumed to have been. Alongside this, there also existed the view I have formulated in the title of this essay. Even if this did not carry the day in the long run, it is still not to be concluded on that basis alone that it was false. It is not simply to be assumed that only correct views ever carry the day. And even if that were not the case, the question about the interest that lay behind a false view is still always worth asking.

Therefore, let me offer a preliminary summary. In earliest Christianity, there are two views concerning resurrection which, to all appearances, cannot be made to agree with each other. According to the one view, the resurrection of the dead is expected only in the future. According to the other view, resurrection may be spoken of as already present. How do we proceed from here?

III.

First, I would like to point out that two problems need to be kept separate from each other. The first problem results from posing the question, "Which of these two views is properly to be called the Christian one?" Since both views can evidently appeal to early Christianity in support of their claims, the answer is hardly a simple one. Texts from the New Testament can be cited in support of both. This shows that it is quite impermissible to ground the Christian character of a true statement by referring to individual biblical texts (which then can be and often are selected arbitrarily). Individual texts never constitute an argument. But then is there any possibility at all of answering the question which view is to be called Christian? I will return to this.

But first, let me mention the other problem which, as I have said, is not to be confused with the first one. It consists in the following. Even if it is a matter of dispute as to which of the two views is properly Christian, we can still (independently of *this* answer) seek to clarify whether each makes sense in itself. At first glance, this does not seem to be the case. Nonetheless, this is just what we want to test out by asking whether we can at least form conceptions of these two views.

We certainly can of one, for, whether we today do or do not regard it as *possible* (we want to prescind from this for the moment), we can all *conceive* of resurrection as taking place at some time and place in the future. However, to speak of resurrection of the dead as already having occurred must seem meaningless to all of us. But in that case, isn't our whole problem actually already settled?

It might in fact seem so. However, before jumping to this conclusion, at least one thing should be considered. If we are of the opinion that it is meaningless to speak of the resurrection of the dead as already having occurred or as now occurring, then were the people in the early church who *made* such claims saying something meaningless? According to 2 Tim. 2:18, Hymenaeus and Philetus asserted that the resurrection had already occurred. If we are to suppose that this really was meaningless at that time, it can only be a matter for amazement that (at least according to the opinion of 2 Timothy) people could fall for it. Were they stupid, or uncomprehending, or dreamers? Who among us would fall for being told that we were already resurrected? We have a simple counterargument against this. We haven't died yet, so we can't have been resurrected, either. But the people at that time must have known this, too. If they speak of a resurrection having occurred anyway, and if such language is supposed to have made sense, then they must have understood something different by resurrection from what we do. This brings us to the decisive point. The dispute is only apparently about whether resurrection is to be understood as future or as present. In fact, it is something deeper. In order to see where the real difference lies, we first have to clarify what was meant by resurrection of the dead at that time. Naturally, *we* can connect a quite definite conception up with this notion. This is not to be disputed in the least. We just need to realize that others who employ the same *notion* conceive of something with a different *content* when they do. However, this is just how misunderstandings so easily arise. The same words are used to express different contents. If we do not make the effort (and unfortunately, we all tend to do this) to specify precisely what we understand by the word in question, and if we do not also struggle to determine how another person understands the same word, we make it impossible to come to any kind of understanding.

In the time of the New Testament, people did not, in fact, all understand resurrection in the same way. And unfortunately, people already frequently did not keep tabs on their language. This is precisely what occasionally led to misunderstandings—even already in the time of the New Testament. I want to indicate briefly how this happened.

In this regard, let me begin not from the conception that is familiar to *us* (resurrection as a calling-back-to-life of someone who is physically dead), but rather from that put forward by 2 Tim. 2:18—more precisely, from the claim that is opposed in that verse. The opponents attacked there were Hellenistic gnostics. I cannot develop the whole problem of what gnosis is here (or even of a Christian gnosis). Neither is this necessary, since what matters for our purposes is only one aspect, namely, that of its anthropology (the doctrine of human existence). This was dualistic. The ancient Greek conception was elaborated and developed, according to which the soul dwells in the body. Body and soul exist alongside each other. The body (thought of as matter, not as creation) is transient. The soul in the body (and only it) is capable of redemption. Redemption can occur by means of gnosis (that is, knowledge) being imparted to the soul. However, it can also happen in other ways: for instance, by means of a baptism, or by participation in cultic observances, and so forth. If then the soul has undergone redemption in one of these ways, it may dwell for some time in the body (the body is then the "prison of the soul"), but it has become immortal and sets off on its heavenly journey when the body has died. The *soul* has been "raised" by means of redemption having taken place. However, the soul is the real "I," not the body (this is precisely only matter). In the framework of this anthropology, it is fully meaningful to say, "I have already been raised. The resurrection has already occurred."

Now for anyone who has a different *conception* of resurrection (in particular, the one with which we are familiar), and who does not realize that the claim of a resurrection that has already occurred has been made in the framework of a different anthropology, such a claim must appear nonsensical. And so misunderstandings result. These already arise in the New Testament and, indeed, in two different forms. I will pursue both, since they will allow us to see what sort of interest is *actually* hiding behind this polemic. Let me name the catchwords in advance. The issue concerns hope for the future and ethics.

The first issue (hope for the future) stands behind 1 Cor. 15:12. In Corinth, as we are told here, there are people who claim that there is no resurrection of the dead at all. However, at the same time, these very people practice so-called vicarious baptism. That is to say, they have themselves baptized on behalf of people who have died (1 Cor. 15:29). Paul says of this what we would presumably also say: This goes against all logic. If there is no resurrection of the dead, a baptism for the dead is meaningless. And yet, precisely this is a mistake.

The Corinthians who denied the resurrection of the dead did so on the basis of their gnostic anthropology. Their *soul* had been redeemed. However, for this redemption *they* do *not* use the notion of resurrection. It does not absolutely *have to* be used, and in gnostic circles it in fact very seldom occurs. One simply spoke of redemption or said, "I am perfected," "I have attained the goal," or something of this sort. This was a statement that concerned only the soul, only the "I" of the person. At this point, one waited for the soul to quit the body. This was to happen when, once the body had died, the soul was freed from it. If one now tells these people that there is a resurrection and means thereby resurrection of the body, then this is precisely for them an expression of utter hopelessness, for then the redeemed "I" has to return to the body and so to the prison. Therefore, it is not because these people have *no* hope that they say that there is no resurrection of the dead; they say this, rather, precisely *because* they have hope. On the other hand, if people whose souls have not been redeemed have died, then the soul (the "I" of these people) is together with the body in the grave. In this case, it is perfectly meaningful for someone to be baptized vicariously at the site of the grave on behalf of such a dead person. To be sure, this is not done so that the *body* of the dead person will be raised, but rather so that the soul (the "I") of the dead person will now be *redeemed*.

It is scarcely worth arguing that Paul does not grasp these connections in 1 Corinthians, for it is only on this basis that he can reproach the Corinthians for their lack of logic. (By the time Paul writes 2 Cor. 5:1–10, he does grasp this and therefore also modifies his statements. Nevertheless, I do not need to say anything more about this.)

What is clear to us is that the *real* interest of this exchange consists not in the question of resurrection, but rather in that of hope for the future. Both sides are interested in this—Paul and the Corinthians. They differ only in this respect: Paul believes that, because the Corinthians deny the expectation of the resurrection, they abandon the hope for the future. However, the Corinthians deny the expectation of the resurrection precisely because they do have hope for the future.

Behind 2 Tim. 2:18, it is the second problem, namely, ethics, that comes into focus. Again, we need to start out from the dualistic anthropology of the text. The soul in the body is redeemed, and in this case the redemption *is* expressed by means of the concept of resurrection, and it can be said in a perfectly meaningful way, "I am already raised." To be sure, a consequence follows from this. The raised "I" dwells in the despised body. However, since the resurrection of the soul has occurred once for all time, the body can now do whatever it wants. This leads to a libertinism that also evidently held sway in Corinth, where the slogan was issued, "Everything is permitted to me." This can be claimed because no action of the body can undo the redemption that has happened to the soul. Indeed, even the precisely opposite conclusion can sometimes be drawn. The raised "I" does not give the despised body permission to do anything at all. This then leads to asceticism, and there is every indication that the opponents that are being fought against in the pastoral epistles (1 and 2 Timothy and Titus) were such ascetics, in the realms of sexuality (up to the point of renouncing marriage) and of food (the use of alcohol was prohibited). On this basis, it is also understandable why, in the pastoral epistles, ethical instructions in favor of self-restraint play a central role against every form of fanaticism. Again the result is that the argument is ignited over the question of whether the resurrection has already occurred. The *real* interest lies in another place, namely, with the issue of ethics.

What have we gained from these reflections? Two things, I believe. On the one hand, an account has to be given of what is *really meant* when the term "resurrection" is employed. On the other, it needs to be seen that, however resurrection is understood, we are never concerned with an isolated issue, but rather with one that occurs in some context. The failure to pay attention to this inevitably leads to oversimplifications.

This is also the case when we take our bearings, not from the gnostic conception that has just been treated, but rather from the one that is more familiar to us. This originates in Zoroastrianism and then comes to us by way of Judaism. Thus, we have to do with a conception that is by no means original to Christianity. This is internally complex in comparison with the gnostic conception, because the resurrection of the dead is expected. However, the conception is as such already an expression of the hope for the future. And another concept, namely, that of a judgment, is generally bound together with it as well. Here too, there are differences. Sometimes it is expected that all people will be raised, but that the judgment determines who will enter into this future salvation. According to another conception, only the righteous will be raised. In other words, the hope for the future is tied to conditions that must be fulfilled in this life. Once again, here we have to do with the issue of ethics—or is it perhaps rather that of faith?

With this, we are in fact faced with a tough problem. Is (always still in the framework of this conception) it faith that is the presupposition of a future resurrection (that is, of making it through judgment)? Or does this not rather depend upon a person's deeds? Or again, if one does not want to make such a distinction, how are faith and deeds related to each other? These very same ideas can be met with today, precisely in Christian circles: since human deeds are always imperfect, faith must be added to them in order to achieve the expected future. Then faith is an additional accomplishment. But this must surely be problematic. The conception of repentance seems to me riskier still. Only the person who has faith is in a position to fulfill by way of deeds the conditions demanded for resurrection and for making it through judgment. Is then perhaps everyone who does not have faith morally defective? Or (and now the matter gets worse yet again) is faith here only being firmly convinced *that* there will be a resurrection of the dead one day? This would mean a state of anxiety for the present. I would have to be scrupulous about fulfilling the scriptures (but which ones?), keeping those that would be checked up on later. And if I don't manage to do this? (And who does?) Then I count on forgiveness for those occasions. But why should this apply just to me? Why not to everybody? Do I now have to accomplish something beyond this, so that I (as opposed to others) can count on forgiveness? And what is that? My faith, perhaps? Then this would be an accomplishment again.

I could continue inquiring in this way and would only end up going around in circles, as I have just been doing. Nevertheless, this process of inquiry was not meaningless, for it has clarified at least one thing for us. However we imagine the future, we can never discuss this topic without relating it to the present. But this is true not just with respect to faith and deeds today (however the two are connected), but (and the earlier reflections showed this) also with respect to our anthropology. Whatever this is, any understanding we might have of a future resurrection of the dead will have to be congruent with it.

We will only get anywhere if we try to clarify the meaning of "faith," because this other term in our title is also anything but clear.

IV.

In the title I spoke not simply of faith, but of Christian faith. It might have seemed natural at that point to inquire into the New Testament, in order to find out what is meant by faith there. Were we to do so, we would rather quickly run up against difficulties similar to those we encountered in the cases of both the concept of resurrection and the way it is presented. The use of language in the New Testament is by no means uniform, for completely different phenomena are referred to by one and the same word. I want at least to illustrate this.

In the Epistle of James, faith and works are contrasted with each other (2:14–26). The author engages in polemic against the claim that faith *alone* makes the individual righteous before God. Rather, this rightwising or justification takes place only when works are added to faith. Paul had previously claimed something completely different. He formulates this explicitly in Romans. "So we are now of the view that the individual is justified before God apart from works of the law and, what is more, by faith *alone*." One must naturally sense this as a contradiction. But is it?

Let us start out not from the difference between the two, but rather from what they have in common. Justification by God is on both their agendas—James' and Paul's. James thinks that faith alone could not suffice for this, and that a doing would have to accompany it. For James, therefore, faith itself in no sense involves something one does. He can say, for instance, that the demons have faith—and shudder (James 2:19). For him, faith is being convinced that God exists. Faith is therefore a "taking-to-be-true." But in this case, we can readily see that James is being a bit sarcastically polemical. Anyone who merely reckons with the existence of the invisible God and then calls this faith, but doesn't draw even a single consequence from this for his or her life, cannot count on being justified by God by means of a mere *sacrificium intellectus*. I think this can be seen straight off.

But then, how can Paul say that faith *alone* produces justification before God? Well, because Paul understands faith as something completely different. For him faith means not something that is limited to the intellect (and that then even excludes the intellect). Rather, faith is for Paul a way of living, a giving oneself over to God that becomes visible in giving concrete shape to one's life. Faith is therefore an occurrence. Only where there is doing is there actually believing. Where nothing is done, however, there there is no faith at all.

I cannot go into the significance of the law for Paul here. That would require an essay of its own. Nevertheless, it remains sufficiently clear, I think, that these are two different understandings of faith. In the one case, faith is a matter of the head, and it remains a matter of the head, even if the intellect is sacrificed. In the other case, faith is an occurrence; it is a trustful giving oneself over to God that becomes visible in the life that is lived. In it, the intellect is in no way switched off, for in the case of this faith the believer must perfectly well consider who it is to whom one gives oneself over, why one does so, and how this is meant to take concrete shape.

Now it is my view that we should speak of Christian faith only in the second case. I emphasize this, because much too often it is the other understanding of faith that is taken to be typically Christian, and this not at all only by non-Christians. People who take this view assume (to put it perhaps too simply) that Christians believe in dogmas that cannot be critically examined and then reproach Christians (often churches as well) for not living according to these dogmas. And many Christians give non-Christians cause for this view, because they themselves regard their faith as *one* thing, and their life as *another*. Naturally, they claim that both have to fit together. However, when their life doesn't work out (and this happens with Christians, too) they are hardly inclined to admit that they no longer have any faith. The conception represented by James has won out. It is (at least in principle) possible to differentiate faith from works.

If I now claim that this way of differentiating the two is not Christian, I could appeal to Paul in support. But is this an argument? I believe it is, on account of the fact that we find the same understanding of faith on the part of Jesus that Paul holds.

(So as not to be misunderstood, I need to modify one thing I said earlier. This does not concern the question whether both conceptions of faith are possible. They are. The coexistence of Paul and James demonstrates this. For this reason, each of us is at liberty to make one of these conceptions our own. However, we ought not to call *both* of them "faith," and we need to ask ourselves whether our *own* conception of faith remains within the framework of what is Christian.)

V.

As I now explain this with regard to Jesus, it will very quickly become clear both that and how the two topics in our title (Christian faith and resurrection of the dead) come into view as an integral whole.

I need to start from the conception that held sway at the time of Jesus, which he could take for granted in his environment and which he can therefore link up with—and which he at the same time decisively invalidates. The Jews of Jesus' time counted on this world (they spoke of "this aeon") soon coming to an end. At that point, God will bring about the turn of the aeons. That is to say, God will replace this world with a new world. The new aeon is inaugurated by the resurrection of the dead. This is followed by the judgment of all people. (Sometimes one also envisages it in such a way that only the righteous are raised.) Those who make it through judgment (or, according to the other conception, the righteous who are raised) will then live in unending fellowship with God. One especially popular conception in this regard was that of fellowship at the table of God. Here the well-being of salvation will finally hold sway. There will be no more want, no crying, no pain. People live among and with each other in perfect shalom (peace). There is no anger. A yes is a yes, a no is a no. Love rules, and enmity is unthinkable. This is the kingdom of God that was expected. And this conception does not derive from Jesus; he finds it already there.

Whether we today do envisage a future beyond this life at all and whether we can envisage it in this way, we can leave aside for now. The substance of what was expected, namely, saving well-being, we can certainly envisage. And so we, too, can at least understand what is meant when someone says, "Where God is present and rules, there saving well-being *happens*."

As we were saying—at the time of Jesus, people expected this from the future, and people who were now living in this evil, old aeon naturally longed for the new one. They longed for the presence of God that would create such saving well-being and, in its absence, they felt all the more intensely the Godforsakenness of the time, which confronted them in the lack of peace, in injustice, in lying, envy, and hate. However (according to the conception), not all will attain to this kingdom of God. Prerequisite to entrance into the kingdom is the fulfillment of the conditions of admission, and this means concretely the keeping of the law. However, just this leads to permanent uncertainty. For who fulfills the law completely? So one starts to keep a tally: good deeds against failures.

But is the account correct? Is there a positive balance of good deeds? And if it is true that, in the coming judgment, God will even cross out a few transgressions, how many is this going to be? The whole thing led to complete nonsense, as becomes clear especially among the Pharisees, who (to give just one example) turned the other way or covered their heads when they saw a woman, in order to avoid a lustful glance or even adultery. The scribes "expounded the law," as this was called. The individual commandments were "amended" until they became casuistic specifications concerning particular actions, so that it became unmistakably clear in each case what God demanded concretely. But who could know all these specifications? The "people of the land," as the "little people" were called, couldn't. So one looked down one's nose at them. They were only sinners. Anyone with any self-respect at all had nothing to do with them. They were not going to come to the table of God, so one was already permitted not to have table fellowship with them even now. Moreover, anyone who had any feeling at all for social justice kept at a distance from people who were engaged in exploitation, thus from the tax collectors, who were collaborators with those who ruled, because the tax collectors had leased their right to collect taxes from the occupying power. This is how people utterly unlike each other, sinners and tax collectors (by way of comparison, we could say "proletarians and capitalists"), came to be mentioned in the same breath. Anyone who was seriously working toward entrance into the kingdom of God had to steer clear of both.

We have to keep this picture of a world bereft of saving well-being very vividly before our eyes in order to understand what Jesus' faith looked like. If this were to be expressed in dogmatic terms, it could be put in this way: Jesus' God is love. He is the father. He is the kindly creator, who has his sun rise over the evil and the good, who sends rain on the righteous and the unrighteous. To be sure, nobody (or hardly anybody) around Jesus would have put this any differently. People were in thoroughgoing agreement with regard to "dogmatic" language. The difference was only this. Although everyone "had faith" *that* God is this way, and although everyone "had faith" *that* God would also (later, to be sure, when he had established his kingdom) act this way toward the righteous (in which case, "faith" is always the expression of an intellectual conviction), it was different with Jesus. He had faith *in* this God.

He had faith in him by *now* giving himself over to him. Jesus' faith in God, Jesus' giving himself to God had the appearance of daring to live in the midst of the old aeon as one would if one were living in God's sight at God's table. For Jesus, God was actually there and was not just a conception.

This came to expression most clearly (and for the people around him most strikingly) in the table fellowship he offered and held. Here no one was any longer excluded. Tax collectors and sinners were part of it. Here, no confession of faith was asked for, either, and for this reason, the pronounced separation between Jews and gentiles no longer played any role. But no accomplishments had to be produced, either. For this reason, even children belonged at it—indeed, on account of this, especially they belonged because, in contrast to adults, they were precisely dependent on receiving gifts. In a word, Jesus believes in his God by now living out saving well-being. This *was* his faith.

The people who experienced this didn't know what was happening to them. Naturally, they could adopt the attitude of consumers and simply let this happen of its own accord. The story of the ten lepers perhaps illustrates this (Luke 17:11–19). Nine of them enjoy being healed; however, one does an about-face. One grasps the extraordinary thing that has happened to him. And it was obviously always only a few who did grasp this. For, isn't this really the way it is when, as in this case, someone actually does good for humanity, someone finally for once does care about a bit more justice on earth? One might then perhaps even resolve to follow his example (at least if possible). And this is just how Jesus is not infrequently understood today.

And yet, anyone who understands him in this way understands him simplistically with respect to what is decisive. Jesus proclaims not a new way of thinking or a new attitude or a program for making the world a better place or for changing society. Of course, this is not to say a single word against all this. All the same, Jesus is concerned not with this, only to a greater degree, but rather with something entirely different. If the question is posed among Christians today whether they do not bear responsibility for social justice, for a better society and the like, the issue is raised on entirely the wrong level. This is a task for every person who shares humanitarian concerns. It is to be hoped that Christians do not exclude themselves in this regard. But this does not identify what is distinctive about their being Christian, and it cannot be a specific task of the church. The real point lies somewhere else entirely.

I was saying that Jesus is concerned not with a "more" to such programs, but actually with something entirely different. More specifically, he brings not less than *his God himself* to this earth. All the other things that so strike us about (as we say) Jesus' exemplary activity are *consequences* of what really concern him.

However, this is just what—at least a few—people understood at that time. They grasped that here *God* had come to them, and this bewildered them. Was it really true that they did not have to produce any accomplishments at all before having to do with God? Yet they were sinners. Therefore, they in no way deserved this. And the idea that they didn't still have time left before having to take seriously the encounter with God—this had never even crossed their minds. Now what they discovered was this: There is no more time. And at the same time, they discovered this: We do not need to fear this encounter, because this encounter is a gift. This turned them inside out, and they now "repented," as we so misleadingly put it. We understand this completely in the sense of John the Baptizer. He preaches repentance, so that people can escape the wrath to come. Here repentance is a precondition, in order to make it through judgment. In Jesus' faith, this looks different. There, repentance (the about-face) is the consequence of the prior encounter with God. For anyone who had this experience that Jesus' activity conveyed and who understood it in the way that Jesus meant it to be understood, that person simply could not remain as before. This person was now personally changed; he had faith. But this means that he now lived in relation to his surroundings as one does at God's table. For him, the saving well-being of the end-time was no longer future (after the turn of the aeons, after the resurrection of the dead, and after the judgment). Rather, through Jesus, the well-being of salvation of the end-time had become possible for him, if he had faith, if he gave himself over to this saving well-being that was given to him as a gift, if he lived it.

I think that now the word of the Johannine Christ can be understood. " 'Truly, truly, I say to you, Whoever hears my word and believes in him who sent me, that person *has* eternal life and does not come into judgment, but rather already has behind him the step

111

from death over into life' " (John 5:24). And I think we can now also make sense of the way our title is formulated: "Christian Faith as Resurrection of the Dead."

VI.

Of the many questions that certainly remain, I would like to pursue one that already came up at the beginning of this essay. If, according to a widespread Christian understanding, resurrection of the dead is above all something to be hoped for, and yet what has been particularly emphasized here is its present character, is there then nothing more that remains to be hoped for? I cannot point directly at the answer to this question. Instead, I have to bring two more concerns to bear on it that are themselves substantively related to each other: the distinctive character and the results of this faith that is lived in the present.

This faith of Jesus and the faith of his followers is at least influenced by its being "u-topian." This word has to be understood quite precisely: "ou topos" (in Greek) means "no place." The world of saving well-being has no place in this evil world. This is clearest with regard to Jesus himself. The old aeon cannot stand it if he lives out saving well-being. Its laws are put at risk.

The *ius talionis* (the law of equivalent retaliation) is a perfectly sensible rule, particularly when one considers that it was established to counteract unrestrained retaliation. "An eye for an eye, and a tooth for a tooth" is not to be understood literally. Substitutions can be made for punishments. But with its rule of punishment that is in due proportion, the *ius talionis* makes social life possible by permitting a person to see through other people's motives and then also to predict how they will react to what one does.

A person who means to live out saving well-being is unpredictable. But then if, as was true in Jesus' time, the rules of social life were regarded as laws *of God*, Jesus was bound to create the impression that, with his behavior, he was acting precisely contrary to God, even though he justified what he did by appealing to God's will. But then this was almost bound to lead to persecution. And this is precisely what Jesus lived out regardless of the consequences.

Here it becomes clear that the faith of Jesus is always a risk. A person can have bad luck with it, and it can lead to one's being taken advantage of. At the same time, it becomes clear that this risk has to be entered into ever anew. It is not as if a turnabout into this faith were something that happens only once. Once it has happened, once saving well-being has broken in, the old aeon gets right back up, and a person faces the question all over again whether to risk his or her faith once more, whether to live God's saving well-being one more time, and then once more, then again and again.

This was no different for Jesus. This rarely occurs to us when we think about the presentation we receive in the gospels. One might get the impression there that Jesus lived this new life as so to speak a permanent condition, from the time of his baptism, according to Mark, or even from that of his birth, according to Matthew and Luke, up until his death on the cross. But we need to realize that the traditions about Jesus were at first independent traditions. There is absolutely no doubt about this. However, this is not a function of people not yet having been in the position to present a life of Jesus in a sequential form. Rather, the fact that we have to do with independent traditions in the beginning is the literary expression of the sort of faith this was. Jesus lives this faith here, he lives it there, he invites people to it through this proclamation, then that, then another, and so forth. Naturally, the individual traditions contain certain developments from a later period. However, the oldest traditions show us in what various and ever-changing situations this faith was lived.

What is characteristic is always this: The person who has once experienced God's saving well-being in the midst of a world that is bereft of this—that is, who has been turned about—has not thereby been taken out of that world. To be sure, this person has now had the experience of saving well-being, has been involved in it. And yet, this experience becomes a matter of the past as soon as it happens. The old aeon now comes upon this person in an entirely new situation and places before her the question whether she will risk faith anew or not.

It even belongs to the essence of this faith that it is either lived completely or is not there at all. It is understandable that precisely Christians do not like to think this through to the end. For, if the Christian has believed (and that means precisely that she has lived God's saving well-being), but does not immediately do so again, can she then still call herself a Christian at all? *Now* she *doesn't* believe.

This is where the temptation becomes great to separate faith from doing, so that one can at least make use of the word "faith" and can enter a claim for oneself if the way life shapes up is nothing like God's saving well-being. People already realized this in early Christianity, too. The gospel writer Matthew deals with the problem by distinguishing faith and "little faith." He knows about all kinds of failure. In order not to have to say that the believer has become an unbeliever (as is still done some twenty years before in the Gospel of Mark), Matthew calls him only a "person of little faith." By doing so, he opens the way for the development that leads to the understanding of faith in the Epistle of James. However, once faith has become a matter of assent to propositions-to-be-believed, it is something completely different from what it originally was.

If we are to avoid taking what I believe to be this wrong road, what it is to be a Christian will need to be defined differently. One might say, for example, that a Christian is someone who has the experience of lived-out saving well-being behind him and who now is waiting for a new inbreaking of saving well-being in his life through his life. Insofar, the Christian life is marked by existing in a mode of ongoing imminent expectation. Christian faith is therefore always a newly expected and newly occurring resurrection of Christians from the dead. Yet, wherever this occurs, saving well-being is wholly there, since God is wholly there in this occurrence. For this reason, the whole of faith ought not to be said to be an affair only of the inner person, and one also ought not to speak of God as working in the life of the Christian in a hidden way. The Christian life happens in the body, and it is a life in fellowship with God. For this reason, it is not a hidden, but rather a visible life. God works visibly. What may remain hidden to others is, however, that *God* is at work here. These two understandings need to be differentiated from each other in a thoroughgoing way.

For this reason, in each moment that she lives God's saving well-being, the Christian is then also at the goal. This must be taken with complete seriousness, and we should not try to soften this claim in any way. In each moment that she lives God's saving well-being, the Christian is at the goal. Jesus says that such a person is perfect, as the father in heaven is perfect. Nevertheless, for as long as she lives in this aeon, she remains on the way. So, on the way to where?

Here I can no longer offer positive descriptions, but only resort to negation. And yet, it can easily be shown that the very same thing is true for Jesus as well. From the perspective of what is visible, as well as from that of the standards of this world, his life of the saving well-being of God ended with the catastrophe of the cross. And on the basis of everything we can determine, this at first drove the circle of people around him to despair. They all fled.

And yet, soon thereafter, these same people found themselves together again. It is very difficult to determine exactly what happened at this point. We hear that a few people claim to have seen Jesus and that they then confess, "He is risen." It can be argued endlessly whether this claim is or is not true and how it can and should be conceived. And, as you know, this was disputed vehemently precisely in the earliest period. And then, taking its bearings from James' notion of faith, what was passed off as decisive for Christian faith was the holding-as-true of events that had taken place.

However, if we take our bearings from the Christian understanding of faith, the matter not only looks very different, it also comes into focus. For what can be clearly seen is this: Occasioned by some sorts of experiences or other (it is still most probable this is a matter of visions), the old faith was risked anew. Jesus' faith was believed once more. And precisely this then led to a new understanding of Jesus.

Because Jesus had risked anew God's saving well-being of the end-time again and again during his earthly life, and because he had risked this no matter what, people proclaimed of him that what was expected to happen at the end-time had now in radical consistency happened to him. "He has been raised."

This was then naturally put forward within the framework of the conceptions of the time: He has been taken up into heaven and sits at the right hand of God. In the Spirit, he nevertheless remains present to his own, who give themselves over again to his risk of faith and who are now once more on the way with the Spirit— which is to say together with Jesus—they who are themselves still in the midst of attack from the old aeon, from which he has been removed.

However, it is out of this experience that Christian hope also finds expression. I have said that this can only be formulated negatively. This is the case because we no longer share the ancient conceptions that are inextricably bound up with the ancient picture of the world. Nonetheless, it is possible to make a positive statement by way of negation.

Let me now link up with our title and with what has just been said. Christian faith is resurrection of the dead. In each moment in which the Christian lives God's saving well-being, she is at the goal. Nevertheless, this perfection of Christian life in the midst of this aeon is a broken one because, once it has been experienced, it has no permanence, but is rather a matter of expectation and meant to take shape ever anew. However, the person who believingly has the experience of perfection is certain *in* this faith that her brokenness is directed toward unbrokenness. The brokenness of faith does not cancel out the previous perfection. The Christian exists on this earth between actual life and continually-falling-out-of this life. Yet this actual life points out beyond itself.

The Christian hope for the future is therefore not an article of faith that the Christian holds as true in the sense of the understanding of faith in James. But Christian faith as a resurrection of the dead that happens again and again implies this hope for the future. And only in this faith, through this faith, through the lived experience of this saving well-being is the believer sure of her future.

No one who has had this experience will let himself be talked out of it by an argument, however it is constructed. And then he will also invite others through his own faith to have this very same experience.

7

THE MEANING OF THE CROSS FOR SALVATION: DISCIPLESHIP AS THE WAY OF THE CROSS*

We may say without being guilty of oversimplifying that the cross is *the* symbol of Christianity. Nonetheless, it would have to be added at once that at hardly any point do Christians turn out to be as embarrassed as they do precisely with regard to the cross. This is true even in view of the discussion about the resurrection of Jesus that has flared up once again in the last decade. Anyone who has not worked this through personally and managed to find a satisfactory interpretation of the statements in the New Testament about the resurrection of Jesus can deny the resurrection if need be, perhaps even argue it away. To be sure, I regard this as a very poor solution to the problem. However, anyone who does not find a solution can still try to "rescue" some version of "Christianity" by bypassing the resurrection. The decisive Christian "principles" (at least in the consciousness of the general public), particularly love of neighbor, are apparently not touched by doing this.

The situation is different with the cross. For one thing, no one can dispute that Jesus was executed on the cross. Also, even though this crucifixion may be vexing, it doesn't have to be an utter scandal. For one can skirt even this, perhaps by understanding the personal defeat of the man from Nazareth as a martyrdom. This creates a slot for him and, along with him, for the principles he stood for. There is always something suspect about the sort of business that one is supposed to go to the wall for (if it comes to this)—at least this applies to the person who introduces this busi-

---

*"Die Heilsbedeutung des Kreuzes—der Kreuzesweg der Nachfolge," *Die Sache Jesu geht weiter* (Gütersloh: Gütersloher Verlagshaus Gerd Mohn, 1976), 82–100.

ness into the world with its heavy demand and expects others to enter into it, too. All the same, if such a person is committed to this business regardless of the consequences, one is at least more inclined to give it a look. There is no doubt that people have occasionally understood Jesus' death in this way and have then spoken of the heroic Christ and of the aristocratic spirit that imbues Christian principles.

But then why is the cross put on the altar? Why do we draw the face of the crucified one with an expression of agony, wracked with pain? This is just not how heroism works. But above all, the death of a martyr never has its meaning in the death itself. However, this is just what seems somehow to be intended, if the cross is the symbol of Christianity. Somehow or other, what finds expression here is that this death itself has a meaning. It is at least more than, perhaps even completely different from a *mere* consequence that the author of the message submitted himself to for the sake of the message itself. The cross is precisely the *content* of the message, and that possibly in a double sense: first, as Jesus' own dying, but then second, as the dying of those who follow him, because it still is part of the (even if often repressed) consciousness of the general public that Christians are on the way of the cross. Whether crosses in the form of pins, pendants, and insignias, and occasionally even as a sign of office still express this does seem questionable. And in any case, the archetype of the cross was carried not on the breast, but on the back, and if we really did want to capture what was meant at that time, we would have to choose a gallows as a Christian symbol. But who would want to get dolled up with that? And how would it be if we were to vary slightly an Old Testament word that Paul writes to the Galatians? He writes, " 'Cursed be every one who hangs on a tree' " (Gal. 3:13). Could we say, "Cursed be everyone who wears the cross"? Paul must have meant something similar to this. He writes to the Corinthians that the word of the cross is stupidity to the Greeks and a scandal to the Jews (1 Cor. 1:23) and that *he* carries the dying of the Lord Jesus in his body (2 Cor. 4:10). It is due to this that he has become a fool for Christ's sake and a "farce" to the world (1 Cor. 4:10).

No. The cross is not just a little vexatious, it is an utter scandal, because it puts an end to life and does so very differently from the "honorable" way in which a martyrdom does. For this reason, the

118

cross again and again poses radical questions, since it calls things radically into question.

I.

The early community knew this. The shameful criminal's death of Jesus on the Roman gallows came as a shock to his followers and drove them to despair and resignation. Nevertheless, a complete transformation occurred among these same people a short time later. I do not want to try to explain how this happened. Perhaps it cannot be explained at all. In any case, statements about the cross of Jesus occur very early on which give meaning to the meaningless event that confronted them, a meaning that could not be read off the occurrence on Golgotha.

We know the formulations. They center on the words "for us." The history of these terms and concepts can be elaborated, since they had been used before and were not inventions or new creations of the early community. Jesus' death was described as an atonement sacrifice ("God publicly put forward Jesus Christ, to make him an atonement for sin by his blood, to be received by faith" [Rom. 3:25]) or a vicarious sacrifice ("One has died for all" [2 Cor. 5:14]). What this means is that Jesus on the cross, by acting on behalf of people whose sin and guilt he has taken upon himself as punishment, has provided the atonement (which God can demand). This then leads on to the thought of the covenant sacrifice, which finds expression for instance in the Lord's Supper traditions ("the new covenant in Jesus' blood" [1 Cor. 11:25]; "Jesus' blood of the covenant" [Mark 14:24]). By means of this sacrifice, the new covenant is established, a humanity reconciled with God. We can summarize all this by saying that, with the help of extant juridical and cultic concepts that were familiar to the world of the time, the puzzling and shameful criminal's death of Jesus was testified to as a salvation-event. The cross, publicly a defeat, was now, explicitly and contrary to all appearances, proclaimed as a victory.

What I have presented briefly here is an example of historical exegesis. There is no difficulty in understanding it, even from a great distance. *This* is how the early community understood the cross of Jesus—not at the crucifixion itself, but very soon afterward. The question is simply whether anything can still be done with this today once we have understood it. This evidently presents difficulties. In this regard, two things need to be distinguished, even if they cannot be completely separated—the *fact* of the interpretation of an historical event, and the *contents* by means of which the historical event is interpreted.

First, the *fact* of the interpretation. It is a daily occurrence that two people who experience the same event nevertheless understand it differently, and *how* a person understands something (or even wants to understand it) is finally a question of her or his own decision. In an extreme case, this might even be a completely arbitrary matter: it is then no longer possible to discuss it at all. In most cases, however, this decision is by no means arbitrary, but rather arises out of an assessment of the event in question in its historical context and in its meaning for the person who is making the judgment. This can be shown directly in the case of our topic. Naturally, the Jewish authorities also interpreted Jesus' execution and, what is more, they could also speak of a victory here. The dangerous troublemaker was finally rendered harmless. The material contents of this interpretation were garnered from the impressions Jesus had made on the Jewish authorities while he was alive. He had caused them all kinds of trouble. Now this trouble was done with. From the standpoint of these officials, not only can we understand this interpretation today, we can even agree with it, if we regard the activity of Jesus as dangerous. However, it follows from this that there can be no objection to the fact *that* the early community interpreted Jesus' cross, and that it is interpretation we have to do with here. Without any interpretation, the cross as a mere historical event (quite literally) wouldn't say a thing.

However, I'm sure we feel difficulties with respect to the *contents* that were used to arrive at this interpretation. Can anything still be made of these? For instance, it has been claimed that we are presented here with a highly objectionable conception of God. What kind of a God is it that requires as cruel a spectacle as the execution of an innocent person (who in addition is also supposed to be his son) in order to be able to bring about reconciliation between himself and human beings (who, after all, are his creatures)? It has been claimed that all these juridical conceptions, including the sacrificial theories, are unsuitable for defining the relation between God and humanity. It has been said that what we have here are mythological conceptions and that, therefore, what needs to be carried out is a demythologizing. Even if, in doing this, the myth is not to be eliminated, but rather (existentially) interpreted, the mythical conceptions themselves end up no longer playing any part in the resulting interpretation. However, if these conceptions are eliminated (N.B.: the conceptions, not what is stated by means of them), then it is claimed that the point itself, which can only be expressed precisely in terms of these conceptions, will have been lost as well.

However, let us put all these objections to one side for the moment, since the last one shows that it is hardly possible to reach a quick consensus on how to make any headway on this subject today. Opinions seem to diverge sharply here. For this reason, let us turn to a question that is a bit more in the foreground. Where did the early community get the contents it used in its interpretation?

II.

I have already said that they come from the Jewish conceptual sphere, and no one will seriously dispute this. These conceptions did not first come to mind at the cross of Jesus, as if they popped up here for the first time and then were put into words. Nonetheless, this correct answer to the question of where the early community got the contents for its interpretation does not suffice. It still remains an open question whether we have to do simply with a makeshift solution on the part of those who were in helpless bewilderment in view of the death of Jesus, and who now, by borrowing what to them were familiar conceptions, came to a "nevertheless" in spite of everything, in order to wrest a meaning from its meaninglessness. Or were these contents developed in the context of Jesus' death, and this means concretely were they developed in response to the actions and life of Jesus himself (as the interpretation of the cross by the Jewish authorities was also developed with regard to their understanding of the activity of Jesus)? Let us look into this question.

In a rather simplified form, this is how things might have stood: If, for example, Jesus himself understood his coming death as an atonement, a vicarious sacrifice, or a covenant sacrifice, such conceptions might remain alien to us and no longer be capable of conveying any meaning to many people today. This can all remain undecided. Nevertheless, this would immediately explain why the early community understood Jesus' death in such ways, for then this death was not really a catastrophe in Jesus' eyes at all, but rather an act of salvation planned by God—even if by way of a cruel execution, whose cruelty is not to be played down in any way. At any rate, this interpretation of the cross would then not have been arbitrary. That would only be true if the life and activity of Jesus had *not* been directed at this sort of death. Only then could it be said that an interpretation of his death as a salvation-event was more or less arbitrary.

Since people have obviously been loath to concede this possibility, they have tried again and again to present Jesus' own understanding of his death as congruent with the early community's interpretation of the cross. On casual inspection, the gospels appear to give one a right to do this. In this connection, reference is made particularly to the predictions of the passion that occur three times in Mark (8:31ff.; 9:30ff.; 10:32ff.). Here there is talk of the Son of Man having to suffer greatly, having to be rejected by the elders, the high priests and scribes, having to be killed, and rising after three days. These predictions of the passion then influence the understanding of the whole gospel. The verses are now emphasized that portray Jesus in lowliness and humility. He is seen as persecuted from the outset in controversies with opponents. Then, not only the last portion of his way (that is, not only the journey to Jerusalem and Jesus' stay in the city) is understood as a series of stations of the cross, but his entire life is portrayed in this way. For, doesn't his lowliness already begin in the manger in which the Son of God is laid? The Christ hymn of Phil. 2:5ff. is then understood as a summary of the way of Jesus. Although originally in the form of God, he emptied himself, took on the form of a servant, became obedient, even obedient unto death on the cross. Seen in this way, everything seems to agree. One may shake one's head that God methodically orchestrates the way of his son as a road to the gallows, because he can only effect the salvation of human beings in this way. And this may then even result in people saying that this brutal God is of no use to anyone. In any event, we would still have to insist on this: when the early community interpreted the cross as a salvation-event, at least *it* did not give meaning to something that was meaningless, because Jesus had already seen the meaning of his life in the cross.

To be sure, this picture of the activity and the way of Jesus has not gone uncontested by historians. So, for example, New Testament scholarship today is nearly unanimous in holding that the evangelists portray the life of Jesus in retrospect. But this means that knowledge of the outcome already determined the presentation. As a literary judgment, the famous formulation of Martin Kähler, who called the gospels "passion narratives with an extended introduction," is credited almost without exception (even if with certain nuances). If the way of Jesus in the gospels is therefore stylized and *insofar* not an historically accurate report, nevertheless, the details of what belongs to the stylization and what is historical are entirely a matter of dispute. I cannot go into this question *in extenso* in these brief remarks, nor in particular can I investigate all the relevant texts. For the time being, let me take my bearings from the predictions of the passion.

Discussion of these texts primarily concerns the question whether we are concerned here with *vaticinia ex eventu*, that is, with predictions that first arose after the event occurred. In this case, the early community's knowledge of the way of Jesus would have been transformed in retrospect into Jesus' foreknowledge of his way. He would then have announced this himself and would even have done so three times. Nevertheless, over against such a conjecture, the historical authenticity of the predictions of the passion, or at least of one of them, has been asserted time and again. To be sure, I myself hold the view that we have to do with *vaticinia ex eventu*. However, in the present context, I do not want to insist upon this. I believe that this controversy, sometimes bitterly pursued ("historically authentic or inauthentic?"), becomes essentially uninteresting the moment one does what one actually should have done beforehand, even if it sounds so banal that I hardly dare to put it this way: One ought to have taken a close look at the texts in the first place. There, the point is that "it is necessary" for the Son of Man to suffer, and this "necessity" indicates that it has to do with the will of God. However, what the defenders of the historical authenticity of these texts almost always want to read out of them is precisely not there. The point at issue is not that the cross, before which Jesus stands, is a salvation-event that Jesus underwent "for us"; the point at issue rather concerns a life that, with some caution, may be called a *way* of salvation, if it is understood as being under the "necessity" of God. Thus, in the predictions of the passion, salvation lies not at the *end* of the way of Jesus, but rather *on* the way itself.

III.

However, in that case, we face this question: What is the relation between the way of Jesus and its conclusion? In order to clarify this, let me formulate it a bit differently. Is it only through the cross that the way of Jesus receives any meaning at all? Or does it already have meaning in itself?

Naturally, one may not (historically speaking) disregard the fact that Jesus' way did end on the cross. At the same time, it is also permissible to proceed from the assumption that Jesus' death was somehow the effect of his way, even if it is not at all directly clear precisely how to formulate the causal connection. For, while Jesus' activity took place among the Jews, the Romans executed him. Nevertheless, there were links here and it is not as if the cross ended Jesus' life in the way that a natural catastrophe or a traffic accident otherwise might. For this reason, the question becomes sharpened into whether Jesus reckoned with a death that was the consequence of his activity.

Three possibilities need to be distinguished in this regard. *First*, Jesus may have desired his death, because he saw in it the absolutely decisive salvation-event. In this case, his activity cannot have been meaningless in itself, but the real meaning consisted not in the activity itself, but in his death. *Next*, Jesus may have understood his death as a necessary consequence of his activity. In this case, his death was an integrating component of his life, and without his death his activity would have been, so to speak, incomplete. *Finally*, Jesus may have acted in such a way that, although he did not desire his death, he knowingly risked death as a possible consequence. Occasionally, the differences consist only in nuances. However, if (working outward from Jesus) the significance of the cross is to be formulated precisely, we have to get involved with nuancing, because otherwise (precisely in view of the uncertainty of the understanding of the cross and the profusion of interpretations that partially overlap each other), what all too readily results are ambiguous expressions.

The decision among the three possibilities that have been mentioned is admittedly not a simple one. We have to remain clear that we are dealing with an historical question, and that to answer it, we need to appeal to explicitly historical criteria. However, our sources are not historical reports; they have been shaped by believers. So if faith expresses itself in various ways, the danger looms that nothing more than taste may end up determining which of the various expressions of faith most nearly corresponds to the historical reality (and that means in this case to Jesus' own understanding of his death).

And yet, perhaps the question is not quite so hopeless as this, for one thing is certain. We can never ascertain Jesus' own view with precision, since not a single line of his own has been handed down. For this reason, we can only ever ascertain how his disciples understood his attitude toward his death. It would therefore be the wrong approach to want to compare the understanding of the cross on the part of the disciples with Jesus' own understanding of his death, for it is just the latter that we cannot ascertain. We have to set out differently, therefore, in our effort at comparison. There was never any possibility of reading off the cross of Jesus that it was a salvation-event. It was understood as a salvation-event by the early community. Then we can compare this understanding with the understanding that Jesus' disciples reached of Jesus' attitude toward his death while he was still alive—that is, the one they later (after Good Friday) state as if it were an impression they had gotten earlier. For the accounts about the earthly Jesus were in any event only *written down* after his death.

One observation is worth making immediately. In the wealth of traditions about what Jesus says and does, his death very rarely plays any role. However, since these traditions were put together only after Good Friday and, therefore, at a time when Jesus' death had to be dealt with, this discovery has considerable importance. If we further consider that we are concerned here with what originally are independent traditions (about which there is no doubt), we realize that it is utterly problematic to want to portray a way of Jesus. The independent traditions are not related to each other in such a way as to require being presented in a sequence. We might rather say that they have a momentary character. Each in itself forms an isolated whole. It is not to be disputed that they complement one another; however, we need to pay close attention to the character of this complementarity. It is not as if we only really have the whole once we have the sum of the independent traditions. Rather, each tradition by itself expresses the whole. The complementarity consists in the fact that the whole is expressed through variations. It is always a particular aspect of the whole that comes to the fore, and the whole evidently has so many aspects that completeness is unattainable.

In contrast, the sequential moment is secondary. This arises only subsequently, as the independent traditions are collected, and only in the process of being collected are the independent traditions brought into relation to each other. It is only at that point that one realizes that it has been a matter of Jesus' *way*. The framework into which the independent traditions were put creates this impression. Nevertheless, this is undoubtedly literary in character and therefore also historically secondary. From here, the predictions of the passion that give a thematic structure to the way of Jesus prove to be secondary, too.

Even someone who is loath to agree with this last implication must concede (insofar as one keeps to the text and does not read into it what is not there) that Jesus' death appears not as a (salvation)-event that has been particularly singled out, but rather as *one* "station of the cross" that is preceded by others (being treated with contempt and abuse, handed over to the chief priests, elders and scribes, and so forth) and followed by yet one more "station" (resurrection after three days).

In the entire corpus of the independent traditions, there are only two traditions that constitute exceptions. In the so-called ransom-saying (Mark 10:45), we read that the Son of Man did not come to be served, but to serve, and to give his life as a ransom "for many." Here death is understood as salvation-event. The same holds true of Mark 14:24, where (in the context of the Lord's Supper narrative) the talk is of Jesus' blood that is poured out "for many." These are actually exceptions, the later origin of which is quite easy to explain. But otherwise, even long afterward and in the tradition as a whole, Jesus' activity is never once presented as if it were directed

toward his death as a salvation-event. On this basis, it may be concluded with certainty that the circle closest to Jesus during his lifetime did not take Jesus to have desired his death.

One occasionally hears that Jesus nonetheless knew of the death
of the Baptizer. From this, it is concluded that Jesus must have had
thoughts of his own possible fate and then also about how his activity and his death were related to each other. This might be the
case, but there is no evidence for thinking that Jesus oriented his
activity to his death and that his activity only really reached its goal
with his death. At any rate, his disciples did not understand him in
this way.

To be properly circumspect, I should like to add that it ought
not to be concluded on the basis of all this that (the historical) Jesus
did not accord some definite understanding to his death. It is only
that we know nothing about this, and conjectures about what Jesus
might have thought, what Old Testament and other conceptions he
might have had of a death as a saving death do not take us a single
step forward. All the conceptions by means of which his disciples
later interpreted his death could have been known to him and most
probably were. However, if he is supposed to have applied them to
his own death, then he must have kept quiet about this. Otherwise,
these words would not have been suppressed right after his death
occurred. To the contrary, these are the very words that would
have been preserved. However, since for all practical purposes we
lack words from the period of Jesus' life about a salvific significance
to his death, his own death was evidently not a "topic" that was
important to Jesus to impart, quite apart from whether it actually
was such a matter for him personally. Finally, this is also confirmed
by the fact that the disciples were utterly at a loss and helpless in
view of this death. The cross hit them unprepared.

Therefore, we simply have to rule out that (in the view of those
around him) Jesus *desired* his death as a salvation-event, or that he
understood it as a *necessary* consequence of his activity. In that case,
it is evidently only the third possibility that is left. Jesus was experienced as one who consciously *risked* his death as a possible consequence of his activity.

However, this might move his death into close proximity with
martyrdom. And what reason is there for disputing that such was
the case? Of course, this has to be defined more precisely. For

instance, we know of early Christian martyrs who went to their deaths singing. They desired death partly because they believed that only there would their work of imitation actually come to completion. However, Jesus' death was certainly no martyrdom in this sense. "Heroic" traits such as these do not occur in the Jesus-traditions. In his activity, Jesus accepted risk regardless of the consequences. That these consequences did take place turned him into a martyr. However, it is not his death, but rather his activity, that is characterized thereby. His activity would have had this character to no less degree if it had not led to a martyr's death.

Thus, what remains problematic about the interpretation of the cross as a saving-event is isolating salvation to just this one event. For, if God reconciled the world to himself *on Golgotha*, then the activity of Jesus loses some of its salvific character. However, if this activity was not understood as salvation (or at best as partial or as leading up to salvation), then the question pops up again whether the early community's interpretation of the cross as salvation-event was not a desperate attempt belatedly to give meaning to something that was meaningless. And this was all the easier to do, because suitable concepts were available for the purpose.

IV.

It cannot be the task of theology to defend answers from an earlier period at any cost. That task can be to make such answers intelligible from an historical point of view. However, what can be made intelligible from an historical point of view is not necessarily right on this account. Indeed, its being intelligible from an historical point of view is the very reason why we may not simply take it over as it stands. On the other hand, we also have to guard against hastily characterizing answers as arbitrary before considering all the possibilities of how they might plausibly have originated. For, how often we label something arbitrary only because we do not understand it!

We might avoid making a old mistake by recurring once more to the life of Jesus. There is no longer any point to trying to demonstrate that the *course* of this life was a way unto death. However much we might be interested in getting an answer to this question, we still have to realize that neither now nor in the future will there ever be an answer to it, because our sources do not permit this. However, if it is certain that a question cannot be answered, we ought to give it up and be content with a "we don't know." As has already been said, our sources do not permit an answer because the framework into which the evangelists placed the independent traditions is secondary and not an historical one. On account of this, we know almost nothing about the course of the life of Jesus in its exact sequential order, nor (as people occasionally used to think) about developments and crises, about a personal formation in terms of being prepared to suffer disappointments, and so forth. Therefore, we may not contrast the *course* of Jesus' life with his cross, but can only take all the narrated incidents independently and inquire of each about its relation to the cross. *Only* such a comparison does justice to our sources, and therefore, only such a comparison is appropriate. What happens when we do this?

You will understand that I cannot lay out the wealth of independent traditions for you in this essay, and that I have to restrict myself to what is representative. Nevertheless, I think it will become clear that I am not proceeding arbitrarily in my selection. So let me proceed by means of what might be called a summary.

There is agreement today that the announcement of God's rule that is now breaking in stood at the center of the preaching and activity of Jesus. Mark 1:15 is characteristic of this: " 'The time is fulfilled; the rule of God has drawn near. Turn about and give yourself over to the message of salvation.' " These sentences very probably do not go back to Jesus verbatim, but they express what he was about. In the circle around Jesus, people were expecting (in apocalyptic terms) the redemption of the present (evil) aeon by a new aeon, which God was to establish as his kingdom. In the meantime, people prepared themselves for this by fulfilling the law, in order to be able to make it through judgment at the turn of the aeons. The present was understood as a time of preparation, in which the individual needed and was able to perform works in order to secure his or her entry into the coming aeon.

Jesus counteracts this extant conception by saying that there *is no* more time. God's rule is breaking in *now*. With this, however, turning about (repentance) receives a new meaning. If it had originally been a condition for entrance into the kingdom of God, it now becomes a result. Since God's rule is now breaking in, immediate turnabout is the only possible consequence. On this basis, we can also understand what faith means in this context. It is the act of giving oneself over to God's rule, announced as good news, as this becomes concrete in the event of turning about. God's rule is an occurrence that takes place where and when God's good will occurs. Therefore, giving oneself over to it means doing God's good will rather than one's own.

This is where the tension becomes clear. Doing God's will means allowing God to triumph in one's own life. Not doing one's own will means surrendering one's own will in favor of God's will, which one lets happen of its own accord. This is just what we now need to make more precise.

The manifold contents of Jesus' message may be organized from various angles. Doing so gives us something like this. Jesus is concerned with the offer of the salvation that breaks in for all people with God's rule. The poor are called blessed. Mourners are to be comforted and the hungry made full. Jesus stands up for the persecuted and goes after the lost. He turns against those who oppress children. Since those in power use the law and the provisions of the cult to do exactly this, he criticizes law and cult. He can sharpen the law tremendously. (Whoever is angry, not just whoever kills, is liable to judgment.) But he can also ease it and virtually abolish it. (Love of neighbor comes before sabbath provisions.)

This is all correct. And yet, in one—and that the decisive—respect, it is oversimplified. This needs to be understood precisely. Specifically, Jesus' message can be turned into doctrine, and this doctrine into a program. When this happens, the Christian message can be said to be about the hungry being fed, prisoners being visited, and the oppressed being freed. Then one can team up with others and try to pursue this program worldwide. The Christian becomes the truly human, Christianity becomes being humane. One needs to guard against saying that this is too little, for it is a great goal that is worthy of everyone's efforts. And yet it is not what is distinctive of Jesus.

A small point will serve to signal this. To be sure, there is a considerable portion of the traditions in the gospels in which the talk is of proclamation. But alongside these are traditions that contain no proclamation at all, but that present Jesus as someone who acts. He sits down at table with sinners. He breaks the sabbath for the sake of people's welfare. He hands out food. He waits on table. He drives out demons—and so forth. People have often reflected on how Jesus' proclamation and activity relate to each other. In the books on Jesus, this often finds expression in the way many of them (for example, the well-known one by Bultmann) restrict themselves completely to the proclamation, while others deal with Jesus' proclamation and activity in two separate sections. Naturally, this can be justified on purely formal grounds. And yet, this needs to be considered: All the independent traditions were formulated by the early witnesses with one and the same end in view, namely, to pass on what had been received from Jesus. They can do this by taking up his proclamation; they can do this by taking up his activity. However, both approaches are materially the same. Each interprets the other—the proclamation the activity, and the activity the proclamation.

When Jesus announces God's inbreaking rule, he announces that it breaks in in his *activity*. When Jesus turns to the children and the hard-pressed, when he drives out demons, he *proclaims*, "In this activity of mine, God's rule comes to you." Therefore, his message may not be detached from his activity (and made into doctrine). However, his activity, his standing up for the oppressed, is understood correctly only when it is understood together with his message—but not as a mere model of behavior to be imitated. If a person says that Jesus engages in social action and in acts of true humanity and is therefore a pattern for humanitarian behavior, this to be sure is not exactly false. Nevertheless, it is a superficial view, in which what is decisive has not yet been perceived at all. To put this pointedly, what is decisive concerns not humanity, but rather God's rule breaking into this world. Still, when one allows this to happen in its own way, what we call humaneness does indeed come out of it. For this reason, if someone develops a social program today, that person is still not pursuing what Jesus had in mind just by doing this. However, if someone lets God's rule come (" 'Seek first God's rule and *its* righteousness' " [Matt. 6:33]), for that person everything else is only a consequence.

This brings us to something further. Now, in this moment, God wants to actualize his rule as saving well-being among people. This is "the Jesus-business," as I once called it years ago. However, this point is only rightly grasped when it is understood that God's way leads to people *by way of* people who themselves *live* the Jesus-business. Whether God has still other ways can be argued about, and it might perhaps be possible to say a good deal about this. It is appealing to do this especially in order to avoid being personally engaged oneself. In any case, it was clear to the witnesses that God's rule comes to us through the person Jesus, and it comes only through him. For this reason, *how* God's rule comes is to be read off him alone, which is to say, in the way *he* gave himself over to it for them. But then, if the Jesus-business continues—if someone awaits God's rule to break in at some later time—this means that, for each person to whom this matters, it does break in. It breaks in only when that person gives herself or himself over to it. Again, whether it does not also break in through other people can be discussed, and of course this may not be ruled out—nor does it need to be. Nevertheless, for the person who is concerned with God's rule, this is (at least in the first instance) of no interest whatever, because such considerations all too easily turn into a self-serving alibi. One who is concerned with the Jesus-business is first and foremost called into question oneself. What does this look like?

It can be read off the earliest traditions. Jesus gives himself over completely to God's rule by asking how God means for one to treat the other person. Since he gives himself over to God as the father who loves him as a son (on account of which, he is later called *the* Son), he counts on God loving others as God's own children as well. Therefore, understanding and doing God's fatherly will as saving well-being means bringing God's saving well-being to the neighbor (and that means whoever one has to do with in the concrete moment). This is how God's saving well-being comes through a person to the neighbor. Still, it remains God's saving well-being only when the person who brings it completely disregards himself. But this is precisely wherein the risk of faith consists.

Two obstacles keep getting in the way of giving oneself over to this risk: the neighbor and people around us—society. Both can make it difficult actually to give oneself over entirely to God and to the inbreaking of God's rule because, in the way they affect us, they themselves lay a claim to rule over us—a rule we for the most part prefer to the rule of God.

Jesus apparently prohibited one question: Is the other person deserving of my love? By human standards, often enough not, especially not if the other person treats me as an enemy. And yet, as God's saving well-being means to break into my life without my having to fulfill any conditions, so too, it means to come through me to the other person without conditions that he or she would have to fulfill, either. Because God's love toward human beings is love toward sinners and, therefore, love of enemy, the distinctive form of the love of Jesus is not simply love of neighbor, but rather love of enemy. However, anyone who practices this naturally risks being disgracefully taken advantage of, for the person who practices love of enemy lays down all his weapons. He offers the right cheek if the neighbor strikes him on the left. She walks her guest home through two miles of dangerous territory, even if the guest has only asked to be accompanied for a mile (already an unreasonable demand and a sign of inconsiderateness). She lets herself be disturbed during his night's sleep, because the neighbor needs (really does need!) bread. She forgives not seven times (which, after all, is already asking for a full measure of self-abnegation), but seventy times seven, which is to say, she always does. I do not need to elaborate. You know the wealth of examples. In becoming concrete through me, God's rule wins out over my own comfort, over insisting on my own (N.B.—justified!) rights. Neither does God's rule allow for helping and giving only when one can count on gratitude. What the other person is like, who the other person is (a poor, oppressed person who lacks the necessities of life, or a rich tax collector, who exploits his own people), and how he behaves is irrelevant to God's unbounded will of love. It is always a question of the saving well-being of the other person, and this always depends on whether I give myself over to God's rule. But then what has become of my own well-being?

Let us leave this question for a moment and turn first to the other obstacle that gets in the way of giving oneself to this risk, namely, the people around us, society. We need to see that the sharing of love may not be codified in such a way that it is made into a set of duties to be fulfilled. This kind of self-denial cannot be expected of anyone who is not convinced that God's inbreaking rule demands precisely this from her in this concrete moment, that it compels her to such action. Without reference to God's rule, and simply as an ethical norm, such action must be described as just plain stupid, if not worse. Anyone who does engage in this sort of action immediately risks being called a fool by society, a coward who will not defend herself, a person with no sense of honor at all, no self-regard, because she gets mixed up with people who are not worth bothering with. It can only be called a stroke of luck if it goes no farther than dismissals of this kind, because something else comes next. People cut themselves off from somebody like this. His family thinks he's crazy, as happened to Jesus, who then carries this to the extreme and says, "Whoever loves father or mother more than me cannot be my disciple." So, after defamation comes isolation. And once again, this is understandable. This person sets himself up over the norms that govern life in society and that have to be obeyed in order to get along with other people. So, Jesus claims to be doing God's will— and breaks the sabbath. He does this not carelessly, but deliberately. The controversy over stoning rests on deliberate violation of the sabbath. Everything that follows is only logical. This man doesn't just teach in a way that's dangerous, he also does what he teaches, and he instigates others (as he says, in God's name) to act in this way. The man has to be gotten rid of. And society is right—this must not be lost sight of for a moment. Society is right. That it then managed to get the death sentence by working in league with the Romans and using a political motive for a pretext is relatively unimportant. Society did what it needed to for its own self-preservation.

I think this little sketch makes one thing only too clear. Jesus did not travel a way of humility with martyrdom as its goal. He never even *desired* suffering and death. To the contrary, he travelled the way of sovereignty. Through each individual word and each individual deed, through his conduct as a whole, he desired to bring God's rule. It is not as if he engaged in a struggle against sinners, and he did not declare war against society. He gave himself over to God's inbreaking rule. Because he did this, he was intolerable, for both sinners and society wanted nothing to do with Jesus' God.

So, was death the *necessary* result of activity like this? This question seems to me an inadmissible one, for who is going to decide what is necessary, and where are criteria to be found for answering it? But this does have to be said. In this world, the only person who can actually live God's rule is someone who is willing to risk death as the ultimate consequence. Conversely, only when death is seriously taken into account as a risk can God's rule be lived without any provisos.

We can understand only too well that the disciples ran into helpless confusion in this situation on the extreme margin. But then their eyes were opened, and they realized that this death was in truth no defeat, but that here the sovereignty of God's rule had been lived out to the bitter end. They then interpreted the cross. However, this did not happen arbitrarily, *in spite of* what had occurred, because ideas that were suited to expressing an interpretation of that kind were also available to them. To the contrary, they interpreted the cross on the basis of their experience of Jesus' activity, because now at the end they had actually understood this activity.

He really was there "for us." He really did set us right with God. He was always doing this during his life (this is just what is meant by "forgiveness of sins"). People who were estranged from God he reconciled to God, by living God's rule toward them (without proviso!). And how consistently he did this is shown precisely by his cross.

If the independent incidents that comprise the activity of Jesus are now placed in a sequence, they appear as a way of the cross. Nor is this false. It is just that this needs to be understood differently from the way it usually is. It was not a way *to* the cross (except in an historical sense), but rather a way *on the brink of* the cross, because each particular act hid the risk of failure within itself. Nor was it that failure at the end was rewarded with majesty, and the resurrection now left the cross behind. The confession of the risen one expresses rather that the *earthly* Jesus lived out the majesty of God's rule in unbounded sovereignty. The logical conclusion of the *majesty* becomes clear in the "failure." And yet, anyone who would still want to speak of failure only shows that he has not understood God's rule.

The disciples now knew themselves to have been freed to travel the sovereign way of the cross even without Jesus' physical presence. The activity of Jesus that had been brought to a close, which they saw in retrospect as a unity, was for them an ongoing offer to take further gambles on God's inbreaking rule, as they had come to know this in following Jesus, as people who through him had been reconciled to God. And of course, it now needs to be said that it is not as if only the person who suffers death at the end for the sake of his being Christian is on the way of the cross for the first time at that point; rather, that person is on the way of the cross who is prepared to take up her cross *on a daily basis* for the sake of God's rule. And anyone who pins on the cross as a symbol has the right to do so only if he does this to express that he is risking giving himself over to God's rule on a daily basis and regardless of the consequences.

V.

In conclusion, let us return to the question that was left to one side earlier. Where is the saving well-being of the person who, having given herself over to God's rule, brings saving well-being to another—and by so doing is always strolling on the brink of catastrophe, because this is precisely a God-less world?

Here are two answers, one theoretical and one practical. The theoretical one is that the well-being of salvation consists, amidst a world that has come unhinged, in letting oneself be granted by God the sovereign freedom to depend neither on this world nor on oneself and—in so doing, in Jesus' freedom—in participating in God's majesty. Perhaps this is capable of being grasped theoretically. But how does a person *come to know* that this truly is freedom?

The practical answer is that it is only on the way itself, and sometimes only in retrospect, when one does not let one's view get obscured by defeats and failures that have gotten and that continue to get in the way, but rather can be glad to be a fellow-worker with God (1 Thess. 3:2). Paul can describe this as God having lighted a beaming lamp in his heart. To be sure, he only ever has this treasure of light in a fragile vessel (2 Cor. 4:6). This is why he always carries the death of Jesus about in his body and yet, precisely by doing so, he brings Jesus' life (2 Cor. 4:10).

8

THE MEALS OF JESUS AND THE LORD'S SUPPER OF THE CHURCH*

In discussions of the meaning of the Christian Lord's Supper, people consistently take their bearings from the New Testament. This seems appropriate, since it is the supper of Jesus that one also wants to celebrate in the church today. However, taking one's bearings directly from the New Testament is problematic precisely if this is what one has in mind. The matter of language already indicates this. The Lord's Supper has its origin in the Palestinian sphere. Here people spoke Aramaic, a late form of Hebrew. However, the New Testament is transmitted to us in the Greek language; therefore, we have to do with a case of translation. Still, this does not mean that the twenty-seven writings collected in the New Testament were originally written in Aramaic and then translated into Greek. Rather (as they are now extant), they were composed by people who had command of Greek and formulated their thoughts directly in Greek. However, this is precisely what makes our problem more difficult. For, if take our bearings from the New Testament in asking about the meaning of the Christian Lord's Supper, we always receive an answer that—because it is formulated in Greek—is also more or less thought out in Greek. Therefore, if I want to know what this was like at the outset, I have to inquire back through the texts we have. But is that possible, if (apart from certain formulaic expressions) what stood behind the Greek text

*"Die Mahle Jesu und das Abendmahl der Kirche," *Die Sache Jesu geht weiter* (Gütersloh: Gütersloher Verglashaus Gerd Mohn, 1976), 63–71. (This was originally delivered as a radio address and published as "Das Mahl—Vorstellungen und Wandlungen," in Hans-Jürgen Schultz, ed., *Die Zeit Jesu* [Kontexte 3], [Stuttgart: Kreuz-Verlag, 1966], 91–97.)

was not an Aramaic text for us to reconstruct, but rather a "state of affairs," a practice, precisely a meal that we should like to envision? The attempt needs to be made.

Let us begin with the purely linguistic problem of translation. Anyone who knows even only one foreign language knows about the difficulties of a translation. Very rarely can something be rendered word for word. One must rather seek to grasp as a whole the sense of what is expressed in one language, in order then to formulate it anew in the other language (and again, as a whole). When it succeeds, therefore, translation is also always a creative process. If this applies to languages that are related to each other, it applies to an even higher degree to those languages that belong to completely different families—such as precisely the Semitic Hebrew-Aramaic and the Indo-Germanic Greek. This can be illustrated by, among other things, the fundamentally incommensurable forms of the verb. The Greek (in a way quite similar to that with which we are familiar) knows specific forms for the pluperfect, past, present, future, and so forth. This is different in Hebrew. A present is lacking. But there are also no true tenses. Hebrew simply looks to the past and states whether what was going on in the past (or what is going on now) was completed or whether it is still uncompleted. In the former case, the so-called perfect is employed, in the other case the imperfect. There are no other tenses.

This grammatical difference certainly presents the translator with considerable difficulties, for which of the various forms of the verb in one's own language is one to choose at any given time? Often only the context can decide this. Yet the problem lies still deeper, and this is where we encounter a certain limit to the possibility of translation at all. No language has been laid out on a drawing-board and then transmitted to the variety of peoples for their use. A language is rather an expression of the thought, experience, and perception of a people at a given time. As thought and perception are impressed upon a child in the course of its learning a language, so the child later expresses the thought and perception that have been impressed upon it with the help of that language. For this reason, we only understand the foreignness of the Hebrew language in contrast to the Greek (and naturally also in contrast to ours) to some extent as a whole, as we become clear about this connection between thought and experience—and speaking.

138

Let us make this clear to ourselves with regard to several mani-
festations of the Israelite cult that stand in close connection with the
forms of the Hebrew verb that are so foreign to us. The origin of
most of the cultic festivals of Israel no longer permits of being illu-
mined with a certainty that is satisfying. For the most part, they
were originally nature festivals, or else they were borrowed from
the religious environment. Nevertheless, it is significant that they
were thoroughly "historicized"—or, we might better say, they were
related to events in the past in a most remarkable way.

Several examples. Before the conquest, the festival of Passover
was celebrated by individual (still nomadic) tribes shortly before
changing pasture (that is, when they were breaking camp). Later,
this setting out was linked to the Exodus from Egypt, in "memory"
of which the festival was now celebrated. The matzo festival (the
festival of unleavened bread) was also connected with the Exodus.
The festival of Booths (originally the autumn harvest festival) later
promoted the "memory" of various events in the history of Yahweh
with his people. The festival of Weeks was linked to the making of
the covenant at Sinai. The festival of Purim (which is probably of
gentile origin) was celebrated in the postexilic period in "memory"
of the killing of the enemies of the Jews at the time of Xerxes, and
so in "memory" of the preservation of the people.

When I link up the term "memory" with particular events in a
way that does not strike our own sense for language as idiomatic,
this is intentional. We would understand all these festivals incorrectly if we were to speak of a memory *of* the Exodus from Egypt,
of the great deeds of Yahweh, *of* the preservation of Israel. It was
rather that these saving events were "brought to mind." What is
distinctive about these "memories" consists in the fact that the temporal distance was, so to speak, bridged, and that those past events
were not thought of in isolated fashion as past, but rather witnessed
firsthand. This is how it is in an ancient regulation from the second
century C.E.: "In each generation, you shall regard yourself as if
you personally had been taken out of Egypt." The particular elements at the meal were then interpreted correspondingly. One now
ate bitter herbs, because the Egyptians had also embittered the life
of one's ancestors. One ate unleavened bread, because one's ancestors had no time to wait for the dough to rise at the Exodus. And
in the case of the festival of Booths, one now built huts and lodged

in them, because the ancestors had lived in huts on the way through the desert. How fully one makes present the past in the framework of Jewish time-thinking (it would be better to say, "in the framework of Jewish time-experiencing") is shown by the Passover liturgy that has been retained and celebrated by the small group of Samaritans up into our own century. The partakers of the meal are girded, carry a staff in their hand, gulp down the lamb with great urgency—for one simply *is in the act of* departing from Egypt. We have some trouble imagining this way of re-presenting the past, and we will not really be able fully to accomplish it.

To the re-presentation, there corresponds an anticipation as well, for the festivals that are now celebrated are also festivals of the end-time. This relation to the future comes to expression, for instance, in the words from the Passover liturgy, "This year here, next year in the land of Israel; this year slaves, next year emancipated." Another sentence reads, "Yahweh our God, the God of our fathers, let us so experience the festivals which *draw near to* us in peace . . . and we will eat there from the Passover sacrifice and the animal sacrifices." The Passover was a major festival of messianic expectations. But something similar may also be said of the festival of Booths. In the book of Zechariah (14:16), the end-time is depicted in this way: "All who survive of all those nations that came up against Jerusalem shall make a pilgrimage year by year to bow low to the King Lord of Hosts and to observe the festival of Booths."

Within this conceptual framework, we can also understand that the end-time could be represented as a meal at the table of Yahweh. This meal of the end-time *drew near to* those who now reclined at table. They celebrated it even now as inbreaking future. But then it stands to reason that every Jewish meal bore a cultic character, that one was not allowed to take part in table fellowship together with gentiles, and that even cultically unclean Jews were excluded. One ate in the sight of God, the God who had entered into the covenant with the ancestors and whose kingdom one encountered there. The meal mediated communion with Yahweh, but it mediated this communion historically. Or expressed still differently, the meal "remembers" Yahweh's past and future saving presence.

Against the background of these conceptions, we can understand how unheard of it was when Jesus invited tax collectors and sinners to his table. This was not simply an act of human friendliness. It was much more. Jesus reintroduced these people into the covenant with God and even now gave a share in the coming kingdom of God precisely to those on whom "correct" Jews looked down. Here we have to do with an essential feature of the message of Jesus. He offers communion with God without tying it to conditions that have to be fulfilled first. Paul will later express this as "justification of the sinner apart from works of the law."

But now let us return to the meal. We know that the early Christian community already gathered at meals soon after Easter. After what we have just seen, this is not only readily understandable, but even the most natural thing in the world. There were not yet any Christian worship services. But there was a Christian community. How was it to discover its own proper form of getting together? If the Jerusalem community was still maintaining (or had reestablished) a certain connection with the temple, these people could not meet there as a specifically Christian community. However, there was gathering at a common meal, which was the distinctive way in which they had experienced communion with God and each other anyway. To be sure, this custom that they had adopted now had to be modified and given new content. How this happened we can still see clearly at many points. An interesting hint is found at one place in the so-called accounts of the institution at the Lord's Supper. In what is probably the oldest formula, which Paul transmits and cites in 1 Cor. 11:23-25, the words over the bread and over the cup do not follow immediately upon each other (as they do in Mark 14:22-24). Rather, they are separated by the meal. At the beginning of the words over the cup, we read, "in like manner he took the cup *after supper*. . . ."

Here we encounter the problem of translation that has been pointed out. Our Greek texts do not go back directly to an Aramaic formulation. Rather, they were directly formulated in Greek and permit us to recognize that (for reasons yet to be discussed), within the Greek-Hellenistic sphere, the Lord's Supper was shortened by eliminating the actual meal. The form of the celebration with which we are familiar has its origin here. The phrase "after supper," however, is a relic from the way the Lord's Supper was celebrated during the Palestinian period and shows that at the outset, the Lord's Supper was actually held as a complete meal.

Meals at Jewish festivals began with the breaking of bread, at which time grace was said. Then the main meal followed. At the conclusion, the so-called cup of blessing was passed around the table, over which the prayer of thanksgiving was spoken. The texts of the prayers are interesting for our purposes. One thanksgiving that has been handed down goes, "We thank you, Yahweh our God, that you have given the beloved good and broad land as an inheritance to our ancestors; that you have led us out of the land of Egypt and have released us from the house of bondage. . . ." Thus, the past is "remembered" here. However, there are also "memories" of the future. A second text concludes with the words, "May the merciful one vouchsafe to us the days of the Messiah and the life of the world to come. . . ." In light of what has been said about the particularity of the Hebrew way of experiencing time, it is immediately clear that these prayers are not to be understood as calling for thought *about* the past and *about* the future. Rather, the meal in the present is bound up with the saving past, and the saving future draws near to those who take part in the meal. The people who are reclining at table are those who belong to the covenant.

It was at precisely this point that the early community was presented with the opportunity to modify certain formulations, in order to express how they understood themselves as they celebrated their Lord's Supper and what it meant to them. We can still discern this most clearly in the formula handed down by Paul regarding the words over the cup. This cup is the new covenant in Jesus' blood. We must pay close attention to the fact that it is not the content of the cup that is spoken about. This is what we are inclined to hear from these words, since this is what fits our form of the celebration. But it is not there. In what respect is the cup the covenant? It is actually not the cup itself, but the cup as it is passed around the table, to which the words refer. The community celebrating the meal in which the cup is being passed around is the community of the new covenant. But this covenant has its basis in Jesus' blood, that is to say, in the sacrificial death of Jesus. Here we actually have to do with a new covenant that has taken the place of the old covenant. This new covenant, which God has concluded in and through Jesus, is "remembered" at the Lord's Supper. The words over the bread must also be understood in exactly the same way. The bread is broken by the head of the house and then passed around, and the words, "This is my body" are spoken. We can no longer ascertain what words were spoken at this point during the Lord's Supper in Jerusalem. The word "body" is already a Greek way of speaking. However, this has an ecclesiological meaning, that is, it denotes the community. "Body" here means "body of Christ," in the sense that Christ and those who belong to him are included in one term. Thus, the motif of "memory" stands behind this word of interpretation, too. The people celebrating the meal, to whom the broken bread is passed around, are precisely the community that "remembers" Jesus. We can now return to what was said previously. I referred to the meals of the earthly Jesus, in which what is distinctive about his message and mission found expression. When the early community gathers at the Lord's Supper after Easter, it now "remembers" just these meals of Jesus, and what was offered to it by Jesus becomes a reality once more.

Whether Jesus expressly instituted the Lord's Supper on the evening before his death I cannot discuss in this connection. As a matter of historical judgment, this is more than improbable. However, one may by no means say on this account that the Lord's Supper therefore no longer goes back to Jesus. Jesus' meals are definitely remembered. Nevertheless, the question remains why, at a later point, the origin of the meal had, so to speak, a date assigned to it. Something happened here that is precisely similar to what we have seen in the way the Jewish festivals emerged. What were originally nature festivals were related to the activity of Yahweh with his people. People wanted to "remember" this saving activity. The early community, which at first "remembered" the meals of the earthly Jesus by means of its Lord's Supper, later linked it with the passion of Jesus, since it saw God's decisive activity of reconciliation in the cross.

However, people now drew attention to the memory in a reverse direction. The early community was expecting the parousia to break in shortly, that is to say, it was expecting the return of Jesus. They now gave expression to this thought in their prayers at meals as well. The words, "until he comes" (1 Cor. 11:26), handed down by Paul in connection with the Lord's Supper traditions, are instructive here. However, even more plain is a liturgical expression that occurs twice in the New Testament (once even in the Aramaic wording) and that almost certainly had its original location in the celebration of the meal. This is *maranatha*, "Come, Lord" (cf. "Come, Lord Jesus!" [1 Cor. 16:22; Rev. 22:20]). It has often been disputed in the scholarship whether the early community prayed in this way for Jesus to come *at the celebration of the meal*, or whether it envisioned the coming of Jesus only *at the end-time* and, therefore, was praying for the imminent parousia.

This set of alternatives is conceived in typically Western fashion. It presupposes our way of thinking about time. We can scarcely speak in any other way here than of an either-or. But what according to our way of thinking about time is a set of alternatives is for the Hebrew way of experiencing time a unity. Of course, the early community also knew that it was living in the period after Jesus. But it celebrated his meals all the same. It "remembered" them by re-presenting them. Of course, the early community also knew that the parousia of Jesus was still outstanding. But Jesus encountered it at its meal nonetheless. It "remembered" his coming in anticipation.

Could this be expressed in Greek? It is clear immediately that word-for-word translation was not possible here. It was necessary rather to try to grasp the whole, in order then to formulate it anew as a whole (in the new linguistic and conceptual sphere). However, this happened not in a conscious (and single) act of translation, but in a more protracted process. For this reason, neither should we now start out by giving an overview of the ways in which meals were conceived of in Hellenism. We must rather try to clarify for ourselves several stages of the translation process, in order to see what the new forms of expression mean in relation to these.

At the time of Jesus, it was very exceptional for Diaspora Jewry (that is, Jewry not living in Palestine) to be fully conversant with Hebrew or, more specifically, with Aramaic. It spoke Greek. The Lord's Supper tradition handed down by Paul was very likely formulated in Antioch, where (so far as we can see) the first Christian communities outside Palestine arose. In this tradition, alongside the originally Jewish motifs (the remark, "after supper," connecting the cup being passed around to the covenant), is also found the Greek-Hellenistic motif to which I referred earlier (relating the broken bread as it is passed around to the body of Christ). We can then ascertain the next stage in Mark. The expression "after supper" is missing. At this point, the word at the breaking of bread is brought together with that spoken over the cup. This is evidently intentional. But what is instructive is the complete transformation of the word over the cup. In Mark we have, "This is my blood of the covenant, which is poured out for many." Here the *content* of the cup is spoken of and, with this, a completely different understanding of the meal comes into view. At the Palestinian Lord's Supper, the words over the bread and cup characterized the meal *as a whole*. It was customary to express the meaning of the entire meal at both of these points. However, these words are now applied to the individual actions and refer to bread and wine. The food is consumed as body and blood of Christ. This decisive transformation of the Lord's Supper is connected up with Greek-Hellenistic conceptions. The mediation of the "divine" to human beings is always thought of here in material fashion. Even "spirit" is the finest possible type of matter on the Hellenistic view. When the Lord's Supper is celebrated in the Greek sphere, Jesus Christ comes to his followers in the sacred food, in bread and wine. A meal, begun by eating bread and ended by drinking wine, no longer has any meaning. Therefore, it drops out. However, since it was later known that the community had earlier held a complete meal, there arose in many places *alongside* the sacramental Lord's Suppers so-called *agapes*, love-feasts, that were pure fellowship meals.

Thus, the Lord's Supper has been translated. The decisive question is, "Did the translation succeed?" Let us be clear about one thing in this regard. Without translation, the Lord's Supper could not have been celebrated in the Greek sphere at all. Translation was necessary. But what is it that was to be translated? It would not do to answer, "a meal," because there could not have been any way of making a Jewish custom at home among the Greek Christians. This would only have been possible if the Jewish way of experiencing time were imparted to the Greeks along with the custom of the meal. In that case, basically only Jews could have become Christians. If, in spite of this, we say that what was to have been translated is what was imparted by way of the meal (that is, the saving well-being that dawned in Jesus and that had been "remembered" in the meal) then the translation may be taken to have succeeded after a fashion, for a Greek was not able to think and experience the imparting of saving well-being historically, but only materially, and that means by way of the food.

To be sure, the limitations of this (as of every) translation also need to be pointed out. It cannot and may not take the place of the original. But unfortunately, this is what has happened all too often. Arguments over the Lord's Supper in church history up to the present have not infrequently been based on a complete failure to include the original form in their considerations. As little as the early Greek-Hellenistic community was able to take its bearings from the Jewish meal in its first translation, but needed rather to translate what the meal was supposed to impart, just as little ought we later to take our bearings from the material conceptions familiar to the Greek, that is, from the sacred food. Here again, a genuine translation must rather keep in view what it is that is supposed to be imparted. If what served to do the imparting could already be replaced in the time of the New Testament, it is not clear why this may not be the case later on as well.

If we understand this first process of translation, this can certainly help us in the task of translation that is ours to perform ever anew—even for the Lord's Supper.

9

TOWARD THE NEW TESTAMENT GROUNDING OF BAPTISM*

Please permit me to begin with a few observations on the way this topic is formulated. The first word "toward" is meant to indicate that I aspire not to any completeness, but rather simply to pull together a few thoughts on the subject that are important to me, thoughts which are certainly in need of completion. But this just in passing.

There is something else that is more important. There is a tension in the way the topic is formulated that permits us to see the real difficulty with which the current discussion of this subject is burdened. This concerns "the grounding of baptism." More precisely, it concerns grounding the practice of baptism as it is engaged in in the church *today*. This grounding is meant to take place *on the basis of* the New Testament and *by means of* the New Testament, that is, by means of an *ancient* document. Is this possible at all?

Perhaps you find this question surprising. It could immediately be retorted, "How else is baptism to be grounded and the way it is administered to be regulated than by recourse to the New Testament?" And this counterquestion is fully justified. I do not intend to appeal to any other authority.

Nonetheless, it does seem to me not unnecessary to examine more closely what is, so to speak, self-evident, and to do this because, up until now, this approach has not been capable of producing a consensus. *Everyone* takes his or her bearings from the

*"Zur Neutestamentlichen Begründung der Taufe," *Der Exeget als Theologe* (Gütersloh: Gütersloher Verlagshaus Gerd Mohn, 1968), 226–45. (This was originally delivered on November 16, 1965, at the Evangelische Akademie Rheinland-Westfalen in Mülheim/Rhein.)

147

New Testament. As things stand, differences of opinion can only be explained in one of two ways. On the one hand, the other person understands the New Testament incorrectly, but I understand it correctly. Naturally, it is clear that, in this case, our opinions about baptism would diverge. (Of course, it could also be the other way around—but who would accept that?) On the other hand, the New Testament has no consistent view of baptism at all. In that case, a justification will have to be provided for giving more weight to the view of baptism in one New Testament passage than in another.

With this, the question concerning whether and how the New Testament is properly to be *used* finally comes into focus. Must one passage be subordinated to another or must differing views of baptism be harmonized?

But this question (concerning the correct *use* of the New Testament) pops up not only if one detects divergent views of baptism in the New Testament. It occurs even if the New Testament takes a consistent view of baptism in all its writings. It is just that we do not usually notice this. And that is why I should like to begin here.

When we reflect on the New Testament grounding of Christian baptism, it is not as if our point of departure were the New Testament; it is rather the way we practice baptism today. This practice does not seem at all controversial to us, since it is what we do. We simply seek to ground it correctly, and the New Testament is supposed to help us with this. Thus, our interest lies entirely in the present. The topic of our conference even shows this—"Should Young Children Be Baptized?" Yet this really means, "Should Young Children Be Baptized *Today*?" and it is only because our views concerning baptism diverge that we question the New Testament. This, in turn, is supposed to ground the practice and also to regulate correctly the way it is administered. If this is possible now, it must *always* have been possible—and not just for baptism. We cannot be so inconsistent as to approach baptism differently from the way we do other such matters. But then, what happens if we are consistent? Let's put this to the test.

James 5:14 reads, "Is any among you sick? Let him call for the elders of the church, and let them pray over him, anointing him with oil in the name of the Lord; prayer and anointing will then make the sick person well." That extreme unction in the Catholic Church has a somewhat different meaning (of course, James 5:14, is precisely *not* about such a *last* anointing) I do not want to debate now. But in the present context I must pose the question why we Protestants do not practice the anointing of the sick. It is commanded quite unambiguously in the New Testament, and there is not a single passage in the entire New Testament where it is prohibited or anything else said on this subject. If what is commanded and ordained in the New Testament is valid, and if this is binding upon us, then we are disobedient if we do not practice it. The anointing of the sick has a New Testament grounding.

I hear two objections. First, this is the case "only" in the Letter of James. But this objection doesn't amount to anything. Its meaning depends on which word is emphasized. If the point is that this occurs only in the Letter of *James*, then what is being said is that there are writings of different degrees of quality within the New Testament and that James is inferior to the other writings. Of course, a case will have to be made for such a view. However, if this succeeds, we will have to stop speaking of the New Testament grounding of a practice such as baptism. Rather, we would perhaps have to put the question like this: How is a practice to be grounded in those New Testament writings which are relatively more valuable (but not in the whole New Testament)? And then, once we had provided the grounding of baptism that was asked for, we would no longer be able to refer to the whole New Testament, but only to its more valuable parts. On no account could one ask for the New Testament grounding of baptism. However, if we did still want to continue asking the question in this way, we would now have to bring in the practice of anointing the sick, even if it were commanded only in the Letter of James. I do not intend to speak here in favor of establishing the anointing of the sick, nor probably do you. However, if we do not, we must be prepared to draw the following conclusion: The fact that a practice is engaged in in early Christianity and that it is attested in the New Testament is still not sufficient justification for our having to engage in it today as well. I think we could agree on this. It is just that we have to be consistent. The fact that baptism was practiced in early Christianity and that this baptism is also attested in the New Testament is still not sufficient justification for our practicing baptism today. So this example makes clear how problematic it is to speak of the New Testament grounding of baptism. It is obviously not so straightforward. And if I do propose a New Testament doctrine of baptism, this still does not say anything directly about our doctrine of baptism today. For once again, I can also propose a New Testament doctrine of the anointing of the sick and still not be prepared to adopt this for our purposes today.

Before I come to the second possible objection to introducing the anointing of the sick among Protestants today, I should like to repeat the first objection once more, only with a slightly different emphasis. This would be that the anointing of the sick is *only* in James. In other words, it is only attested once. But can the number of times something is attested be what is decisive here? Wouldn't this have to apply to *everything* that is only attested and commanded once? In that case, we should have to do without extended passages from the Sermon on the Mount, for instance. But then this means that the frequency of regulations, explanations, and so forth can't be made to count as a relevant consideration. This holds true for baptism as well. One could never argue, "To be sure, this understanding of baptism glimmers through here and there, but another one is more common." This is no argument! Counting is not to the point here.

Let me now turn to the second possible objection. It could be said that the anointing of the sick is not a sacrament. A sacrament can only be an action instituted by Jesus, and this is not true of the anointing of the sick. Is this really an argument? I hardly think so. For one thing, we could immediately refer to John 13:14–15. After the footwashing, Jesus says, " 'If I then, your Lord and teacher, have washed your feet, you also ought to wash one another's feet. For I have given you an example, that you also should do as I have done to you.' " So here, according to the wording of the text, we have not only a practice instituted by Jesus himself, but even a command to "go and do likewise." Wouldn't it at least be consistent to adopt the practice of footwashing ourselves? If it should be retorted that what belongs to a sacrament is that the visible sign mediates a gift, and that this is lacking here, then one would have to ask in reply whether in this case the gift were not the sharing of the love of Jesus. This could quite readily be shown to be the case from the context. But enough of this. Who is it that actually determines what a sacrament is? The concept is not found in the New Testament—in any case, not in the sense in which we mean it. It only developed later in the church. However, this means that there is no way to check this or to take one's bearings concerning it from the New Testament, but that a dogmatic interpretation is intruding into the process. The New Testament is not the norm we adhere to; it is a norm only when and to the extent that a practice has been shown to fulfill the conditions of what constitutes a sacrament laid down by dogmatic theology. Once more, put differently, one is not consulting the New Testament, but rather first establishing the concept of sacrament and then, once this concept has been formulated and defined, employed it so to speak as a filter. Only that in the New Testament which passes through this filter is then to be considered normative. We need to be clear that this ought not to be called "grounding in the New Testament."

These examples ought to have shown that grounding baptism in the New Testament is a tricky business. For, if we do not want to proceed arbitrarily, if we do not concede a privileged position to baptism from the outset, we have to be ready to draw conclusions that extend far beyond baptism. If we are not prepared to draw these far-reaching conclusions, then we may not apply the methods we normally use to the task of grounding baptism, either.

So we find ourselves in a rather embarrassing situation, and I think this is just as well, for this situation needs to be dealt with. And just so that there will be no misunderstanding, perhaps I might add that it is not as if I created these embarrassments. I have only exposed an embarrassing situation that was already there but that is usually overlooked. We have not noticed it because of the bias that is built into our angle of vision. We have not started out from the New Testament, but have searched for a practice that we regard as obviously legitimate because we already engage in it. Looking backward, we have interrogated the New Testament with our own questions. We have claimed that the justification is to proceed in the opposite direction (from the New Testament forward to ourselves), but we are not prepared to allow this opposite direction to determine how we practice baptism. Now, of course, this just will not do!

Let me state this one more time. The direction in which justification was undertaken was restricted and, more particularly, narrowed down—first by the question of frequency in the New Testament, then by the question of the value of one writing as compared to others, and finally by the search (imposed throughout the New Testament) for something instituted by Jesus, and this as influenced by the concept of a sacrament. In each instance, a demonstration of what is in the New Testament does not yet constitute a justification.

I might now draw attention to the fact that the New Testament contains no uniform doctrine of baptism. There are a wealth of motifs connected with baptismal statements—cleansing from sins, sealing with the name of Jesus Christ, bestowal of the Spirit, granting a share in the death and resurrection of Jesus, incorporation into the body of Christ as a rite of initiation. However, alongside these the bestowal of the Spirit is also separated from baptism (which then grants only forgiveness of sins), since the Spirit is mediated in connection with the laying on of hands. Above all (and this is not unimportant), the relationship of baptism and faith is entirely unstable.

If I were to go into this more closely, I should have to provide a much fuller account than is possible in this context. Nor do I want to lay out the individual motifs here, since (as I have already tried to indicate) this does not take us any further. For instance, if I were to succeed in proving that in one place (or even in several places) faith is presupposed by baptism, the question would still remain whether this is decisive for us today, for there are other places which say nothing at all about this. If baptism presupposes faith, it will hardly be permissible to baptize young children. But if baptism is incorporation into the body of Christ, then it is difficult to see why young children should not be baptized. I could discuss this more fully, except that (once again) it would not *prove* a thing. It is not possible to *justify* anything in this way.

It is simply time that we gave up citing *dicta probantia* (prooftexts) in the discussion of how we are to understand baptism today. It is time to abandon talk of a New Testament doctrine of baptism. There is none, and this is not only because its statements about baptism cannot be harmonized, but also because not all its writings even talk of baptism. I cannot assume that the writings that are silent about baptism recognize the same view of baptism that is found elsewhere. To be consistent, anyone who claimed this would have to assume that Paul always and everywhere thought exactly as did James about the anointing of the sick.

Thus, if we carry on in this fashion, we go from one embarrassment to another. And it seems to me that we need for once to look for a way out of this situation. So let me proceed from a consideration that has already come up and that will prove important for our purpose. It is the issue of *direction*. We look *back* as we inquire—and this inquiry is now meant to provide justification for *us*. However, it is not as if these two directions (inquiring backward and justifying forward, from earlier to us) applied only in our situation today; they also already apply within the New Testament. We need to pay a good deal more attention to this than we have done previously. Indeed, I should say that this question about the direction in which statements are made has all but gone unasked up to now.

However, if this already occurred in the New Testament, then there was already a question concerning baptism at that time, and this seems to me worth noting, for asking questions already presupposes either that one is uncertain or at least that there is unclarity. Therefore, if both of these directions were already at work in the New Testament, then the situation within the New Testament bears a certain resemblance to ours. There was at that time a practice that was engaged in, but whose meaning and grounding were still questioned, and the direction of this process of questioning and answering now needs to stand at the center of our further reflections.

Let me proceed step by step and begin to clarify the problem by comparing it with the Lord's Supper. There is not (and about this there can be absolutely no doubt) *one single* doctrine of the Lord's Supper in the New Testament. It is therefore impossible to develop the doctrine of the Lord's Supper for today by means of a direct interrogation of the New Testament. For this reason, I also regard it as mistaken (as the Arnoldshain theses put it) to ask about the "decisive content of the biblical testimony about the Lord's Supper," which we discover when we listen to the Bible. For who determines what is "decisive" in this case? Here the texts are so to speak placed alongside each other—and a selection is made. But this is just what won't work, for within the New Testament itself (and immediately thereafter) we already have to do with a history of the Lord's Supper. Precisely what this looked like (concretely speaking, in what historical relationship the individual traditions that have been handed down stand to each other) is disputed in the scholarship, to be sure. But *that* there is a development, *that* historically determined modifications are to be recognized, is not a matter of dispute—as it is likewise not a matter of dispute that what people intended to celebrate at a later time was the Lord's Supper of *Jesus.* Therefore, the various formulations state how the Lord's Supper is to be celebrated (and how it is to be celebrated in the future as well)—and yet each grounds its Lord's Supper in the institution of Jesus. Since we have to do with a history of the Lord's Supper within the New Testament, it is not permissible to place different strata of this development alongside each other and then to relate these *directly* to ourselves. In other words, we have to take seriously the fact that the New Testament is not a book of dogmatic recipes for today, but one that traces the history of the theological development of early Christianity. I invariably read and make use of the New Testament incorrectly if I, so to speak, "take it straight," that is, if I place all its writings alongside each other. I need to allow the writings to stand in succession and always ask at precisely what point in this development a given statement was made. Thus, attention needs to be paid to the movement, the direction.

Correspondingly, one might attempt to trace a history of baptism within the New Testament. Certain points of reference could be specified, since several motifs carry on through and recur in later texts in the same or even in modified form (and then often combined with others).

I want to illustrate this by means of a few examples. In Romans 6:3f., it is said that Christians have died with Christ in baptism—not, to be sure, that they have been raised (the resurrection here remains a matter of the future), but that, just as Christ has been raised, they are also to walk in newness of life. This motif recurs in Col. 2:12, if naturally in a changed fashion. "And you were buried with him in baptism, in which you *were* also raised with him through faith." Colossians comes from a follower of Paul. He takes up Pauline conceptions, but Paul would never have put it in this way because, if baptism brings about resurrection, as Colossians 2 says it does, the danger might arise of falling into a form of perfectionism. Indeed, there were in (and alongside) the early community such perfectionistic enthusiasts—gnostics—with whom especially Paul had to do battle. They could say that the resurrection had already occurred—as, in effect, we find in 2 Tim. 2:18. If baptism does bring about resurrection, then one would have to agree with these people. Thus, it is conceivable either that Paul has modified a view commonly shared by Christians (that is, in order to say something against the gnostics) or that the author of Colossians has carried on a Pauline initiative.

One other example. In Rom. 2:29, Paul speaks of spiritual circumcision. It is not the person who is outwardly circumcised who is a Jew (a *real* Jew), but the one who has experienced the circumcision of the heart, which takes place in the Spirit, not in the letter. Whether Paul is thinking of baptism here is rather uncertain.

Now, according to Col. 2:11, "In him you were circumcised with a circumcision made without hands, by putting off the body of flesh in the circumcision of Christ." Here (as can be clearly seen) thoughts are taken up that we also meet in Paul, and they are at least moved nearer to baptism, of which the author of Colossians speaks in the next verse, that I just cited.

But now consider 1 Peter 3:21: "What happened to the people who lived at the time of Noah is taking place now in baptism for your deliverance. For in baptism, the impurity of the flesh is *not* done away with; but we rather appeal to God to bestow upon us a good conscience through the resurrection of Jesus Christ." What has happened here? Here baptism is interpreted by means of a conception that was originally joined to spiritual circumcision, so that precisely the antithesis between bodily and spiritual circumcision is carried through to the point that baptism does *not* do away with the impurity of the flesh, but is rather an appeal for a clean conscience.

Naturally, these texts would have to be examined much more closely. This would allow us to recognize how motifs which at first were not joined to baptism at all were drawn to baptism as time went by and then served the purpose of saying what baptism means. Further examples could be given. What is characteristic is that, over the course of the history of baptism within the New Testament, a consolidation of motifs connected with baptism occurs, and therewith clearly a development of the conceptions of baptism.

Once this is seen, it must immediately be conceded that the fact that one can demonstrate that there are differences among statements in the New Testament regarding baptism becomes less important. For one may now no longer speak of contradictions.

What at first glance cannot be reconciled (for example, that baptism *resembles* the resurrection and that it *is* resurrection) is the result of an historical development, and each statement needs to be understood in its own context. Thus, something can have been said in one context that would be quite out of the question in another.

If we can distinguish earlier and later strata, we must nevertheless state that our texts are very fragmentary and that for this reason it is not possible (because of the lack of sources) to write a genuinely complete history of baptism in New Testament times. Moreover, it has to be borne in mind that themes which only occur late in the literature are not necessarily late in origin. The uncertainty that prevails here can never be eliminated completely.

For all this, if we now want to try to sketch a history of baptism at least in outline, we must start out with what, from a literary point of view, are the oldest traditions, and this means with the writings of the New Testament that were written down first. These are the Pauline letters.

However, in this case, we need to take note of what in my judgment is a very important difference between the directions of the statements concerning the Lord's Supper and baptism. From the so-called words of institution, the understanding that was linked to the celebrations of the Lord's Supper can be read off without difficulty. Here we have to do with something like liturgies, and these liturgies have what we might call a "programmatic" character. The Lord's Supper can be repeated, and by stating how one understands the celebration today, one says how one means to conduct it and understand it in the future as well. In contrast, the statements about baptism are not programmatic. Paul does not tell the communities, "when you baptize, such and such happens," or "you should regulate your baptism in such and such a way." But with the Lord's Supper things are quite different. There we read (in connection with the words of institution in 1 Cor. 11:26), "For as often as you eat of this bread and drink of this cup, you proclaim the Lord's death until he comes." In contrast, when Paul speaks of baptism, he is speaking to Christians who have already been baptized. The baptism that *has already taken place* and that now lies in the past is the starting point for what Paul says about baptism.

This is naturally connected with the fact that baptism (as distinct from the Lord's Supper) takes place only once. But this is connected with the fact that, at the time of Paul, the way baptism was practiced was not a matter of dispute. So, Paul has no intention at all of giving the communities instructions for how to baptize. The point is rather to tell the communities (and this means baptized Christians) how they have understood and ought now to understand their own baptisms *that have already taken place.* Thus, whereas Paul does treat the Lord's Supper thematically, baptism never becomes a topic in its own right for Paul.

This needs to be noted—and (on the basis of what is said in the letters) one simply must challenge the view—that we can make general statements about a Pauline doctrine of baptism. When I speak of a "doctrine of baptism" here, I intend this in the programmatic sense. In this programmatic sense (and this is what concerns us when we ask about the justification of baptism or when we ask how we should regulate baptism and the practice of baptizing), we cannot draw out any doctrine of baptism from the letters of Paul.

We also need to distinguish one other set of considerations from this. Since Paul himself did baptize (even if, as he says, very seldom), *he* must naturally have attached some understanding or other to this. But what that understanding was is precisely what we do not learn from his letters—or at least not directly! Now, since (as I mean to show presently) Paul does lay out how he understands baptisms that have taken place previously, we ought not to insert this sort of understanding into an expressly programmatic conception of baptism. It can also be shown that Paul's statements about baptism undergo a process of development.

But let us now take a look at a few texts. In Rom. 6:1ff., it is not baptism that is the subject (as one learns in "Bible study," for example, and hears time and again), but ethics. At the beginning of the chapter, Paul poses the question, "Are we to continue in sin that grace may become correspondingly more powerful?" (He had previously been speaking of the superior power of grace.) However, if grace is so central, then (so it could be reasoned) what one does no longer matters. If everything depends on grace, one may simply remain content in sin. And this (as Karl Barth once called it) "idiotic" question, which does imply an answer (if a stupid one), is now rejected. "How can we who died to sin still live in it?" (v. 2). Paul says this is impossible! And now he traces the "having died to sin" back to baptism. "Do you not know that all of us who have been baptized into Christ Jesus were baptized into his death?" Finally, he demonstrates that, "In baptism you were buried with Christ (and this means 'died to sin'), and you have been called to a new life (just as Christ was raised from the dead)." Ethics! Paul wants to show the Romans that *despite* the grace that was given, it is *new life that matters*. In order to show this, he *appeals to* the baptism that has already been performed among the Romans. In this way, Paul means to lead the Romans to a better understanding of their own baptism, and he appeals to the process of baptism (immersion and coming out of the water) in order to ground the necessity of the new way of life.

1 Cor. 10:1ff. is an analogous case. Here Paul introduces the comparison with Israel. The ancestors were under the cloud. They all went through the sea, and they were all baptized into Moses in the cloud and in the sea. They all drank the same spiritual drink. It is not as if Paul were saying that there were sacraments even at the time of the ancestors. The context again makes clear that what is at stake is ethics! For the *tertium comparationis* (point of comparison) consists in this. The Israelites had "something like" sacraments; they relied upon them, but they did not conduct themselves according to God's will. Therefore, God punished them. And now there are people in Corinth who rely on baptism (and the Lord's Supper) and, by so doing, they fall into libertinism. So Paul tells them, "If you understand the baptism *you have already undergone* in such a way that it gives you a guarantee, then you are deceiving yourselves just as the ancestors deceived themselves." The sacrament does not exclude, but rather precisely demands ethics. The point is to counter a misunderstanding to which the baptism they had already undergone has led. People had a guarantee and were now indifferent to the Christian life. This is the situation. And since the Corinthians justified this with reference to baptism, Paul introduces the history of the ancestors as an example and shows that the situation is quite the opposite. The sacrament does not make ethics superfluous; it demands it. Here, too, the necessity of ethics is proven from baptism, from the sacrament. The topic is ethics.

1 Cor. 6:11 is similar. In its context, it concerns the question whether people should press for their own rights and whether they may live as they want. Paul lists in a catalog of vices those who will not inherit the kingdom of God—the covetous, thieves, drunkards,

and so on. And then verse 11 reads, "And such were some of you. But you *were* washed, you *were* sanctified, you *were* justified in the name of the Lord Jesus Christ and in the Spirit of our God." Here, to be sure, the language is not *expressis verbis* that of baptism, but this is very probably what is meant. For our purposes, it is again important that baptism (or else terminology that suggests baptism) is appealed to in order to ground ethics. "Since you were washed, and so forth, you may no longer live as you did before! Unfortunately, this is what you are doing. But don't you see that at that point you were made new?" These are examples of how Paul grounds ethics (*this* is the subject, *not* baptism) by means of a baptism that has already taken place.

However, Paul can also appeal to a person's having previously been baptized to point out another feature of this topic. Consider 1 Cor. 12:12–13. In Corinth, there were divisions in the community. We do not need to elaborate here what these were connected with. Paul wants to eliminate these divisions. He does this by acknowledging a thoroughgoing differentiation of individual gifts. Even in a single community not all people are alike. Each person has his or her own gifts. The gifts are also in their differentiation all gifts of *one* Spirit. And then Paul continues, "For just as a body is *one* and still has many members, yet all the members of the body, though many, are still *one* body, so also this is how Christ is. For by *one* Spirit we were all baptized into *one* body—whether we are Jews or Greeks, slaves or free." Once more, it is clear that the topic here is *not* baptism, but the unity of the church, which in Corinth is endangered by division. In order to ground this unity, Paul makes use of, among other things, the *one* baptism that has taken place.

Finally, Paul argues in exactly the same way in 1 Cor 1:11f. Here he even speaks of a quarrel in the community, of divisions. One group wants to be Pauline, another Petrine, the third counts itself as belonging to Apollos, and others to Christ. (What is meant is probably a pneumatic Christ of the gnostics.) Paul asks, "Were you baptized in the name *of Paul*?" Paul again points to the *one* baptism and from this he argues *ad absurdum* with respect to the divisions.

What these statements have in common is this. In each instance, determined as it is by context or the situation in the community, Paul *makes use of the fact of his readers' baptism* in the way he argues.

He interprets this fact. By doing this, he leads his readers to a better understanding of the fact of their baptism. He lifts up *the particular* feature that is important to him in relation to the Christian existence of his readers in each case.

We may speak here of a "cognitive moment." This consists in Paul's desire for a more comprehensive understanding, a more comprehensive *insight* into the meaning of the fact of having been baptized. The readers must not yet have been aware of all that their own baptism meant. And doubtless there was a great deal they were not aware of at all. But it is essential to be clear about this: What their baptism meant could also be developed in other directions. It is not only a lack of ethical action, a false guarantee, or the division of the community that Paul could struggle against by appealing to the fact of baptism. For instance, he might also have been able to overcome despondency by pointing out that baptism that *really had* occurred. "Just as you *really have* undergone baptism, so now you *really are* children of God—and therefore you have no cause at all for anxiety and despondency." Baptism may therefore be appealed to for many different purposes. The readers are precisely *introduced* to the meaning of their own baptism. They do not receive catechesis *in preparation for* baptism, but rather instruction subsequent to it. Baptism is therefore appealed to for cognitive purposes. That is, it is appealed to as a basis for explaining the meaning of Christian existence. It is appealed to in order to grasp what Christian existence means.

I have now used the term "cognitive" twice. This plays a role in the more recent discussion, in which the cognitive sense of baptism is set over against a causative sense. What is meant is more or less this. "Cognitively," baptism is something like a means of proclamation, through which people are told of the salvation that has happened to them in Christ; "causatively," baptism effectively places a person into the new reality.

The question is whether this was a happy distinction. However, once it is drawn, one cannot pretend that it does not exist. I should just like to point out one thing. I have spoken twice of the appeal to baptism for cognitive purposes. This is not to be confused with a cognitive *sense* of baptism. Which of these two senses (the so-called cognitive and causative) is the correct one we must still discuss. To "appeal to baptism for cognitive purposes" is not to say anything about baptism itself, but to teach someone better to understand his or her Christian existence *by means of a baptism that has already taken place.*

I certainly believe that one must speak of a causative understanding of such baptism in Paul's case. (It is obvious from what has been said thus far that this does determine how baptism is to be understood today.) For what *Paul* thinks of baptism is still in no sense the New Testament view of baptism and, therefore, one may not appeal to any passage in Paul to ground the New Testament conception of baptism today. Let me reemphazise this. *No* passage from a letter of Paul can ground what is to be said about baptism today. From an *historical* point of view, I am indeed of the opinion that Paul took baptism to have what we have called a causative sense, because only in that case could the Christian live out of a baptism that had already taken place.

I should like to show this by means of yet one other example. "For you are all God's children through faith (this you are) in Christ Jesus" (Gal. 3:26). This means that faith (and in the context of the argument of Galatians, one must add "not circumcision") has made you God's children. Faith has therefore (causatively!) effected something. And the next verse is strictly parallel to this. "For as many of you as were baptized into Christ have put on Christ" (3:27). Again—your own baptism *did* effect this at the time when it occurred.

In this passage, it is striking that faith effects nothing different from what baptism has also effected. But according to Paul, faith comes in response to the proclamation (Rom. 10:17). If we combine the two statements, we can put it like this: Paul speaks to people (here to the Galatians) who have become Christians and who now need to live as Christians. He gives them the help they need for this by placing them anew into the beginning that has already occurred, so that they can begin to live anew from this beginning. However, Paul can describe this beginning in a wide variety of ways. Pointing back to a baptism that has already occurred is but *one* among several possibilities. To be sure, Paul assumes that his readers have been baptized. This is a practice that was standard and that was taken for granted in the early community. But nothing gives one the right to claim that Paul understood baptism as *the* decisive locus or *the* decisive point in time at which one becomes Christian. One may not speak in Paul's case of baptism being necessary for salvation. 1 Cor. 1:17 even speaks against supposing that Paul had thoughts that point in this direction. He says there that he doesn't know exactly whom he has baptized in Corinth, and then he explicitly states that, "Christ did not send me to baptize but to preach the gospel." However, there is no doubt that Paul meant to lead people to faith by the preaching of the gospel and, thereby, to Christ. To be sure, they were then baptized as well. By whom, remains unclear. There is little point in trying to systematize the relation of preaching and sacrament, of faith and baptism in Paul. To be sure, we sense a tension here (I will come back to this directly), but—let me quote Dinkler—"Paul obviously did not sense a tension between word and sacrament and, on account of this, he did not treat the problem."

Let me now go one step further. We have taken our bearings from the baptismal texts that occur in what, from the point of view of literary criticism, are the oldest documents of the New Testament, namely, the Pauline letters. It is impossible to determine the origin of Christian baptism from these. There is not a single passage in which this is even suggested. However, attempts to work back to the origin of baptism starting from other, later texts also demonstrate that we get mixed up with very uncertain hypotheses here. Most of this remains (at least at present) obscure. All that can safely be said is that Jesus did not baptize (in spite of John 3:22; 3:26; 4:1, since the statement is explicitly retracted in John 4:2). All the same, it may safely be said that Paul already met with baptism. Thus, we can narrow down the time of origin of Christian baptism to within a very few years. That the so-called baptismal command at the end of the Gospel of Matthew is a secondary development is shown not only by the trinitarian formula (initially, one baptized in the name of Jesus), but also by the fact that here different units of tradition have been joined together. As for what remains, this scarcely contributes to our line of questioning either, because here it is only the *practice* of baptism that is commanded, and nothing is said about the content of this practice.

In view of this (historical) uncertainty in uncovering the origin of Christian baptism, it may perhaps be worth risking a constructive attempt in place of proceeding in analytical fashion. There seem to me to be a few secure starting points for this. Once again, let us start from a comparison with the Lord's Supper. I said that, at a later point, people wanted to celebrate the supper of *Jesus*. (They wanted to celebrate the supper of *Jesus*, even if the meal itself and the original understanding of it had already changed greatly.) The early community after Easter was concerned to hold fast to Jesus. They were concerned to press on with what Jesus had brought. This could happen in the meal. After this, it happened in the proclamation. Baptism is not to be classified with these, at least not directly, since its beginning lies after Easter. In the case of baptism, a practice that is well known in the surrounding world has "come in between". With regard to this practice, it was also known that John the Baptizer had baptized Jesus. (However, this was of course not a Christian baptism!) Various and heterogeneous conceptions and understandings were attached to this practice in the different areas in which it was practiced in the milieu of early Christianity. Baptism was employed as an initiation rite. It could mediate removal of sin and, as such, could naturally be repeated. Baptism could effect redemption; it could effect new creation, communication with the divinity, and so forth. The practice as such was in no way unambiguous. I think there is little prospect of success in seeking (as has frequently been done) to trace Christian baptism (by means of a history-of-religions approach) back to *one* completely determinate understanding among those in the surrounding milieu. For, on the one hand, the motifs I have mentioned are already present within Christianity very early on. On the other hand, they also occur there with modifications that are characteristic of early Christianity.

What is certain is only that a practice was taken over which, *as a practice*, had already been well known for a long time. What remains uncertain is the understanding of this practice that shaped this process. That the baptism of John played an important role here is not to be disputed. How far its influence extended is as hard to make out as it is because of the fact that the *depictions* of the baptism of Jesus are not historical reports, but rather Christian accounts that for their part already presuppose the baptismal practice of the Christian community.

So this is where we stand. A practice is borrowed which (on account of its disparate origin) is now open to different understandings. And these very understandings were transferred to Christian baptism—*to the extent that they admitted of being filled with content from the Christian kerygma.* That this is what was intended in each case becomes clear from the fact that one baptized "in the name of *Jesus.*" To be sure, this is in the first instance only a name, a formula. But this formula could now be filled in and interpreted. And this took place in such a way that traditional conceptions of baptism were claimed as having come from Jesus. Perhaps we can make this clearer if we speak of *effects* of baptism, instead of conceptions of baptism.

One effect of baptism was that of cleansing from sins. This "bath of purification" is well known in many religions. Since it was *Jesus* who had brought forgiveness of sins, the kerygma of forgiveness of sins could also be applied to baptism. Thus, Christian baptism (baptism in the name of Jesus) *effects* forgiveness of sins.

Since it was Jesus who had brought redemption, the new creation, Christian baptism in the name of Jesus could also don these effects. Since baptism (as in the mystery religions) bound the participant together with the fate of the divinity, it could now be said of Christian baptism that it grafted a person into the "body of Christ," that the person who was baptized thereby went through Jesus' death and resurrection. Thus, (if I may summarize it in this way) baptism conferred the "effects" of Jesus. To the extent that these effects could be summed up by means of the conception "gift of the Spirit," the gift of the Spirit could also be linked with baptism, for the early community (or better, parts of the early community) regarded being endowed with the Spirit as its decisive understanding of being Christian. In the Spirit, Jesus was at work—and to the extent that baptism was now conceived as an effect *of Jesus*, it could be said that baptism confers the Spirit. (However, this means nothing essentially different from saying that baptism effects a new creation for the person, that it grafts into the Christ-body, or whatever.) All these conceptions are so to speak interchangeable, since—on the basis of Jesus—they mean to say essentially the same thing, and just do so by means of different conceptions of the time, conceptions that have different origins in the history of religions.

So this was the situation. A borrowed practice was interpreted and filled in with the aid of the kerygma—and in utterly different conceptual directions. Here again, something like a cognitive moment is present. But at the same time, we ought not to speak of a cognitive *sense* of baptism here, either, because being baptized is immediately understood as being effectively and (naturally also efficaciously) taken into the new situation brought through Jesus—into the eschatological existence of the eschatological community.

There is one thing we need to note. Insofar as it was Christian, baptism would never again be in a position to confer anything other than the kerygma that this practice interpreted. Furthermore, it needs to be said that it was an historical coincidence that the early community took up just *this* practice. It is just as conceivable that the early community might have availed itself of another practice from its environment with the same function.

But if baptism had at first been a custom that was self-explanatory (which was then traced back to a command of the risen one—in doing which one was essentially correct, since it was *his* kerygma that determined the content of baptism), and if baptism had then been interpreted in different directions, then it was quite self-explanatory that programmatic statements should have developed. They must have been implicit from the start—in fact, nascently explicit as well, even if we cannot recognize them, since programmatic statements about baptism are the exceptions in the New Testament. Even in the post-Pauline period, those who have been baptized are consistently addressed with the fact of their baptism in the New Testament writings.

Here are a few examples. "You *were* buried with [Christ] in baptism, and with him you *were* also raised through the faith that is worked by the God who raised him from the dead" (Col. 2:12). Or Eph. 4:4: "There is *one* body and *one* Spirit, just as you were called to *the one* hope that belongs to your call: *one* Lord, *one* faith, *one* baptism." But we do not find any fundamentally different direction even in Acts, for Luke seeks to understand the church of *his* time on the basis of its beginnings. For this reason, statements about baptism are only apparently programmatic for the situation to which they apply. They have to be interpreted in the context of the work as a whole.

In contrast, the other direction in which statements may be made (the programmatic one), does not enter the picture so clearly. Texts such as Mark 16:16 do not provide any further help. "Anyone who believes and is baptized will be blessed; anyone who does not believe will be condemned." The reason this text provides no further help is that hardly anything is said about how baptism is *understood*. If faith is mentioned first, this is at best a reference to the *practice* of adult baptism. But it just cannot be maintained exegetically that the relation between word and sacrament is reflected here (as if the word led to faith and so was the *prerequisite* for baptism). Besides, an exegetical finding would not provide any dogmatic justification (as has already been mentioned several times).

However, I should like to point to two more examples before concluding. Within quite a few New Testament writings, formulations occur that scholars refer to as liturgical expressions. These originally existed independently and have been worked into the texts, and (when they are reconstructed) they allow us to see that here we have to do with confessional formulations in these cases. If we have to do with baptismal confessions, as is often supposed, then a confession was presumably linked with baptism. Naturally, this is significant (for a programmatic understanding of baptism). Thus, if the supposition is correct that behind 1 Pet. 1:3–4:11 stands an ancient baptismal paranesis, we would have here the first point of reference we could really get hold of for a programmatic development of statements about baptism. It would thus be clear that the intent was to avoid a magical understanding of baptism, for 3:21 reads, "in baptism, the impurity of the flesh is not done away with [that is, as if we were now perfect], but we rather appeal to God for a clear conscience." Here, baptism may be characterized as setting the newly baptized person off on the way she or he is to travel as one who has been reborn.

Later, every motif is taken up, formulated, and made use of in programmatic fashion. And only then (long after the New Testament) does there arise a really comprehensive *doctrine* of baptism that attempts to connect the independent motifs with each other. At *this* point, one asks, "What happens when *we* baptize?"

This has been a quick stroll through New Testament texts about baptism. I did not intend to achieve completeness. It was more important to me to indicate directions and movements, to draw attention to those in which we find the evidence for baptism in the New Testament and in which the history of baptism played itself out. If these have been understood correctly, the question finally faces us once again whether we shall succeed in getting anywhere systematically (that is, dogmatically or theologically) on the basis of historical and exegetical findings. To put it another way, we now need to ask once more about the grounding of baptism—to ask whether such a thing can succeed, even though we know that historical findings as such do not suffice to provide such a grounding.

In my judgment, we need to start out by realizing that we cannot justify the necessity of baptism for salvation. Rather, we have to do with a practice that was taken for granted, the meaning of which was to be filled in on the basis of the kerygma. To put it rather pointedly, we may state quite definitely that the church would lack nothing if it did not have baptism and no longer practiced it. It is always a point of interest in this regard that the "twelve" very probably were not baptized. (Even a Catholic exegete like Schlier admits this, even though he would like to salvage the necessity of baptism for salvation.)

What has just been said ought in no way to be taken to mean that I am speaking in favor of abolishing baptism. It is not only ecumenical considerations that prohibit this. One neither can, may, nor should try to leap thoughtlessly over the tradition in which one stands. The ecclesial practice of baptism belongs to this tradition. It is just that—and this is now important—in baptism, we have to do with the unity of a *practice* that is understood very differently in the individual churches (and also by individual theologians). We make the issue too easy for ourselves if we say that the common bond that continues to unite all Christian churches despite all their various differences is baptism. We make it too easy by talking only about the practice and declining to say anything about the *content* of the practice. For what difference does it make if all churches have a common practice, but they have neither a common doctrine nor a common order of baptism?

Once we realistically concede this, it immediately becomes clear that (ecumenically speaking) we do in fact live in a situation that is very similar to that of the early community. Baptism came to the early community as a practice, and the early community confronted the question whether it could fill this practice (which belonged to various religions) with the kerygma. So also today, baptism comes to us as a practice (through the tradition), and we also confront the question whether *we* can fill this practice. But this can only be done properly on the basis of Jesus, and that means on the basis of the kerygma. This is the task we need to set for ourselves.

However, we run up against a variety of issues right away. The adult who has come to faith through the *sermon*, who has become a new creature through the sermon, who is now "in Christ," who has been justified—however we want to identify and describe this new being of the Christian (more precisely, the having-become-new through the sermon which led this person, as an adult, to faith)—such a person does not need baptism in order to *become* what he or she already *is*.

This is not to say anything against adult baptism (as one might take me to be doing). We merely need to ask what we *may* and what that we may *not* use to fill the practice of baptizing adults. We need to ask how adult baptism is to be understood.

What we may not do is fill adult baptism with contents that, for the person being baptized, are already there. Baptism does not bestow yet again what is already there. However, it may be understood to some extent as a confession of faith. Its concreteness can be an aid to the person who is being baptized as a comprehensive expression of the complex process of becoming Christian. (However, it is never to be understood as this process *itself*!) The Christian sets himself visibly and publicly on the way. In this sense, baptism can be an aid for him subsequently. Therefore, it is by no means impossible to fill the practice of adult baptism with meaning. However, it does seem to me incomparably more difficult to do this than to fill the practice of infant baptism with meaning. What we must avoid at all cost in the case of adult baptism is the impression that what has already been received by someone who *came to faith* through the message, through the sermon, is only now made into a reality for that person by baptism. For us, the coexistence of word and sacrament is no longer unproblematic. But once the problem exists, it may not be side-stepped. Still, what we must not do is turn a coexistence that was unproblematic at the outset (in the New Testament) into one that is *necessary* today.

The situation is different with regard to infant baptism. A child cannot yet even hear. Nevertheless, in baptism it is "declared" to her that through Christ she has been enlisted by God and set on a new way. It is "declared" to her that, although she has been born physically, she now belongs to God in a different relationship; that, while she is a child of her parents, as a child, she is God's creature; that she—through Jesus—is God's child. And (as she grows up) she can be called back to this path ever anew, and ever anew be set back on this starting point. The cognitive *function* (but not a cognitive sense) that is linked to baptism throughout the New Testament can be transferred much more directly in the case of infant baptism than can be done in the case of adult baptism. Here being baptized may be interpreted in a variety of ways.

On no account may one argue that the person who is baptized has to *know* what happens to him or her in baptism. No, the baptism that has taken place is precisely open to being explained (as in the New Testament, people who were baptized consistently had their baptism explained to them). It goes without saying that the issue of the character of the proclamation that is to follow needs to be thought through. However, that this can only occur after the fact is no reason for rejecting infant baptism. What is at stake here are questions about the order, but not about the essence of baptism. Naturally, the problem of the relation of church and state plays a role. However, this is not a theological problem in the proper sense, but rather a sociological one. I do not want to go into this here. I do want to point out that, if we pay attention to the direction in which statements about baptism are usually made in the New Testament, we simply have to insist (and this is surprising, in view of the current state of the discussion) that it is not infant baptism, but rather adult baptism that presents the real problem. This is connected with the fact that the unproblematic coexistence of word and sacrament in early Christianity is no longer unproblematic for *us*. In early Christianity, things could be said in connection with baptism that could just as well be said in connection with preaching. Being possessed by the Spirit could be explained by the hearing of the word (to give just one example) *and* it could be explained by the fact of a person's baptism. This coexistence is no longer unproblematic for us and, as a result, statements about baptism in the New Testament can no longer be directly converted into ones for use today.

It is also not possible to clarify the relation of word and sacrament *on the basis of the New Testament*. However, if we ask about the meaning of sacrament (in this case, about baptism), we can manage quite successfully to fill this practice with meaning (and in a way that is strictly parallel to the way things developed in early Christianity). Baptism came into early Christianity as a practice, and it was filled with meaning on the basis of the kerygma.

In conclusion, I need to register one more criticism of how our issue is formulated. (Incidentally, I should add that this formulation is my own. I formulated it in the way it is generally put today, as a way into our subject.) In order to be in a position to correct how the issue is stated, I have to modify my last sentence. I said that baptism came into early Christianity as a practice; it was filled with meaning on the basis of the kerygma. More precisely, the sentence should read that *adult* baptism came into early Christianity as a practice; it was filled with meaning on the basis of the kerygma. Naturally, no one would have spoken of "adult" baptism in early Christianity. Baptism simply *was* adult baptism. All attempts to provide evidence from the New Testament for infant baptism I regard as hopeless. However, as the doctrine of baptism developed later on, the question arose *out of this later doctrine of baptism* whether children and infants ought not to be included. And that is then what happened.

So today in the Christian church we have the practice of adult baptism *as well as* that of infant baptism. For this reason, we cannot ask about the New Testament grounding of baptism *as such*, because this question makes it sound as if there were only *one* practice, and as if the meaning of this *one* practice either were unambiguous—or could be made to be so by theological means. And this is just what won't work.

If we have been confronted once more with the problem of deciding between a combination of adult *and* infant baptism, on the one hand, and a choice of adult *or* infant baptism, on the other, then we must face up to it. And so the situation is this: We have to ask whether *either* practice can be justified on the basis of the New Testament. And we have to pose these two questions *independently of each other*. Therefore, we have to ask whether both infant and adult baptism can be filled with meaning on the basis of the kerygma. And I believe I have shown that *both* can be done. To be sure, this works out differently, for we have to think through the relation between word and sacrament *today*, and this is different in each case.

Once again, we find ourselves dealing with the issue of *direction* that has occupied us all along. If sacrament is related to word (as in the case of adult baptism), then baptism has a *different function*, even a *different content* than it does if word is related to sacrament (as in the case of infant baptism).

I hope to have made clear that this is not an insignificant issue. I have probably not presented you with any ingenious solution. It is clear to me that questions remain. But of this I am convinced: The discussion about the New Testament grounding of our practice of baptism (in its various forms) would be clearer if, in the exegesis of New Testament texts regarding baptism, as well as in systematic theological reflection, attention were consistently paid to the direction of what is being said.

I have explained that I have nothing to say against adult baptism. But it does seem certain to me that the New Testament statements about baptism—better, that its statements by way of interpreting baptism *that has already taken place*—that nearly all of these (and nearly always quite directly) apply to people *who have already been baptized* (and today this would mean, primarily, to people who have been baptized as infants). For in the New Testament, it is without exception people who have *already* been baptized who are subsequently told how, and especially how inclusively they are to understand this baptism.

INDEX

172

INDEX

twofold, xxvii, xxviii, 53, 84, 86
  See also Christianity, Church
Christianity
  essence of, 36, 37
  beginnings of, xi, xiv, xv, xix, xx,
    76–95
  See also Church, Christian commu-
    nity
Christology, xxiii–xxv, 23, 31, 36, 37,
    43, 90
  and soteriology, 25, 33, 65
  as functional, 33
  classical, xxiii–xxv
  deductive, xxiv, xxv, 89
  development of, 13, 56, 89, 94
  explicit, 19, 21, 23, 24, 32, 54, 65,
    90, 92
  implicit, 20, 23, 91
  inductive, xxiv, xxv
  liberal or revisionary, xxv
  point of, xxv, 33
  terminus a quo for, 21
Church, originating events of, ix, x,
    xiv, xv, xix, 83
  See also Christianity, Christian com-
    munity
Circumcision, 155, 161
Creed, 14, 15
Cup
  as new covenant, 142, 144
  content of, 142
  words over, as passed around, xxx,
    141–45

Doctrine, xii, xxx, xxxi, 130, 131
Dinkler, Erich, 162
Dogma, 40, 42, 45, 107

Easter, xiii, 10, 21, 22, 49, 53, 54,
    55, 61, 78
  as *terminus a quo* of Christ-kerygma,
    50, 53
  "business" of, 79
  -experiences, xxvii, xxx, 33, 34, 53,
    82, 84, 87, 90
  events of, xiii, 85
  faith of, 84
  -kerygma, xii, xxvi 78, 79, 80, 86,
    87
Ernst, J., 83

Ethics, xvii, xxx, xxxi, 25, 71, 72, 91,
    104, 109, 112, 130, 133
  baptism and, 157–71
  resurrection and, 102, 103–5, 154
Exorcism, xv, xix, xx, 29, 60, 61, 131
Extreme unction, 148

Faith, xiii, xviii, 32, 161
  and deeds, 104–7, 114
  as being moved (*betroffen*), xxv,
    xxvii, 27, 32, 52, 88, 89, 90, 91,
    93, 94
  as eschatological existence, 91, 165
  as freedom, 136
  as giving oneself over (*sich einlassen
    auf*), xxv, 16, 24, 29, 32, 33, 51,
    53, 54, 59, 64, 69, 70, 72, 73,
    74, 82, 89, 93, 94, 106, 107,
    130
  as imitation of Jesus, 91
  as initiated by Jesus, xxvii, 52, 74,
    88, 90, 92, 93
  as resurrection of the dead, xxv,
    96–116
  as risk, xxv, 6, 13, 29, 34, 48, 49,
    51, 54, 70, 112, 113, 115,
    132–36
  as taking-to-be-true, 106, 114, 115
  as visible, 107, 114, 168
  Christian, 76, 85, 90, 92, 96–97,
    105–116
  beginning of, xxxii n.7, 92
  in Jesus (Christ), xxvi, 14, 37, 38,
    39, 44, 46, 50, 52, 53, 85, 86,
    88, 89, 92
  Jewish, 85
  like Jesus', 37, 38, 44
  little, 114
Footwashing, 150
Form criticism, x, xi, xii, xiii, xiv,
    xxvi, 47, 50, 65, 77, 80, 81, 82,
    86, 87, 88

Geertz, Clifford, xix
Gnostics, dualist anthropology of,
    101–105
God
  activity of, 133
  as enacted by Jesus, 60, 68, 70,
    74, 75, 93, 131, 143

INDEX

as hidden, 68, 73–74, 114
as visible, 68, 73–74, 114
as Father, 30, 36, 109, 114, 132
as king, 30, 140
children of, 12, 169
encounter with, 64, 111
finger of, xviii, xix, xxvii, 60, 61, 63, 67
judgment of, 63, 64, 104, 108, 109, 111
kingdom of, xviii, xxviii, xxxi, 24, 26–30, 62, 63, 67, 74, 108, 109, 129, 140, 158
"performance of," 12, 13
rule of, xviii, xix, xxii, xxiv, xxviii, xxx, 19, 24, 28–34, 51, 52, 60, 61–75, 108, 129–36

Hahn, Ferdinand, 83
Harnack, Adolf, 36, 37, 38, 43, 44, 46, 52, 77
Heidegger, Martin, xii, 44
Holtzmann, H. J., 77
Hope, 97, 102–3, 115–16
Hymenaeus, 98, 100

Ius talionis, 112

James, 106, 107, 115, 116
Jesus
appearances of, xxviii, 16, 115
as "bearer" of the gospel, xxiii, xxv, 36–54
as Beelzebub, xxvii, 3, 4, 60, 67
as blasphemer, 3, 4
as bridegroom, 67
as "content" of the gospel, xxiii, xxv, 36–54
as crazy, 3, 6, 134
as criminal, 119
as criterion of interpretive validity, xxi
as deed, xxx, 5, 6, 31
as earthly, 54, 55, 90
as Elijah, 1, 2, 6, 68
as event, xvi, xvii, xxii, xxv, xxvi, 3, 55–75
as example, xxv, 20, 67, 68, 110, 131
as first Christian, 95

as forerunner, 4
as God, 9, 15, 35, 56, 73
as God who raises the dead, 56
as head of the body, 15
as hero, xxv, 118, 128
as High Priest, 8
as incarnation of God, 56, 68
as judge, 30
as King of the Jews, 7, 8
as Lord, 20
as martyr, xxv, xxix, 117–18, 127–28, 134
as messenger of God, 11, 13, 15
as Messiah, xiv, 1, 4, 6, 7, 8, 9, 13, 14, 21
as Messiah of God, 13
as miracle worker, 5, 33
as mouth of God, 6, 11, 13, 15
as person, xxi, xxii, xxiii, xxv, xxx, 3, 34, 52, 53, 55, 56, 132
as pioneer of faith, xxxii n.7, 94, 95
-as-praxis, xv, xvii, xxii, xxiii, xxv, xxx
as preexistent, 12, 20
as proclaimed or as proclaimer, 32, 43, 46, 47, 49, 51, 52, 85
as prophet 1, 2, 6
as revolutionary, 20
as risen, 34, 53, 54, 55, 57, 87, 88, 90
as servant, 122
as Son of David, 7, 14
as Son of God, xxx, 3, 11, 13, 15, 21, 122, 132
as Son of the living God, 9, 14
as Son of Man, 30, 122
as subject-matter of Jesus-kerygma, xvii, xix, xxi, xxii, xxvii, 50, 82, 168
as subject-term of Jesus-kerygma, xiii
as teacher, 20
as word, xviii, xxx, 5, 6
before his death, xiii, xxvii, 12, 87, 89, 115
as immediately present, xxi, 10
as corporeally absent, xxi, 89, 135
blood of, xxx, 119, 126, 142, 145
career of, xxix, 77, 78, 113, 122, 123, 128, 129

INDEX

175

INDEX

INDEX

INDEX OF PASSAGES

INDEX OF PASSAGES

Messiahship was
open + available
to all comers,
who read, + understood.
Although, + wise, to understand
+ were willing
to make the
sacrifice.

We confer Messiahship
on him just we choose,
Not a cosmic act.

all
"Jesus
the Man Names"